Language, Literacy & Vocabulary!

NATIONAL GEOGRAPHIC
Windows on Literacy®

TEACHER'S GUIDE
Fluent

NATIONAL GEOGRAPHIC

School Publishing

Produced through the worldwide resources of the National Geographic Society, John M. Fahey, Jr., President and Chief Executive Officer; Gilbert M. Grosvenor, Chairman of the Board; Nina D. Hoffman, Executive Vice President and President, Books and Education Publishing Group.

**PREPARED BY NATIONAL GEOGRAPHIC
SCHOOL PUBLISHING**
Steve Mico, Senior Vice President and Publisher; Marianne Hiland, Editor in Chief; Chris Jaeggi, Executive Editor; Michael Murphy, Senior Editor; Barbara Wood, Senior Editor; Carol Kotlarczyk, Editor; Nicole Rouse, Editor; Jim Hiscott, Design Director; David Dumo, Art Director; Shanin Glenn, Designer; Margaret Sidlosky, Illustrations Director; Matt Wascavage, Director of Publishing Services; Sean Philpotts, Production Manager.

MANUFACTURING AND QUALITY MANAGEMENT
Christopher A. Liedel, Chief Financial Officer; Phillip L. Schlosser, Director; Clifton M. Brown III, Manager.

TEACHER'S GUIDE DEVELOPMENT
Navta Associates

Published by the National Geographic Society
1145 17th Street, N.W.
Washington, D.C. 20036-4688

Product No. 4X52465

ISBN-13: 978-0-7922-6320-3
ISBN-10: 0-7922-6320-0

2010 2009 2008 2007 2006
1 2 3 4 5 6 7 8 9 10 11 12 13 14 15

Language, Literacy & Vocabulary!

NATIONAL GEOGRAPHIC
Windows on Literacy®

About the Program

Content and Literacy Development for Diverse Language Learners

National Geographic's *Windows on Literacy: Language, Literacy & Vocabulary* program is designed for today's classroom—diverse, challenging, and complex. Many students come to school without the basic background knowledge and oral language development needed for academic success. *Language, Literacy & Vocabulary* provides the extra support young learners need to experience success from the start.

National Geographic's *Language, Literacy & Vocabulary* program offers rich opportunities for learners to build background knowledge, develop vocabulary and oral language, and learn grade-level content. Throughout the nation, teachers told us they needed materials that scaffolded the learning so that students from diverse language backgrounds, at-risk readers, and students with learning challenges would have opportunities to achieve their full potential. The *Language, Literacy & Vocabulary* program meets this need through:

- Thematic units built around essential key concepts in science, social studies, and math
- Academic vocabulary development
- Age-appropriate and engaging nonfiction texts
- Considerate text with strong picture-text match
- Scaffolded, multilevel instruction for students at different levels of language proficiency
- Springboards to related reading and writing
- Customized instruction for English language learners (ELLs)
- Research-based instructional strategies
- Rich and varied teacher support and tools

Consulting Author: Linda Hoyt

Linda Hoyt is an educational consultant who strives to help teachers and school districts implement best practices in literacy instruction. She has had a rich array of experiences in education, ranging from classroom teaching to working as a reading specialist, curriculum developer, Title 1 teacher, staff developer, and Title 1 District Coordinator. She is the author of numerous books, articles, and videos and conducts presentations and workshops on literacy throughout the country.

Program Advisor: Mary Hawley

Mary Hawley is an educational consultant who has worked with teachers, educators, and publishers to implement best practices for teaching students with diverse language backgrounds. She has taught English as a Second Language in Mexico, worked with migrant and refugee children in Indiana, and studied in Latin America. In recent years, she has been instrumental in developing Spanish reading programs and products for English language learners.

Program Reviewers

Susan Brandt, Director of Staff Development and Support Programs, Arlington Heights School District 25, Arlington Heights, Illinois

Theresa Castelan, English Language Development Resource Teacher, Clovis Unified School District, Clovis, California

Dr. Beverly Ann Chin, Professor of English, University of Montana

Danielle Clayton, Director of English Learners, Kings Canyon Unified School District, Reedley, California

Paula Olson, retired teacher, Fairfax County Public Schools, Fairfax, Virginia

Sheryl Powell, Pre-Kindergarten Teacher, Wells Branch Elementary School, Austin, Texas

Accessible Academic Content

Success From the Start!

Achieving academic success is essential for students to make adequate yearly progress and for continued academic growth. Conclusive data and research show that students who fall behind on their acquisition of academic content and vocabulary during the K–3 years will fall further behind as they advance through the grade levels. To help students achieve success from the start and prevent them from falling behind, *Windows on Literacy: Language, Literacy & Vocabulary* gives students access to the core grade-level content they need for standards-based academic success through these features:

- Explicit instruction in core academic content and vocabulary to build a foundation for future success
- Focused, targeted, standards-based content
- Alignment with TESOL standards
- Multiple exposures to and applications of academic vocabulary
- Carefully leveled developmental texts
- Picture glossaries of key content vocabulary
- Simple, engaging, and visually striking student book pages
- Strong picture-text match
- Familiar language and simple sentence structures
- Multiple opportunities for oral language development
- Theme Builders for building background and developing oral language
- Opportunities for writing and related reading

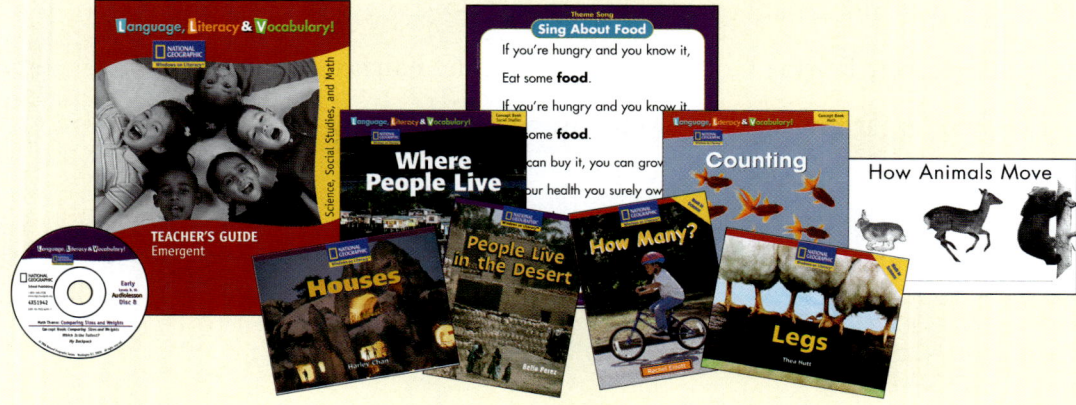

One Program for Your Diverse Classroom

Windows on Literacy: Language, Literacy & Vocabulary recognizes that every classroom includes diverse language learners as well as students whose background knowledge and oral language require development. Teachers told us they wanted one program that they could use with English language learners, students with reading and vocabulary challenges, and students with learning issues that affect their ability to acquire and process language. With appropriate modifications for different needs, *Language, Literacy & Vocabulary* gives teachers a sound, research-based instructional plan to meet the common needs among diverse language learners.

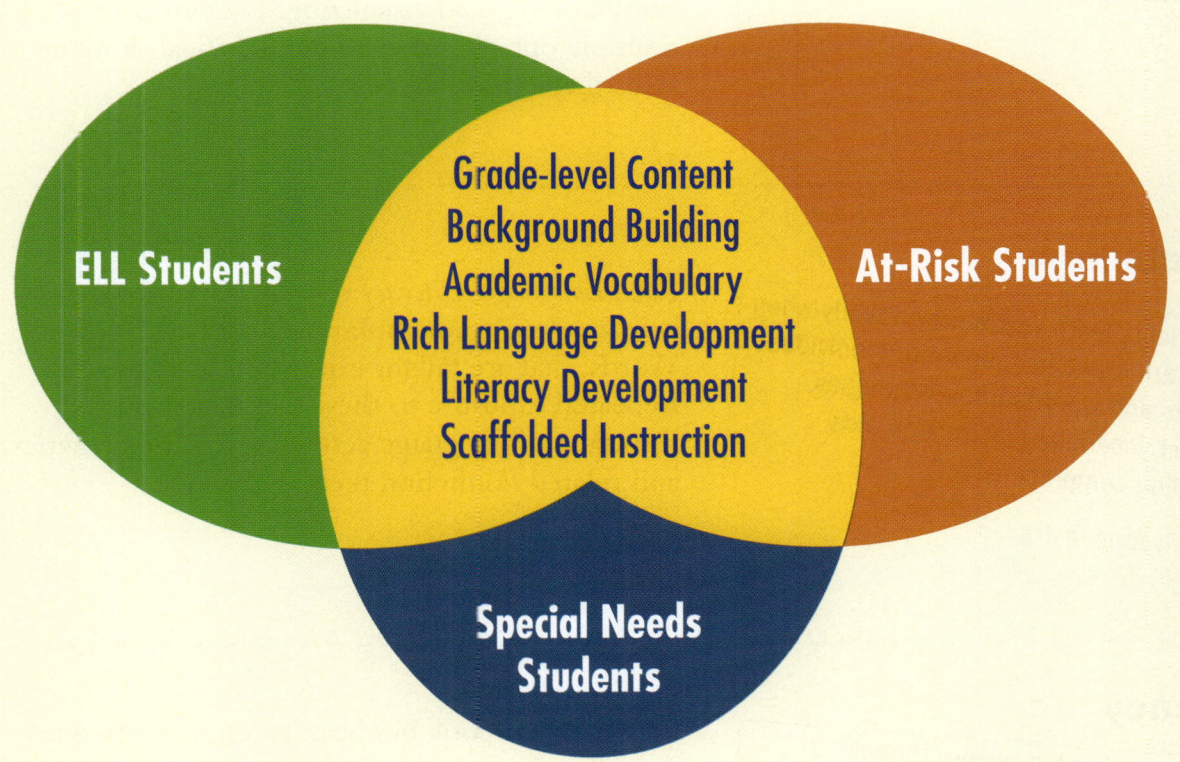

ELL Students

At-Risk Students

Grade-level Content
Background Building
Academic Vocabulary
Rich Language Development
Literacy Development
Scaffolded Instruction

Special Needs Students

Research-Based Instruction

Windows on Literacy: Language, Literacy & Vocabulary incorporates best practices that have been identified through research. Practices that are critical to academic success are highlighted below.

Comprehension

> "Text comprehension can be improved by instruction that helps readers use specific comprehension strategies."
>
> *Put Reading First, p. 49*

The lesson plans for each title provide explicit instruction, practice, and applications of one of the following seven **Comprehension Strategies:** asking questions, determining importance, making connections, making inferences, predicting, summarizing, and visualizing. Lessons include multiple opportunities to build critical thinking skills through discussion.

Vocabulary

> "Students learn vocabulary directly when they are explicitly taught both individual words and word-learning strategies. Direct vocabulary instruction aids reading comprehension."
>
> *Put Reading First, p. 35*

Each *Language, Literacy & Vocabulary* theme has core **academic vocabulary,** called Key Concept Words, that are taught explicitly before reading. Repeated exposure to these words is provided through oral language activities, writing activities, and related nonfiction texts.

Fluency

> "Students develop fluency through focused and deliberate engagement with a range of uses of language—both oral and written—together with many opportunities to practice newly learned structures in different contexts."
>
> *Dutro, S. & Moran, C. (2003). Rethinking English language instruction: An architectural approach.*

Each student book has been carefully crafted to provide content in an engaging and accessible way. The **Concept Book,** paired with related nonfiction titles, provides extended reading opportunities for gaining fluency. Multiple opportunities for speaking about and listening to text support students' growth as fluent readers.

Strategic Reading

"When learners are carefully coached and supported, they can simultaneously develop strong skills as decoders, excellent fluency, AND comprehension."

Hoyt, L. (2005). Spotlight on comprehension: Building a literacy of thoughtfulness (p. 155).

The Teacher's Guide provides repeated, explicit instruction and application of **Comprehension Strategies.** Additional support is included in the **Audiolessons,** through which students gain fluency and build comprehension by listening to modeled, strategic readings of the text.

English Language Learners

"English learners develop both English proficiency and reading ability in classes in which teachers present reading as a meaning-making activity."

Freeman, D. & Freeman, Y. (2003). Teaching English learners to read: Learning or acquisition?

The Teacher's Guide provides suggestions for teaching **forms and functions of English.** Repeated exposure to and practice of these language forms and functions ensure students' continued development as speakers, readers, and writers of English. The sheltered content in the theme materials serves to create meaningful reading by showcasing concepts essential for future academic success.

At-Risk Readers

"Schools need to assist at-risk students by providing experiences that show abstract concepts are drawn from and applied to the everyday world."

Center for Research on Education, Diversity and Excellence (CREDE) Standards

Students have the opportunity to apply concepts in theme materials to the real world by discussing theme-related realia as they draw on—and then continue to build—their background knowledge. Related materials, including a student-written **Take-Home Book,** extend the meaning of the texts as students apply their knowledge of concepts and vocabulary to other situations.

Program Components

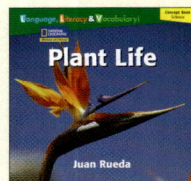
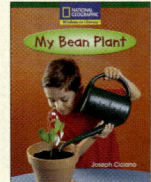

Thematic Student Books

Each developmental stage includes 36 books organized into 12 themes. Each theme includes one Concept Book and two related nonfiction books.

The **Concept Book** introduces the theme and develops key concepts and academic vocabulary.

The **Related Nonfiction Books** support and develop key concepts and academic vocabulary.

Each stage includes science, social studies, and math themes, which develop grade-level content and academic vocabulary.

- Five science themes
- Five social studies themes
- Two math themes

See pages 12–15 for a complete list of Fluent themes and content.

Teacher's Guides

One Fluent Teacher's Guide, featuring:

- Step-by-step lessons and lesson planner
- Explicit instruction
- Reading comprehension strategies
- Vocabulary instruction
- Oral language development opportunities
- Customized instruction notes for ELLs
- Opportunities for rich assessment in reading, fluency, vocabulary, and oral language

Theme Builders

One Theme Builder per theme, ideal for small-group instruction to build understanding:

- Think and Discuss Scene
- Oral Language Activity
- Graphic Organizer

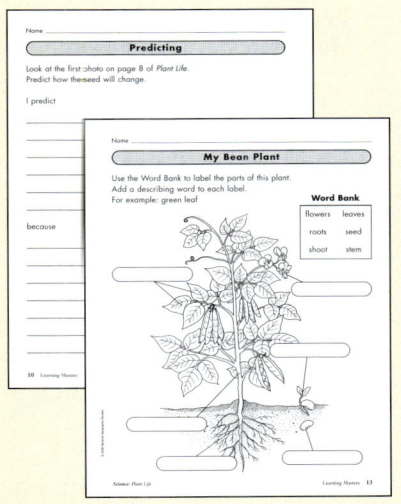

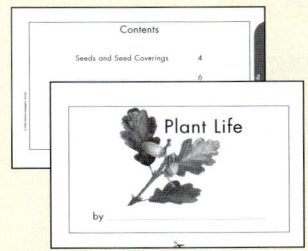

Learning Masters

A collection of reproducibles for each theme:

- Home-School Connection
- Oral Language Activity
- Reading Strategy Masters
- Comprehension Master for each student book
- Self-Assessment Tools
- Graphic Organizer to plan writing

Take-Home Book Masters

Reproducible Take-Home Book Masters to accompany each theme:

- Provide visuals for writing prompts
- Reinforce concepts of theme
- Allow for assessment opportunities
- Celebrate learning of key concepts
- Can be shared with family

Audiolessons

An audiolesson to accompany each title— ideal for independent practice:

- Contains complete audio of Concept Book and related nonfiction texts
- Provides fluency practice
- Builds content and understanding
- Provides detailed practice with text features and reading strategies

Fluent Stage Themes

Concept Books	Related Nonfiction Books	Key Concepts	Key Concept Words	Comprehension Strategies
Plant Life Levels 13–14		**Life Science** • Plants grow and change following a specific sequence. • The basic parts of a plant have functions that help plants live and grow. • People and animals need plants.	flowers fruit leaves root seeds shoot soil stem	Predicting
Then and Now Levels 13–14		**Technology** • There are many information sources people can use to find out about the past. • Comparing the past with the present shows how things have changed over time. • Different kinds of technologies can be improved and changed over time.	change invent long ago machine the past school	Making Connections
Providing Goods Levels 13–14		**Economics** • People grow and make products that other people want. • The distribution of goods involves a sequence of steps. • The distribution of goods involves different forms of transportation.	buy goods move sell stores transport truck warehouse	Making Inferences

Concept Books	Related Nonfiction Books	Key Concepts	Key Concept Words	Comprehension Strategies
Measurement *Levels 13–14* 	 	**Measurement** • People use measurement in daily life. • Length, height, weight, and volume can be estimated and measured. • People can measure the sizes, weights, and volumes of things using nonstandard, U.S. customary, and metric units.	inch foot/feet centimeter meter ounce pound gram kilogram teaspoon tablespoon cup pint quart gallon liter	Asking Questions
Wind, Water, and Sunlight *Levels 15–16* 	 	**Physical Science** • Wind, water, and sunlight are powerful forces. • Wind, water, and sunlight can change nonliving things. • People and other living things use wind, water, and sunlight.	heat melts power sunlight water wind	Visualizing
Prehistoric Life *Levels 15–16* 	 	**Science** • Scientists study fossils to learn about plants and animals from the prehistoric past. • Many plants and animals that lived long ago are now extinct. • Fossils are formed over a long period of time.	dinosaur extinct fossil paleontologist prehistoric remains skeleton	Asking Questions

Fluent Stage Themes

Concept Books	Related Nonfiction Books	Key Concepts	Key Concept Words	Comprehension Strategies
Maps — Levels 15–16 — Maps, Ari Brennan	All Kinds of Maps, Stevie Prince; Mapping North America, Kate McGough	**Geography** • Maps represent landforms, bodies of water, and places. • People can use maps and their symbols to identify and locate continents, oceans, lakes, rivers, mountains, countries, cities, roads, and buildings. • Maps that show the same place in different ways can be used for different purposes.	border continent country highway lake landforms mountain ocean river road	Determining Importance
Patterns, Shapes, and Symmetry — Levels 15–16 — Patterns, Shapes, and Symmetry, Susan Long	How to Make a Paper Frog, Jan Pritchett; Looking for Symmetry	**Math** • There are patterns, shapes, and symmetry in many living and nonliving things. • People can look for patterns, shapes, and symmetry. • People can create patterns, shapes, and symmetry.	circle half line of symmetry pattern rectangle shape square symmetry triangle	Making Connections
States of Matter — Levels 17–18 — States of Matter, Mary Garcia	Water Can Change, Brian Birchall; Everything Is Made of Matter, Rowan Sellers	**Physical Science** • Matter can take the form of a solid, a liquid, or a gas. • Each state of matter has its own unique properties. • Changes in temperature can cause matter to change from one state to another state.	change gas heat ice liquid matter melt solid steam temperature	Making Inferences

	Concept Books	Related Nonfiction Books	Key Concepts	Key Concept Words	Comprehension Strategies
Animal Habitats	Levels 17–18 Animal Habitats Michelle Kramer	Life in the Ocean George Hoxley The Rain Forest Pat Malone	**Life Science** • Animals live in many different kinds of habitats. • Animals live in habitats that provide for their basic needs, which include food, water, air, and shelter. • Animal adaptations help animals survive in their habitats.	Arctic desert habitat level ocean prairie rain forest zone	Summarizing
Producing Goods	Levels 17–18 Producing Goods Charlie Walker	Wool Keeps Me Warm Mario Lucca Cotton Comes From Plants Norman Yu	**Economics** • People take raw materials found in nature and turn them into finished products. • Workers follow a sequence of steps to turn raw materials into finished goods. • There are special words to describe the process of turning a raw material into a finished product that can be sold in stores.	factory goods harvest machine product raw material	Asking Questions
United States Geography	Levels 17–18 United States Geography Ruth Wong	Places to Visit More Places to Visit Nick Bruel	**Culture** • There are many famous places in the United States of America. • Some of these places are natural landmarks, and some are landmarks made by people. • People can use maps to identify the locations of landmarks.	canyon cave geography landmark monument national park volcano waterfall	Asking Questions

Thematically-Organized Student Books

Scaffolded Literacy and Content Development

Each theme in *Windows on Literacy: Language, Literacy & Vocabulary* offers opportunities for students to explore grade-level science, social studies, or math concepts across a variety of texts. Reading across texts invites students to compare texts and learn from multiple sources.

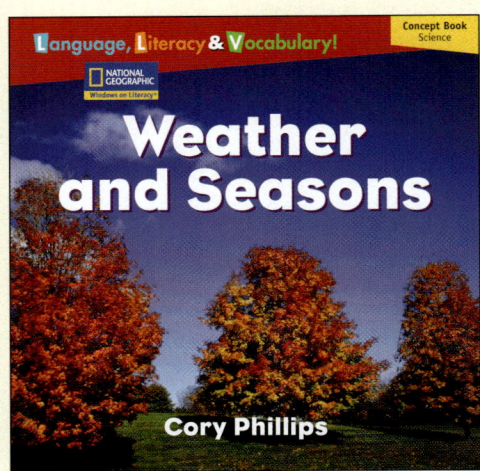

Concept Books

Many students come to school with limited background knowledge, vocabulary, and oral language development. Concept Books give these students the extra support they need to build background knowledge and develop the oral language and academic vocabulary essential for success in school.

Concept Book Features:

- Every Concept Book begins and ends with strong images that prompt talk about the basic concepts covered in each theme.

- Key Concept Words are provided to give students access to the academic vocabulary they will need to understand and discuss basic content.

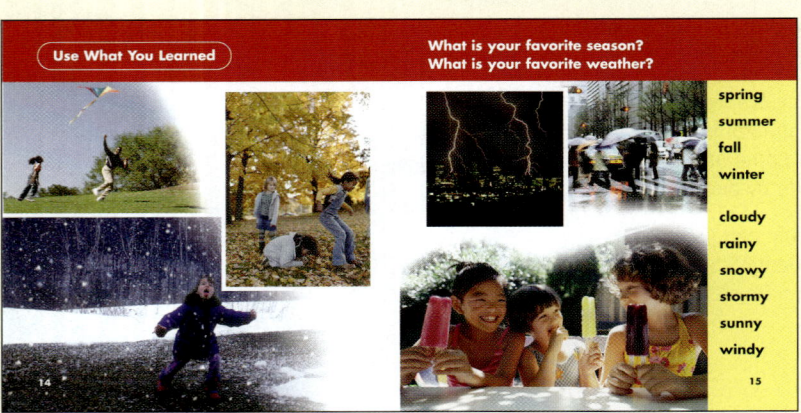

Related Nonfiction Titles

Each theme has two related nonfiction titles that expand on the basic concepts of the theme. Text features and the academic vocabulary introduced in the Concept Book are featured and provide students with an opportunity to apply new concepts, vocabulary, and knowledge.

Optional Fiction Titles

For each theme, two optional fiction titles extend the learning. These content-based fiction books provide additional reading and invite comparison of similarities and differences between fiction and nonfiction. Reading similar content across texts provides opportunities for students to use reading strategies in different contexts.

Teacher Support

Teacher's Guide

The *Windows on Literacy: Language, Literacy & Vocabulary* Teacher's Guide uses a sheltered-content instructional approach in which students are taught basic concepts, academic vocabulary, language forms, and comprehension strategies to provide them with the tools they need to achieve their full potential. The strategies, materials, and activities are modified so that all learners can be successful. The easy-to-manage five-lesson plan for each theme offers the flexibility to fit into every busy schedule.

The **Overview** provides all the tools needed to help plan and manage instruction.

The **Theme Materials** show what you need at a glance.

Instructional Highlights focus on Key Concepts, academic vocabulary, and target skills and strategies.

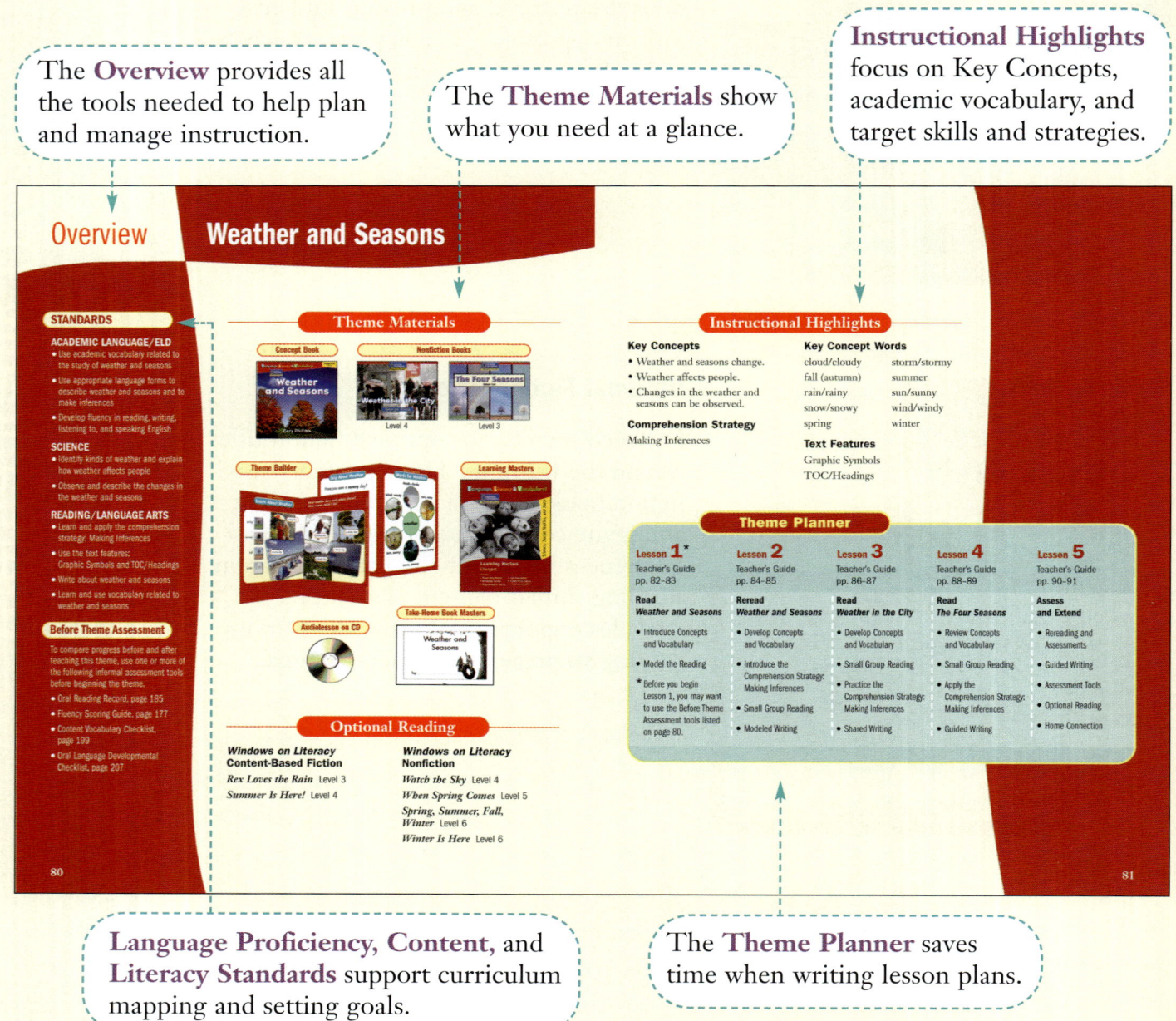

Language Proficiency, Content, and **Literacy Standards** support curriculum mapping and setting goals.

The **Theme Planner** saves time when writing lesson plans.

The **academic vocabulary** for each theme is taught before reading.

Teacher modeling demonstrates fluent reading. Partners read, building understanding of concepts while practicing to achieve fluency.

Lesson 1 — Read *Weather and Seasons*

OBJECTIVES
- Understand that weather and seasons change and that these changes affect people
- Learn and use vocabulary related to weather and seasons
- Use photographs to predict vocabulary
- Use text features, such as graphic symbols and TOC/Headings, to comprehend text

Materials
Realia: umbrella, sunglasses, mittens
Theme Builder
Weather and Seasons
Learning Masters page 37
Audiolesson 5

Theme Builder (Song)

Theme Builder (Scene)

Introduce Concepts and Vocabulary

Introduce Theme Question
Ask children: How would you talk about the weather today? Explain that they will learn about the weather and seasons. They will also learn the language to use when describing weather and seasons.

Have children look outside. Then have them draw what they see, including weather elements, such as the sun, rain, or clouds. Talk together about words that name or describe the weather they have shown.

Develop Oral Language
Open an umbrella and hold it over your head. Model a sentence using the phrase *a rainy day*: I use an umbrella on a rainy day.

Then put on a pair of sunglasses. Ask children when you would use sunglasses. Then model: I wear sunglasses on a sunny day.

Finally, put on a pair of mittens. Ask children when they would wear mittens. Then model: I wear mittens on a snowy day.

Have partners take turns pantomiming and using the model sentences. One partner pantomimes using the umbrellas, sunglasses, or mittens, and the other partner says:

You use _____ on a _____ day.

Introduce the Theme Song
Display the Theme Song on the *Theme Builder* (tune: "The Muffin Man"). Sing the song, putting on a pair of sunglasses. Repeat, inviting children to sing as you point to the picture of a sunny day. Have pairs

of children use *Learning Masters* page 37 to practice using the language forms for describing the weather.

Introduce Key Vocabulary
Use the Think and Discuss scene on the *Theme Builder* to teach Key Concept Words and model language forms.

I see rain on a rainy day.

I see a blue sky on a sunny day.

Repeat with other weather words and the names of the seasons. As you introduce words, jot them down on chart paper. Display this Word Bank throughout the theme. Have children work with conversation partners to practice using the language forms for describing the weather.

WEATHER	SEASONS
cloud/cloudy	spring
rain/rainy	summer
snow/snowy	fall
storm/stormy	winter
sun/sunny	
wind/windy	

Build Background
Display the Think and Discuss scene on the *Theme Builder* again. Ask children what they notice. As children share observations, guide them to use the correct names for the seasons and the weather. Have pairs of children talk about the scene and practice using language forms for describing the weather, such as: The weather is *(cloudy)*.

Model the Reading

Preview the Book
Distribute copies of *Weather and Seasons*. Read aloud the title and the author's name. As you page through the book, point out:
- Arrows show the order of the seasons.
- Graphic symbols on most pages show the kinds of weather.
- Each page about weather begins with the word *sometimes*.

Predict Vocabulary
Encourage children to use pictures to predict vocabulary: Which words do you expect to see in this book?

Display a page and cover the words: Which words do you expect to see on this page?

Children may mention objects or activities on the page—such as trees, walking, and playing. Add these words to the Word Bank. Have children work in pairs to use words in the Word Bank to describe the weather or the season in the picture. Continue with other pages as time allows.

Read Aloud
Invite children to follow along as you read *Weather and Seasons* aloud. As you read, pause to think aloud. Encourage children to ask questions and make observations.

Pages 4–5
Think Aloud This is like the Think and Discuss scene on the *Theme Builder*. Look at the labels. They tell me about each of the seasons and different kinds of weather.

Pages 6–7
Think Aloud The labels tell what the seasons are. The arrows show that the seasons are always in the same order—spring, summer, fall, and winter. The picture of winter shows snow. It's usually cold in snowy places. Winter must be cold.

Pages 10–11
Think Aloud Here are two symbols. One is for sunny weather. The other is for cloudy weather. I see the word *sometimes* used on each page. The weather isn't always the same. It changes.

Pages 12–13
Think Aloud The symbol for snow is a snowflake. What's the symbol for storms? It's a cloud with rain and lightning. It's a lot like the symbol for cloudy weather.

Page 16
Think Aloud The Picture Glossary helps me remember the words for different kinds of weather. It reminds me that the weather can change. The pictures also remind me of different seasons.

Reread for Fluency
Have children reread the entire book independently to build fluency. See *Customize the Reading*.

Customize Instruction for ELLs

Newcomers/Beginning Point to each page and have children act out what they do during different kinds of weather. *(open an umbrella, put on sunglasses, and so on)*

Developing Ask questions, such as: "What do you see on a windy day?" "What happens in a storm?" Children should use language forms to answer.

Expanding/Bridging Have children use Key Concept Words and language forms in complete sentences to describe their favorite seasons.

Learning Masters/page 37

Customize the Reading
Children reread and talk about Weather and Seasons on their own to build fluency.
- Children who are not yet able to read the book can look at the photos and name the different kinds of weather.
- Children who need extra support can reread the book while listening to the audiolesson.
- Children who can read the book might read independently or aloud with partners.

82   83

Each theme begins with rich **oral language activities,** as well as activities that build background, to develop the language and understandings needed to learn key concepts.

Comprehensive lesson plans include specific recommendations for **customizing instruction** for varying language proficiency levels.

Teacher Support

Teacher's Guide

Each lesson includes opportunities for reading, writing, academic vocabulary and language development, and assessment. Suggestions for tailoring instruction to students' needs are provided.

Oral Language activities develop the forms and functions students need to learn and use the academic vocabulary.

Small Group Reading offers the support students need as they access the Key Concepts and become comprehending, fluent readers.

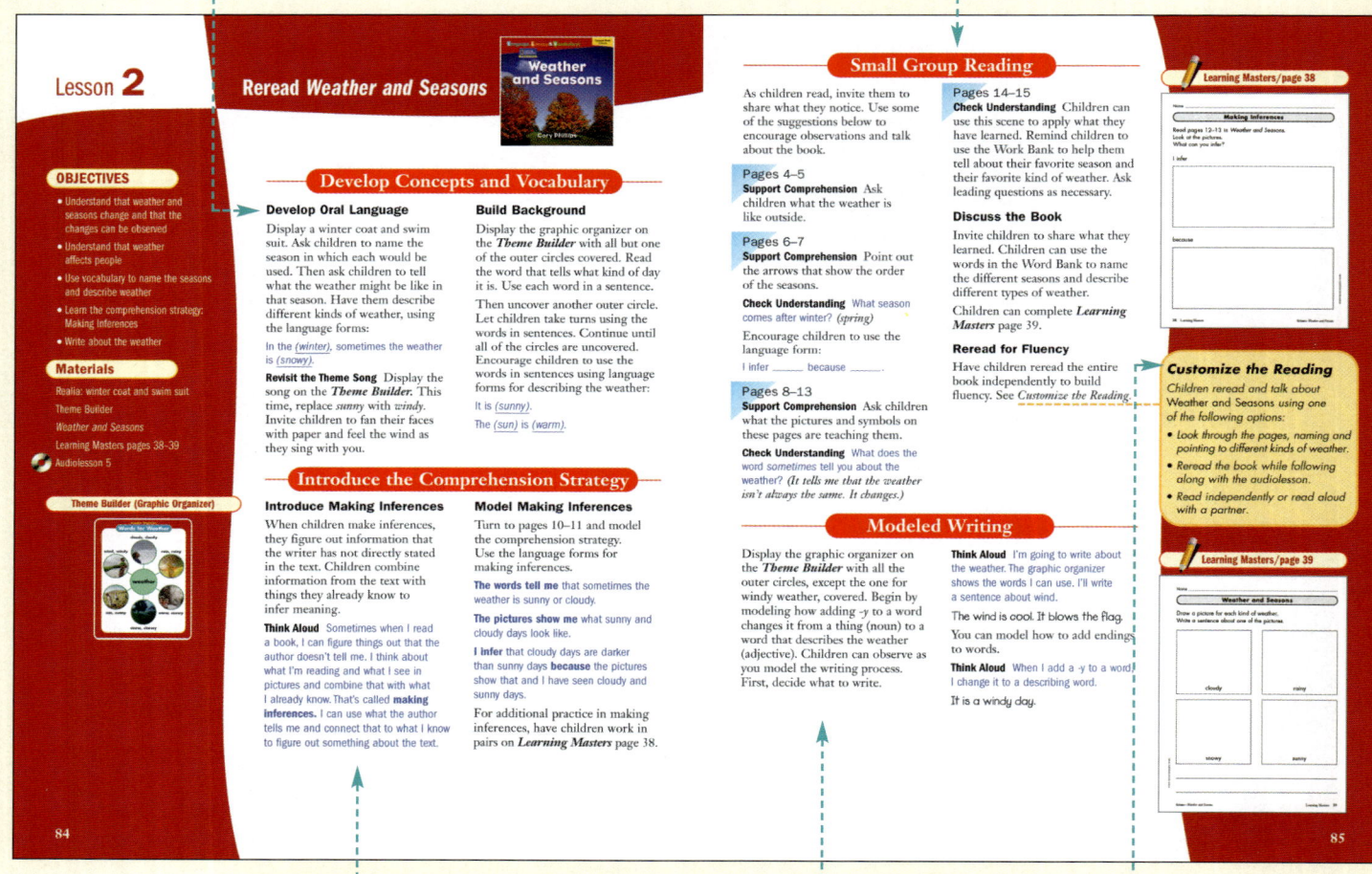

Explicit instruction and practice in **comprehension strategies** provides students with the skills they need for understanding.

Within each theme, students participate in **modeled, shared,** and **guided writing.**

Customize the Reading suggests varying levels of support as students reread books to develop fluency.

Guided Writing lessons invite students to develop content knowledge through the **Take-Home Book** and provide an opportunity to monitor comprehension.

A variety of **Assessment Tools** offer opportunities to assess reading, writing, content-area learning, academic vocabulary, and oral language development.

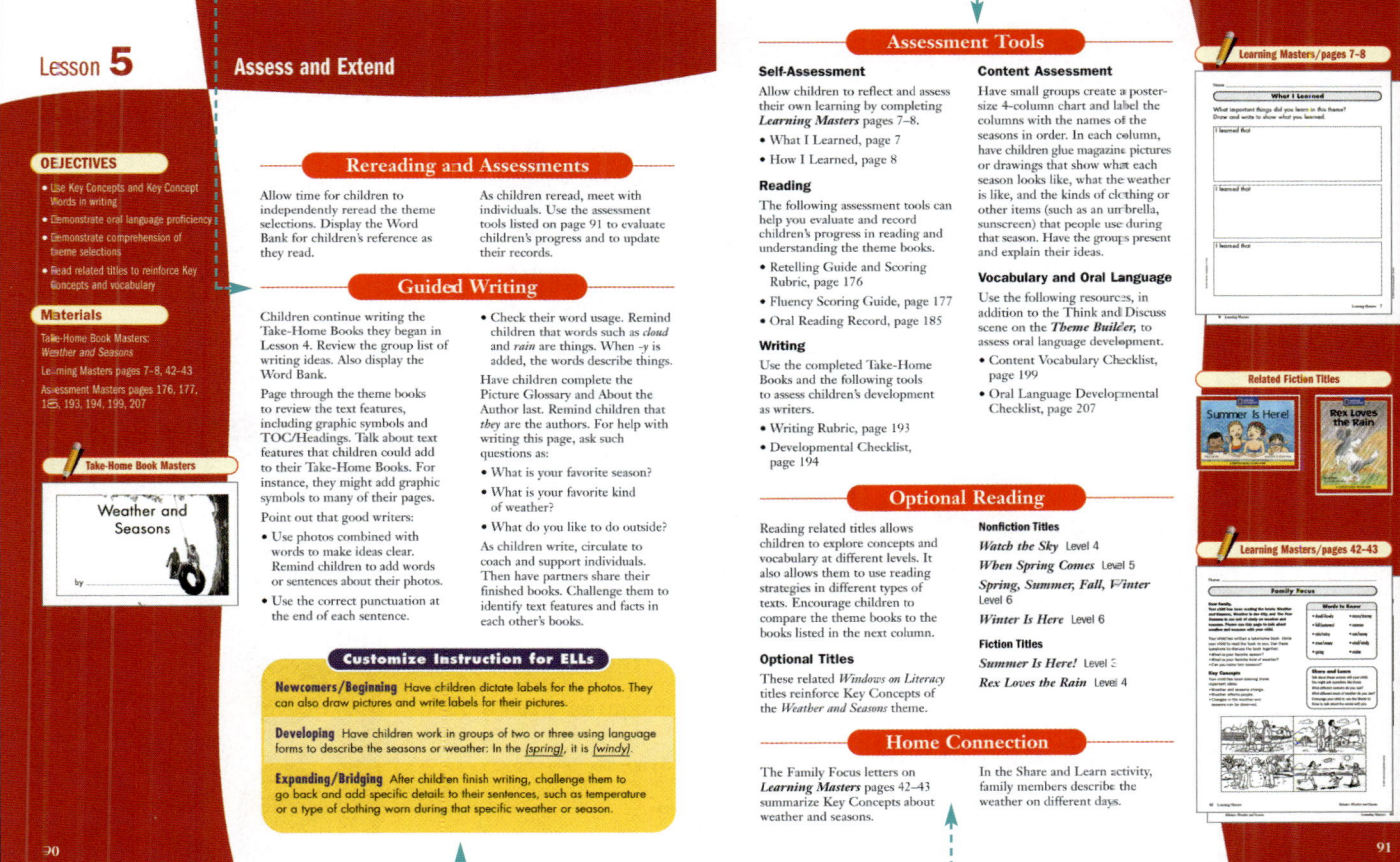

Lesson 5 — Assess and Extend

OBJECTIVES
- Use Key Concepts and Key Concept Words in writing
- Demonstrate oral language proficiency
- Demonstrate comprehension of theme selections
- Read related titles to reinforce Key Concepts and vocabulary

Materials
Take-Home Book Masters: *Weather and Seasons*
Learning Masters pages 7–8, 42–43
Assessment Masters pages 176, 177, 185, 193, 194, 199, 207

Take-Home Book Masters

Weather and Seasons
by _____

Rereading and Assessments

Allow time for children to independently reread the theme selections. Display the Word Bank for children's reference as they read.

As children reread, meet with individuals. Use the assessment tools listed on page 91 to evaluate children's progress and to update their records.

Guided Writing

Children continue writing the Take-Home Books they began in Lesson 4. Review the group list of writing ideas. Also display the Word Bank.

Page through the theme books to review the text features, including graphic symbols and TOC/Headings. Talk about text features that children could add to their Take-Home Books. For instance, they might add graphic symbols to many of their pages.

Point out that good writers:
- Use photos combined with words to make ideas clear. Remind children to add words or sentences about their photos.
- Use the correct punctuation at the end of each sentence.

Check their word usage. Remind children that words such as *cloud* and *rain* are things. When -y is added, the words describe things.

Have children complete the Picture Glossary and About the Author last. Remind children that *they* are the authors. For help with writing this page, ask such questions as:
- What is your favorite season?
- What is your favorite kind of weather?
- What do you like to do outside?

As children write, circulate to coach and support individuals. Then have partners share their finished books. Challenge them to identify text features and facts in each other's books.

Customize Instruction for ELLs

Newcomers/Beginning Have children dictate labels for the photos. They can also draw pictures and write labels for their pictures.

Developing Have children work in groups of two or three using language forms to describe the seasons or weather: In the *(spring)*, it is *(windy)*.

Expanding/Bridging After children finish writing, challenge them to go back and add specific details to their sentences, such as temperature or a type of clothing worn during that specific weather or season.

Assessment Tools

Self-Assessment
Allow children to reflect and assess their own learning by completing *Learning Masters* pages 7–8.
- What I Learned, page 7
- How I Learned, page 8

Reading
The following assessment tools can help you evaluate and record children's progress in reading and understanding the theme books.
- Retelling Guide and Scoring Rubric, page 176
- Fluency Scoring Guide, page 177
- Oral Reading Record, page 185

Writing
Use the completed Take-Home Books and the following tools to assess children's development as writers.
- Writing Rubric, page 193
- Developmental Checklist, page 194

Content Assessment
Have small groups create a poster-size 4-column chart and label the columns with the names of the seasons in order. In each column, have children glue magazine pictures or drawings that show what each season looks like, what the weather is like, and the kinds of clothing or other items (such as an umbrella, sunscreen) that people use during that season. Have the groups present and explain their ideas.

Vocabulary and Oral Language
Use the following resources, in addition to the Think and Discuss scene on the *Theme Builder*, to assess oral language development.
- Content Vocabulary Checklist, page 199
- Oral Language Developmental Checklist, page 207

Optional Reading

Reading related titles allows children to explore concepts and vocabulary at different levels. It also allows them to use reading strategies in different types of texts. Encourage children to compare the theme books to the books listed in the next column.

Optional Titles
These related *Windows on Literacy* titles reinforce Key Concepts of the *Weather and Seasons* theme.

Nonfiction Titles
Watch the Sky Level 4
When Spring Comes Level 5
Spring, Summer, Fall, Winter Level 6
Winter Is Here Level 6

Fiction Titles
Summer Is Here! Level 5
Rex Loves the Rain Level 4

Home Connection

The Family Focus letters on *Learning Masters* pages 42–43 summarize Key Concepts about weather and seasons.

In the Share and Learn activity, family members describe the weather on different days.

Learning Masters/pages 7–8

Related Fiction Titles

Summer Is Here!
Rex Loves the Rain

Learning Masters/pages 42–43

Family Focus

90 91

Customized Instruction for ELLs provides multilevel instruction and assessment options for students at varying levels of English language proficiency.

The **Family Focus Learning Master** connects school and home, encouraging students and their families to discuss and extend learning.

For more detailed notes and assessment options, see the corresponding pages in this Teacher's Guide or use our online guide at www.ngschoolpub.org

21

Teacher Support

Theme Builder

The Theme Builder that accompanies each theme is a valuable tool for small group instruction.

The interior scene reproduces the **Think and Discuss** page of the **Concept Book** to stimulate student talk using the academic vocabulary.

A **Graphic Organizer** for each theme supports thinking, oral language development, and writing.

An **oral activity** scaffolds learning through poems, readers theater, and other oral responses.

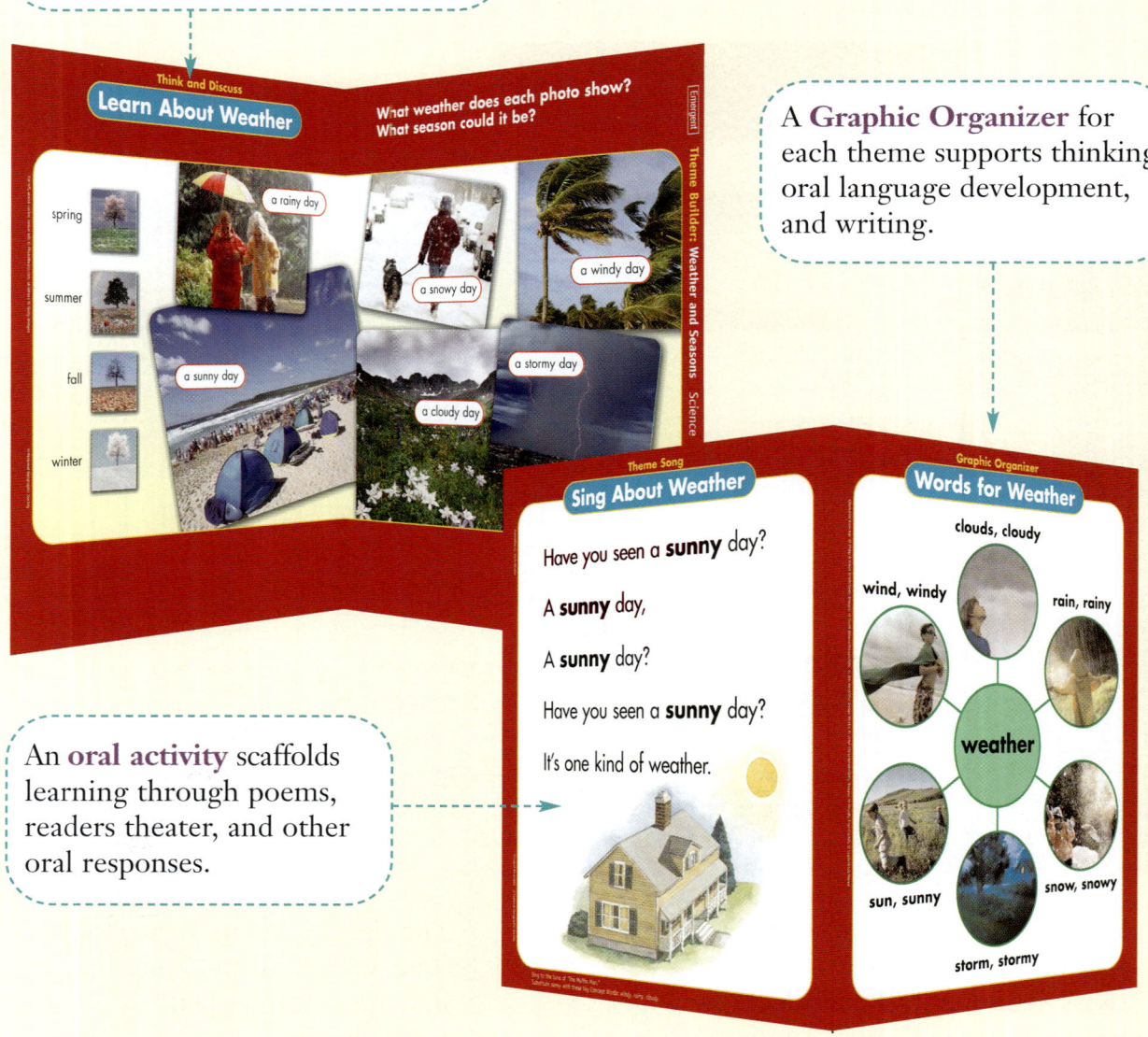

Audiolessons on CD

The three books in each theme are read aloud as the narrator provides additional support and questions during the readings. Students can reread books with this extended support.

Take-Home Book Masters

Students become authors as they create their own theme book. For each theme, blackline masters are provided for students to write about what they learned in the theme. These can be shared with family and friends to celebrate learning.

Pictures serve as prompts for writing and drawing.

Learning Masters

Each theme offers a rich array of Learning Masters to support collaborative and independent learning.

- A Comprehension Master offers the language forms needed to apply the theme's comprehension strategy.

- An Activity Master for each of the three student books in the theme provides support and an opportunity to explore the content of each book.

- The oral activity is reproduced to provide repeated use throughout the theme.

- Self-Assessment Masters help students reflect on both what they learned and how they learned.

- Family Focus letters in both English and Spanish help connect school with home.

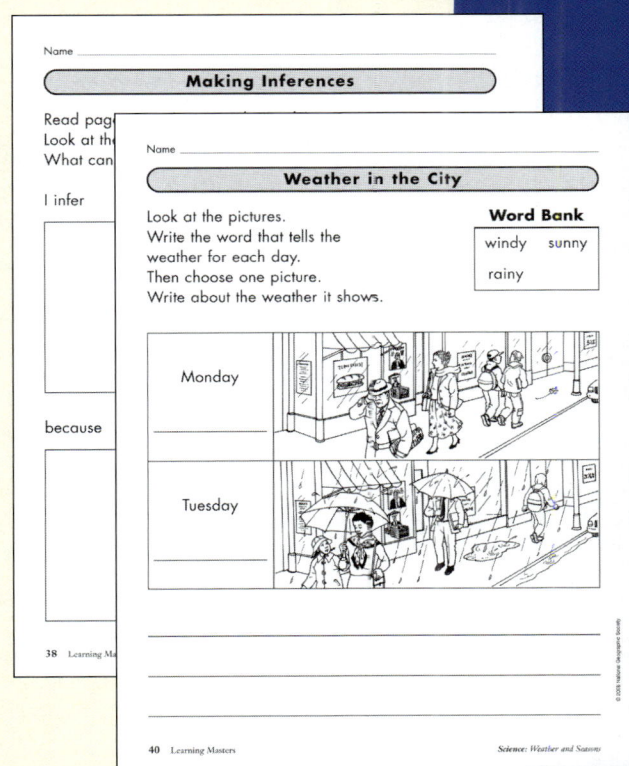

For more detailed notes and assessment options, see the corresponding pages in this Teacher's Guide or use our online guide at www.ngschoolpub.org

23

Assessment

Assessment provides teachers with valuable information they need to plan instruction and sets benchmarks that allow them to measure students' progress. An assessment program needs to be ongoing so that changes over time in students' learning can be noted. An assessment program includes tools to use before, during, and after reading so that evaluation of performance and planning for instruction are reliable and informed. Each theme in *Windows on Literacy: Language, Literacy & Vocabulary* offers rich opportunities for assessment.

Name _____

What I Learned

What important things did you learn in this theme?
Draw and write to show what you learned.

I learned that

I learned that

I learned that

Self-Assessment

After each theme, students reflect on what they learned while reading and the strategies they used to comprehend the material. As students monitor their own strategy use, they become more aware of what good readers do—and build their reading skills in the process. What I Learned allows students to fine-tune their understanding of key theme concepts. How I Learned provides an opportunity for students to reflect on the strategies they used during reading.

Name _____

How I Learned

Good readers do these things when they read.
Draw an *X* by the things you did when you read this text.

☐ I made connections.

☐ I thought about what would happen next.

☐ I asked questions before I read.

☐ I asked questions while I read.

☐ I made pictures in my mind.

☐ I picked out the most important ideas.

☐ I figured things out without the author telling me.

Give advice to another reader.

_____

_____

8 Learning Masters

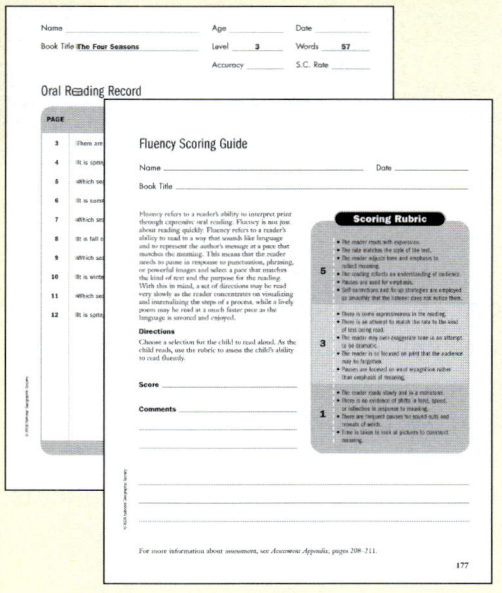

Assess Reading and Fluency

The Oral Reading Record focuses on a theme selection and provides insight into individual growth while informing instruction, while the Fluency Scoring Guide measures students' reading behaviors as they build fluency. The Retelling Guide encourages students to tell the main concepts from the reading, allowing teachers to gauge comprehension of key ideas.

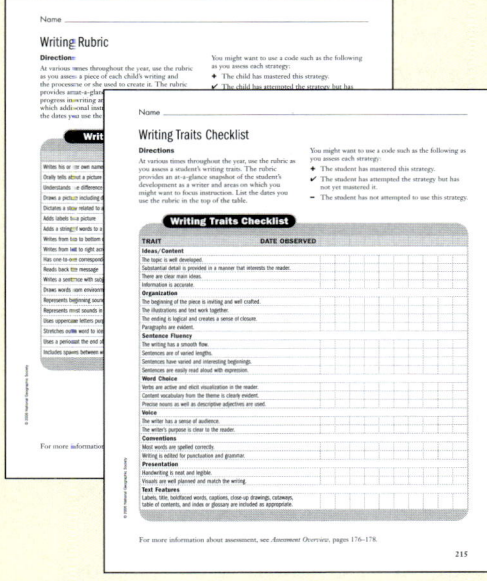

Assess Writing

Two valuable tools—the Writing Rubric and Writing Traits Checklist—allow teachers to measure students' progress in writing. The Rubric provides the opportunity for teachers to assess individual pieces of writing, while the Checklist is an ongoing snapshot of the qualities of strategic writers.

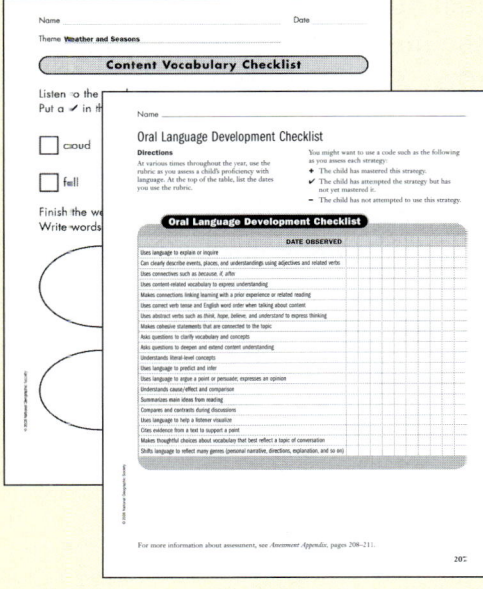

Assess Vocabulary and Oral Language

The Content Vocabulary Checklist can be used both before and after the theme to measure students' progress in understanding the academic vocabulary. As students learn language forms and functions, they become more adept at using oral language. The Oral Language Developmental Checklist measures students' progress in using oral language.

For more detailed notes and assessment options, see the corresponding pages in this Teacher's Guide or use our online guide at www.ngschoolpub.org

25

Diverse Language Learners

"What is most important for ESOL learners [English language learners] is to function effectively in English and through English while learning challenging academic content."

Teachers of English to Speakers of Other Languages (TESOL) Standards

Meeting Diverse Needs

Many students come to school without the background knowledge and language experiences they need for academic success. National Geographic's *Windows on Literacy: Language, Literacy & Vocabulary* program is designed to provide these young students with the support they need to achieve success from the very beginning. Today's classroom presents a demanding combination of student needs. While some students may be at-risk readers who lack prior knowledge of academic topics, others may be English language learners from diverse first-language backgrounds and experiences. Our goal as educators is to help all students reach their highest levels of achievement, particularly those students who need extra support. The *Language, Literacy & Vocabulary* program offers support for building basic background knowledge, oral language development, academic vocabulary, and content-area learning, helping these diverse groups of learners achieve success right from the start.

At-Risk Readers

Students enter our classrooms with a wide variety of academic needs. Some bring strong background knowledge and rich experiences to their learning while others have limited language development and exposure to topics that will support their learning in school. These students are often quite challenged by the daily tasks required of them and face frequent obstacles in their pursuit of literacy and content-area learning. For students struggling to acquire essential literacy skills, the challenges are compounded. As they grapple with the literacy tasks, they often fall behind in acquiring content-area vocabulary and concepts as well.

For at-risk readers, the challenges of literacy and content-area learning can be extremely demanding. These students need a scaffolded instructional plan that is designed to promote their academic success from the start. Instruction should offer explicit support for language, comprehension, fluency, vocabulary expansion, and content-area learning—the type of support provided by *Language, Literacy & Vocabulary*.

English Language Learners

Similarly, English language learners face distinct academic challenges. English immersion requires English learners to simultaneously acquire the English language while they are under pressure to learn English literacy. English literacy is a challenging learning task for many native English speakers. It is an extremely demanding undertaking for most English learners. We know that English learners can acquire conversational English quite rapidly, and some students become quite accomplished in conversational English in a couple of years. However, these same students also face the challenge of acquiring the academic forms of English grammar and vocabulary necessary for their academic success, which may take seven years or more to develop. As these students confront the demands of language learning, they must also acquire the grade-level academic content required of them, even in the face of gaps in their knowledge of the language.

The *Language, Literacy & Vocabulary* program accommodates the unique needs of English language learners by addressing individual levels of English language proficiency. Each Customize Instruction for ELLs feature provides options to support students at various proficiency levels: Newcomers/Beginning Students, Developing Students, and Expanding/Bridging Students.

LANGUAGE PROFICIENCY LEVELS

Newcomers/Beginning Students	Developing Students	Expanding/Bridging Students
• Have limited knowledge of English language	• Use English language purposefully	• Have strong conversational skills
• May use gestures, actions, and one- or two-word responses to communicate	• Produce complete sentences	• Can read, write, and speak effectively in English
• Primarily observe during classroom instruction	• Successfully use English to participate in small-group activities	• Participate more fully in classroom activities
• Benefit from activities that build listening comprehension and vocabulary	• Benefit from lessons that develop vocabulary and encourage higher levels of English language use	• Benefit from explicit strategy instruction, contextual support for academic tasks, and continued affirmation of their home cultures

Diverse Language Learners

English learners and at-risk readers alike need ample, daily instructional opportunities to develop language through explicit instructional activities designed to provide effective practice. Beneficial for all students, such explicit instruction promotes language practice and growth in at-risk learners and students who struggle with language acquisition and processing as well. *Windows on Literacy: Language, Literacy & Vocabulary* supports the needs of these diverse groups of students with an instructional plan that features an effective combination of English language development and research-based strategies:

- Extensive front-loading for concept and skill building combined with interactive use of visuals to support vocabulary, concepts, and comprehension development

- Teachers and students working together in collaborative activities that promote student interaction and maximize student talk

- Explicit and scaffolded instruction of academic forms and vocabulary

- Modeling, guided practice, and application of academic language forms and vocabulary

Four Seasons

There are four seasons every year.

spring   summer

winter   fall

3

Front-Loading, Concept Development, and Visual Support

Through front-loading, linguistic demands of the text are analyzed prior to the lesson by previewing and preteaching vocabulary and language forms and functions. Front-loading concepts and skills through use of the Theme Builder helps students build background and activate prior knowledge. Strong picture-text match throughout student materials makes abstract concepts more concrete. Visuals are combined with well-written text and graphic aids to deliver grade-level content in an engaging, understandable format.

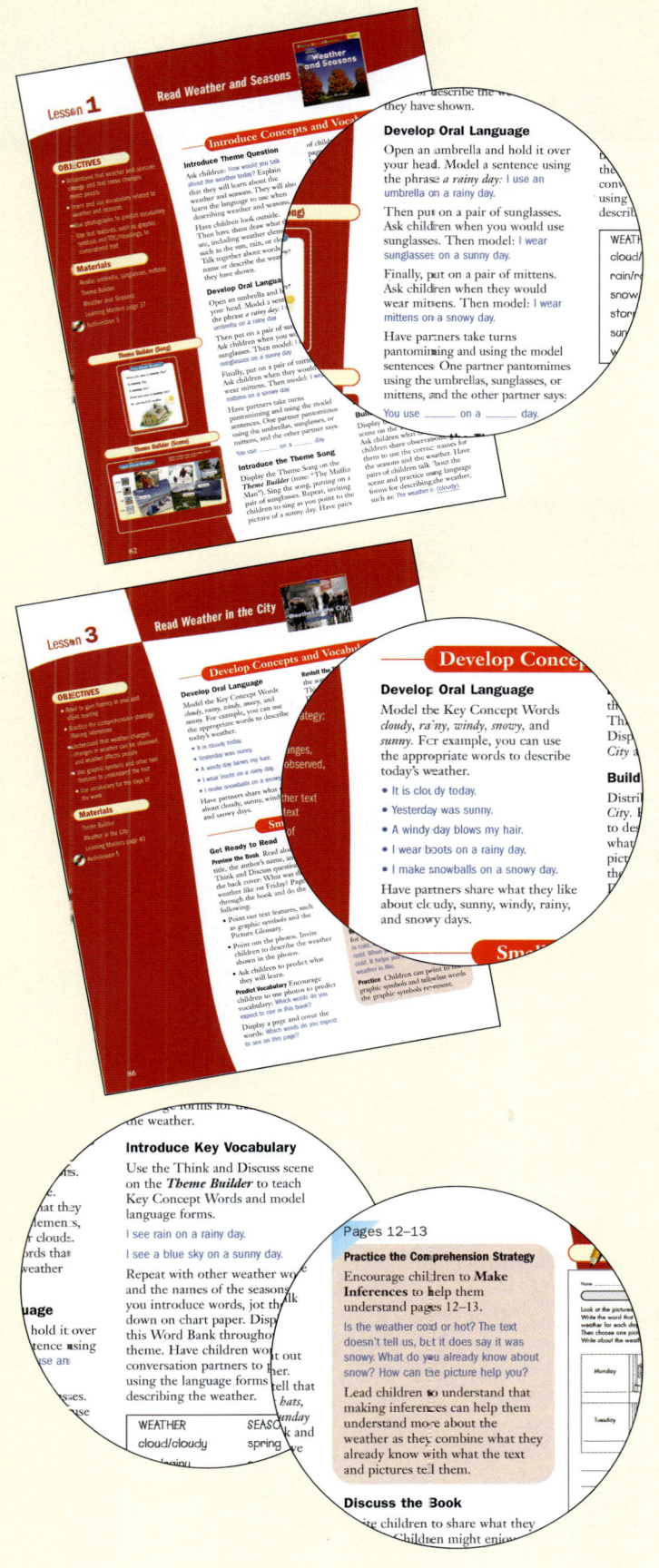

Promoting Interaction and Student Talk

Concepts and strategies are reinforced through meaningful opportunities for listening, speaking, reading, and writing. In this Develop Oral Language activity, students use realia to reinforce key concepts while building oral language. The Customize Instruction for ELLs feature accommodates various language acquisition levels.

Guided Practice and Application of Language Forms

Guided practice and application of language forms and vocabulary, modeled in sentence frames appropriate for students' language acquisition levels, are essential for their successful use of the functions of language. Students learn to use their developing oral language skills in appropriate contexts and for the correct purposes.

Explicit and Scaffolded Instruction

Explicit instruction in academic vocabulary, reading comprehension strategies, and language forms provides students with the knowledge and skills needed to access core content as they read. Strategies and skills for reading nonfiction and learning language are revisited throughout the lesson sequence, providing continuous support as students learn.

Flexible Use

Windows on Literacy: Language, Literacy & Vocabulary is designed to be used in a variety of classroom situations. This flexibility allows you to custom fit the program to match your scheduling and program needs.

Regular Classrooms

The chart below shows the suggested pacing for use in the regular classroom. Each theme can be completed in five days.

Pacing Guide: One Week for One Theme	
Day 1 · Lesson 1	Read Concept Book Introduce Concepts and Vocabulary Model and Share the Reading
Day 2 · Lesson 2	Reread Concept Book Develop Concepts and Vocabulary Introduce Comprehension Strategy Small Group Reading Modeled Writing
Day 3 · Lesson 3	Read First Related Nonfiction Book Develop Concepts and Vocabulary Small Group Reading Practice Comprehension Strategy Shared Writing
Day 4 · Lesson 4	Read Second Related Nonfiction Book Review Concepts and Vocabulary Small Group Reading Apply Comprehension Strategy Guided Writing
Day 5 · Lesson 5	Assess and Extend Rereading and Assessment Guided Writing Assessment Tools Optional Reading Home Connection

After-School Programs

Language, Literacy & Vocabulary works within a variety of after-school programs. Whether your after-school program meets every day or only three days a week, the program can easily be adjusted to meet your scheduling needs.

- For programs that meet every day, one theme can be completed each week of the summer school program. Use the Pacing Guide on page 30 for use within the regular classroom.

Pacing Guide:
One Week for One Theme

- For programs that meet three times per week, one theme can be completed every two weeks. Use the suggested plan shown below.

Pacing Guide:
Two Weeks for One Theme

Week 1 · Day 1 · Lesson 1	Week 2 · Day 1 · Lesson 4
Read Concept Book Introduce Concepts and Vocabulary Model and Share the Reading	Read Second Related Nonfiction Book Review Concepts and Vocabulary Small Group Reading Apply Comprehension Strategy
Week 1 · Day 2 · Lesson 2	**Week 2 · Day 2 · Begin Lesson 5**
Reread Concept Book Develop Concepts and Vocabulary Introduce Comprehension Strategy Small Group Reading Modeled Writing	Assess and Extend Rereading and Assessment Begin Guided Writing
Week 1 · Day 3 · Lesson 3	**Week 2 · Day 2 · Complete Lesson 5**
Read First Related Nonfiction Book Develop Concepts and Vocabulary Small Group Reading Practice Comprehension Strategy Shared Writing	Complete Guided Writing Assessment Tools Optional Reading Home Connection

Summer School Programs

Language, Literacy & Vocabulary is the perfect fit for your summer school program. When time is short and results matter, your class time must be productive. The five-day lesson plan allows you to complete one theme during each week of your summer school program. Whether your summer school plan includes a four-, five-, or six-week program, you can select developmentally appropriate themes that focus on the content areas of math, science, and social studies while developing strong literacy skills.

Four-Week Program	Five-Week Program	Six-Week Program
Choose four themes.	Choose five themes.	Choose six themes.

Overview

Plant Life

STANDARDS

ACADEMIC LANGUAGE/ELD

- Use academic vocabulary related to the study of plant life
- Use appropriate language forms to discuss and describe plants and to make predictions
- Develop fluency in reading, writing, listening to, and speaking English

SCIENCE

- Describe the specific sequence of steps that occur as plants grow
- Name and identify the basic parts of a plant and their functions
- Explain how people and animals need plants

READING/LANGUAGE ARTS

- Learn and apply the comprehension strategy: Predicting
- Use the text features: Picture Glossary and Labels
- Write about plant life
- Learn and use vocabulary related to plant life

Before Theme Assessment

To compare progress before and after teaching this theme, use one or more of the following informal assessment tools before beginning the theme.

- Oral Reading Record, page 185
- Fluency Scoring Guide, page 180
- Content Vocabulary Checklist, page 216
- Oral Language Developmental Checklist, page 228

Theme Materials

Concept Book

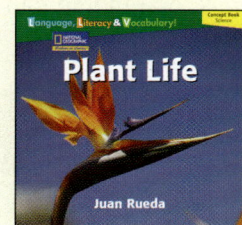
Plant Life
Juan Rueda

Nonfiction Books

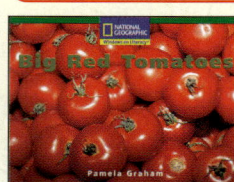
Big Red Tomatoes
Pamela Graham
Level 13

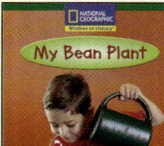
My Bean Plant
Joseph Ociano
Level 14

Theme Builder

Learning Masters

Language, Literacy & Vocabulary!
Learning Masters
Fluent

Audiolesson on CD

Take-Home Book Masters

Plant Life
by _____

Optional Reading

Windows on Literacy
Content-Based Fiction

A Tree of Her Own Level 13
The Mystery Seed Level 14

Windows on Literacy
Nonfiction

Seeds Grow Into Plants Level 10
Plants on My Plate Level 10
Peanuts Level 17
Cactuses Level 18

Instructional Highlights

Key Concepts

- Plants grow and change following a specific sequence.
- The basic parts of a plant have functions that help plants live and grow.
- People and animals need plants.

Comprehension Strategy

Predicting

Key Concept Words

flowers	seeds
fruit	shoot
leaves	soil
root	stem

Text Features

Labels

Picture Glossary

Theme Planner

Lesson 1*

Teacher's Guide pp. 34–35

Read
Plant Life

- Introduce Concepts and Vocabulary
- Model and Share the Reading

* Before you begin Lesson 1, you may want to use the Before Theme Assessment tools listed on page 32.

Lesson 2

Teacher's Guide pp. 36–37

Reread
Plant Life

- Develop Concepts and Vocabulary
- Introduce the Comprehension Strategy: Predicting
- Small Group Reading
- Modeled Writing

Lesson 3

Teacher's Guide pp. 38–39

Read
Big Red Tomatoes

- Develop Concepts and Vocabulary
- Small Group Reading
- Practice the Comprehension Strategy: Predicting
- Shared Writing

Lesson 4

Teacher's Guide pp. 40–41

Read
My Bean Plant

- Review Concepts and Vocabulary
- Small Group Reading
- Apply the Comprehension Strategy: Predicting
- Guided Writing

Lesson 5

Teacher's Guide pp. 42–43

Assess and Extend

- Rereading and Assessments
- Guided Writing
- Assessment Tools
- Optional Reading
- Home Connection

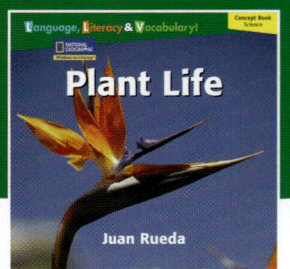

Plant Life

Juan Rueda

OBJECTIVES

- Understand the basic parts of a plant and how each functions to help the plant live and grow
- Learn and use vocabulary related to plant life
- Use photos to predict vocabulary
- Use the Picture Glossary to find the names of specific plant parts

Materials

Realia: small potted plant or photo of a small potted plant

Photos: a variety of plants

Theme Builder

Plant Life

Learning Masters page 9

Audiolesson 1

Theme Builder (Poem)

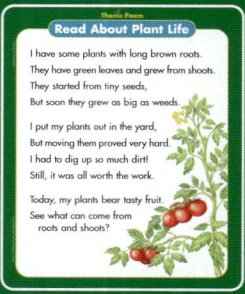

Theme Builder (Scene)

Introduce Concepts and Vocabulary

Introduce Theme Question

Ask students: What makes a plant grow? How are all plants similar? Explain that students will learn about plant life. They will also learn the language to use when describing plants and how they grow.

Turn and Talk Ask learning partners to describe kinds of plants they have seen at home or in other places.

Develop Oral Language

Hold up a potted plant or a photo of a potted plant. Ask students to describe the plant by counting the number of leaves they see and telling the color of the leaves. Model a sentence that includes nouns and adjectives. This plant has (five) leaves that are (green).

Then ask students to name something else they notice about the plant. Model another sentence that includes nouns and adjectives. This plant has leaves that are different sizes.

Remind students that describing words tell about a person, place, or thing.

Turn and Talk Have partners take turns describing plants in pictures you provide. Ask them to include nouns, such as *plant* or *leaf*, and adjectives to describe the plants.

Introduce Theme Poem

Display the Theme Poem on the *Theme Builder.* Have students say the poem in unison. Tell partners to use *Learning Masters* page 9 to practice reading the Theme Poem.

Introduce Key Vocabulary

Use the Think and Discuss scene to teach Key Concept Words and model language forms.

This plant has flowers that are yellow.

This plant has roots that are long.

This plant has delicious fruit.

Continue to model sentences, using the words listed below to help identify objects in the scene. As you introduce words, jot them down on chart paper. Display this Word Bank throughout the theme.

Turn and Talk Have students work with partners to describe other objects in the scene, using the words and language form for describing.

This plant has _____ that are _____.

This plant has a _____ that is _____.

flowers	leaves	seeds	soil
fruit	root	shoot	stem

Build Background

Display the Think and Discuss scene on the *Theme Builder* again. Ask students to tell what the people are doing. Have students tell how the actions of the people help them understand more about how plants are used.

Turn and Talk Ask partners to talk about what both the woman and panda are doing. For example: The woman has an orange carrot that she is eating. The panda has green leaves that it is eating.

Model and Share the Reading

Preview the Book

Distribute copies of *Plant Life*. Read aloud the title and the author's name. As you page through the book, point out:

- Captions and labels provide information.
- The boldfaced words are vocabulary words.
- The Picture Glossary helps with learning the meanings of words.

Predict Vocabulary

Encourage students to use photos to predict vocabulary: Which words do you expect to see in this book?

Display pages 6–7 and cover the words: Which words do you expect to see on these pages?

Students may mention objects on the page, such as *hose, woman, hands,* and *water*. Add these words to the Word Bank. Have students describe these items to partners. Continue the activity with other pages as time allows.

Model the Reading

Invite students to follow along as you read aloud pages 4–7 in *Plant Life*. Read fluently, modeling smooth, accurate reading with appropriate expression. After reading each pair of pages, pause to think aloud. Encourage students to ask questions and make observations.

Pages 4–5

Think Aloud This is like the Think and Discuss picture we talked about earlier. The labels tell me the parts of the plants and what plants need to grow. The panda is eating leaves. The woman is eating a carrot. This tells me that humans and animals use plants for food.

Pages 6–7

Think Aloud As I read the *caption*, the words under the pictures, I can match what I read to the pictures. I read *water* and see a woman watering a garden. I read the word *soil* and see a picture of hands in dirt.

Share the Reading

Now have partners complete the reading. Encourage students to pause after reading one or two pages and have conversations about what they have read. Ask them to share questions they have about the pages, as well as ideas about what they will read next.

Reread for Fluency

To have students practice fluent reading, read aloud the first few sentences of *Plant Life*. Be sure to pause after each comma. Have students read subsequent sentences in unison, imitating how you read. Then have students reread the entire book independently to build fluency. See *Customize the Reading*.

Theme Poem

I have some plants with long brown roots.
They have green leaves and grew from shoots.
They started from tiny seeds,
But soon they grew as big as weeds.

I put my plants out in the yard,
But moving them proved very hard.
I had to dig up so much dirt!
Still, it was all worth the work.

Today, my plants bear tasty fruit.
See what can come from roots and shoots?

Science: Plant Life   Learning Masters **9**

Customize the Reading

Students reread and talk about Plant Life *on their own to build fluency.*

- *Students who are not yet able to read the book can point to and name the objects they recognize on each page.*
- *Students who need extra support can reread the book while listening to the audiolesson.*
- *Students who can read the book might read independently or aloud with a partner.*

Customize Instruction for ELLs

Newcomers/Beginning Hold up the potted plant and point to each part. Ask, "What is this part?"

Developing Hold up the potted plant. Ask students to name the plant parts you point to, using the following sentence frame in their answers: This part of the plant is the _____.

Expanding/Bridging Hold up the potted plant. Ask students to suggest sentences to describe the plant's parts.

Lesson 2

Reread *Plant Life*

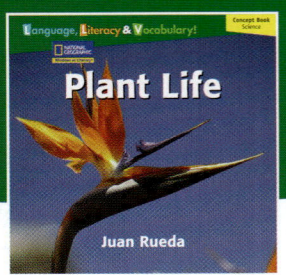

Language, Literacy & Vocabulary!
Plant Life
Juan Rueda

OBJECTIVES

- Understand that people and animals need plants
- Use vocabulary to name parts of a plant
- Learn the comprehension strategy: Predicting
- Read to gain fluency in oral and silent reading
- Write about how humans and animals use plants

Materials

Theme Builder

Plant Life

Learning Masters pages 8, 10, 11

 Audiolesson 1

Theme Builder (Graphic Organizer)

Develop Concepts and Vocabulary

Develop Oral Language

Display the graphic organizer showing photos of humans and animals using plants and plant products. Ask students to describe what they see. How are the humans and animals using plants?

Turn and Talk Ask learning partners to choose one of the photos and further discuss how the plant is being used.

Revisit the Theme Poem Display the theme poem on the *Theme Builder*. Have a group of students stand and read the poem together. Have them emphasize the plant parts by saying those words louder.

Build Background

Display the graphic organizer on the *Theme Builder*. Discuss the photos. Ask students to tell how humans and animals use plants in similar ways. Next, have them tell how humans and animals use plants in different ways. Point out that people and animals need plants.

Turn and Talk Have partners choose one of the photos from the graphic organizer and discuss it further, describing how the plant is being used.

Begin Vocabulary Log As students read, encourage them to use sticky notes to tag words they would like to save. After reading, students can record the words and their notes about them. Model tagging a word and recording it on the Vocabulary Log for students.

Use *Learning Masters* page 8.

Introduce the Comprehension Strategy

Introduce Predicting

Students use their prior knowledge, as well as illustrations and text, to tell what they think an entire reading selection—or parts of a reading selection—will be about.

Think Aloud Before I read a book, I use what I already know plus what I see and read. Then I can make a prediction. I can tell what I think the book will be about. I can also predict what will happen next as I read. Then I read on to see if I was right about my predictions.

Model Predicting

Turn to pages 4–5 and model the comprehension strategy of predicting.

I see questions at the top of page 5, so **I can predict** that the book will answer these questions on the next pages.

I predict that I will learn more about plant parts and how they grow **because** the pictures show parts of plants. The pages also show a woman eating a carrot and a panda eating leaves. **I predict** that I will learn more about how humans and other animals use plants.

For additional practice in predicting, have partners work on *Learning Masters* page 10.

Small Group Reading

As students read, invite them to share what they notice. Use some of the suggestions below to encourage observations and talk about the book.

Pages 6–9
Support Comprehension Guide students to look at the photos and read the text on pages 6–7. Have them make a prediction about what may happen when someone plants a seed and gives it warmth, water, and light. *(A plant grows.)*

Pages 10–13
Check Understanding After reading these pages, what can you figure out is true about most plants? *(They grow the same way. They have a way of making seeds in order to make new plants.)*

Pages 14–15
Support Comprehension Point out the diagram in the right margin. Ask students why the information might be shown in this way. Invite a volunteer to point to parts of the diagram while explaining the process they show.

Pages 16–19
Check Understanding Have students use the Word Bank to help them describe the photos. What do the photos show about how plants can be used?

Discuss the Book
Invite students to share what they learned. Ask them to tell, in their own words, how all plants are alike. Then have them tell ways plants are used by humans and animals. Encourage students to use the words in the Word Bank to discuss what they have read. Remind students to add words to their Vocabulary Logs.

Students can complete *Learning Masters* page 11.

Reread for Fluency
Have students follow along as you read aloud the four sentences on page 12 without taking a breath. Ask why it was hard for them to understand you. *(You didn't pause, and you ran everything together.)* Point out that punctuation helps you know when to pause. Remind students that a period means to pause before reading the next sentence. Ask a volunteer to read the sentences, pausing appropriately at the periods. Have partners reread pages 8–11, focusing on pausing for punctuation. For additional suggestions, see *Customize the Reading.*

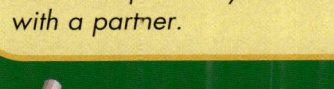

Learning Masters/pages 8, 10

Name _____

Vocabulary Log

List words you want to remember. Tell what each word means. Add notes or drawings about the word.

Word	What It Means	Notes or Drawings

8 Learning Masters

10 Learning Masters   *Science: Plant Life*

Customize the Reading
Students reread and talk about Plant Life, *using one of the following options:*

- *Look through the pages, identifying as many plant parts as possible in each of the photos.*
- *Reread the book while following along with the audiolesson.*
- *Read independently or read aloud with a partner.*

Learning Masters/page 11

Name _____

Plant Life

Write two questions you might find on a test about plant life. Then exchange papers with a partner. Answer each other's questions. Discuss your questions and answers.

Example: What plant part grows underground?
  A. leaf
  B. stem
  C. root
  D. flower

1. _____
  A. _____
  B. _____
  C. _____
  D. _____

2. _____
  A. _____
  B. _____
  C. _____
  D. _____

Science: Plant Life   Learning Masters **11**

Modeled Writing

Use the graphic organizer on the *Theme Builder* to review some Key Concepts of the theme. Prepare to model writing an interesting beginning.

Think Aloud I'll write about how a plant grows from a seed. My beginning should get readers' interest. I'll use interesting words that help the reader picture a seed changing and a plant beginning to grow.

The soil is warm and moist, and a little seed begins to grow.

Think Aloud Saying that something is starting to happen can catch readers' interest. Describing words, like *warm* and *moist,* can help readers picture the scene.

White roots stretch down from the seed, and a thin green shoot pushes up. The shoot breaks through the top of the soil. It stretches up in the sunlight.

Lesson 3

Read *Big Red Tomatoes*

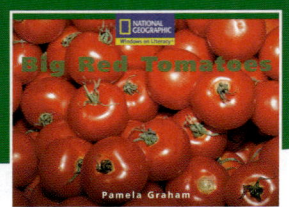

OBJECTIVES

- Read to gain fluency in oral and silent reading
- Practice the comprehension strategy: Predicting
- Develop an understanding that all plants have parts that help them live and grow and that plants change in a sequence as they grow
- Use labels to comprehend text
- Use the information and photos in the text to make an inference about who uses tomatoes for food

Materials

Realia: tomato plant with flowers, sliced ripe tomato, whole tomato; assortment of vegetables

Theme Builder

Big Red Tomatoes

Learning Masters page 12

Audiolesson 1

Develop Concepts and Vocabulary

Develop Oral Language

Model the Key Concept Words *seeds*, *soil*, *leaves*, and *flowers* as you show the tomato plant and sliced tomato. Ask volunteers to use three words to describe each of the parts you named. What three words can you use to describe the leaves? The soil? The flower? The seeds?

Turn and Talk Have learning partners use some of the describing words from the discussion to make up a sentence for each part of the plant. For example: The leaves on this tomato plant are *small* and *white* and *pretty*.

Revisit the Theme Poem Display the poem on the *Theme Builder*. Help students write two more rhyming lines for the poem.

Build Background

Distribute copies of *Big Red Tomatoes*. Show students the tomato plant and other vegetables you have brought in. Ask students about their experiences with vegetable gardens, and have them describe what they have seen in them. Find out how many students like to eat raw tomatoes and how many like tomatoes cooked in foods, such as pizza sauce.

Small Group Reading

Get Ready to Read

Preview the Book Read aloud the title, the author's name, and the Think and Discuss question on the back cover: How does a tomato grow?

Page through the book and do the following:

- Point out the labels in the book. Discuss how they are different from those in *Plant Life*.
- Discuss the photos, and ask students why the author may have included them.
- Ask students to predict what they will learn as they read the book.

Predict Vocabulary Encourage students to use photos to predict vocabulary: Which words do you expect to see in this book?

Display a page and cover the words: Which words do you expect to see on this page?

List the words students provide. Add Key Concept Words in the book that students do not mention.

Text Feature: Labels

Introduce Point out the label on page 3. Labels tell us what we see in a photo. Labels may also point out what the author wants us to notice.

Model On pages 4–5, I see three labels: *salad*, *sandwich*, and *sauce*. I recognize the salad. I'm not sure what the second picture shows, but the label tells me: *sandwich*. The third label says *sauce*.

Practice Have students read the labels on page 9. Ask what the author wants them to notice. *(the plant's leaves and the soil)*

Read the Book

As students read, invite them to share what they notice. Use the suggestions below to encourage observations and talk about the book.

Pages 2–5

Support Comprehension Poll students to see how many eat tomatoes in a salad, how many on a sandwich, and how many in a sauce. Ask students what they learned as a result of their poll.

Pages 6–13

Key Concept Words *flowers*, *leaves*, *seeds*, *soil*

Support Comprehension As students read these pages, ask them to point out the labels and read them aloud. Have students predict how the tomato seeds will change.

Pages 14–19

Support Comprehension Have students confirm their predictions. Then make certain they understand the meaning of *ripen* on page 16. Point out that other vegetables, such as bell peppers, start out one color and change to another color as they ripen.

Pages 20–21

Practice the Comprehension Strategy

After reading pages 20–21, encourage students to predict how the tomatoes will be used. Have them think about what they have already read and then **Make a Prediction.**

Pages 22–23

Support Comprehension Have students confirm their predictions. I predicted we would see tomatoes used in food. I was right. The foods are the same ones shown in the beginning of the book.

Discuss the Book

Invite students to use the Word Bank to discuss the book and to share what they learned. Then have students name something they found interesting. Tell students to add words to their Vocabulary Logs.

Use *Learning Masters* page 12.

Reread for Fluency

Have students reread the entire book independently to build fluency. See *Customize the Reading.*

Name _____

Big Red Tomatoes

Here are chapter names and numbers in a book about tomatoes.

Chapter 1: How Tomatoes Grow
Chapter 2: Tomato Flowers
Chapter 3: Where Tomatoes Grow
Chapter 4: Picking Tomatoes
Chapter 5: From Farm to Market

Where could you find the answer to each question?
Write the chapter number on the line.
Then talk about the answers to the questions with a partner.

1. What is a seedling? Chapter _____

2. What color is a tomato flower? Chapter _____

3. How does the grocery store get tomatoes for me to buy? Chapter _____

4. How are tomatoes taken out of the field? Chapter _____

5. What is the best place to grow tomato plants? Chapter _____

6. When does the tomato plant get leaves? Chapter _____

12 Learning Masters   *Science: Plant Life*

Customize the Reading

Students reread and talk about Big Red Tomatoes *using one of the following options:*

- *Look through the pages, using the photos to tell what is happening on each page.*
- *Reread the book while following along with the audiolesson.*
- *Read independently or aloud with a partner.*

Shared Writing

Review the writing you modeled in Lesson 2. Invite students to help you continue to write about a growing plant. Review the Key Concept Words for suggestions of other plant parts. Help students list interesting words to describe the plant parts and the actions of the plant as it grows. You may wish to draw a plant to include with the writing and add labels to your drawing.

Customize Instruction for ELLs

Newcomers/Beginning Have students draw a plant and label the plant parts, using words from the Word Bank.

Developing Encourage partners to list words that could describe a plant's actions as it grows.

Expanding/Bridging Ask students to suggest an interesting beginning that will catch readers' interest.

Lesson 4

Read *My Bean Plant*

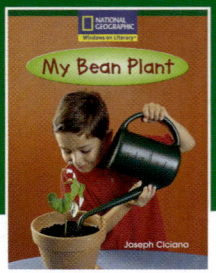

OBJECTIVES

- Read to gain fluency in oral and silent reading
- Apply the comprehension strategy: Predicting
- Understand that plants grow and change in a specific sequence
- Use a Picture Glossary to understand new words
- Use photos to aid in determining word meaning

Materials

Theme Builder

Photos: sunflower plant, African violet

Realia: green beans and other green vegetables, such as broccoli, Brussels sprouts, and lettuce

My Bean Plant

Learning Masters pages 13, 14

Take-Home Book Masters: *Plant Life*

Audiolesson 1

Take-Home Book Masters

Plant Life

by _____

Review Concepts and Vocabulary

Develop Oral Language

Review the meanings of the Key Concept Words *soil*, *seeds*, *root*, *shoot*, *stem*, *leaves*, and *flowers*. Display a photo of a giant sunflower plant and then of an African violet. Model using each word in a sentence.

Here are the seeds on the giant sunflower plant.

The leaves on this plant are purple.

Turn and Talk Assign two words listed above to each pair of learning partners. Have partners create sentences for their words. Have all share their sentences in a group.

Revisit the Theme Poem Display the poem on the *Theme Builder*. Have three students stand and each read one stanza of the poem. Then read it aloud again as a class.

Build Background

Distribute copies of *My Bean Plant*. Invite students to share what they know about vegetables. Ask them to name and discuss green vegetables you display. Point out how all these plants are alike.

These plants are all vegetables. The plant in the book we will read is a bean plant. A bean is a vegetable.

Small Group Reading

Get Ready to Read

Preview the Book Read aloud the title, the author's name, and the Think and Discuss question on the back cover: What plant would you like to grow?

Page through the book and do the following:

- Point out the labels on the pages.
- Point out that the photos show the steps in a process.
- Ask students to predict what they will learn.

Predict Vocabulary Encourage students to use photos to predict vocabulary: Which words do you expect to see in this book?

Display a page and cover the words: Which words do you expect to see on this page?

List the words students provide. Add Key Concept Words in the book that students do not mention.

Text Feature: Picture Glossary

Introduce Have students turn to page 16 in *My Bean Plant*. This is a Picture Glossary. It shows important words from the book. The words are in alphabetical order. The pictures help you know what the words mean.

Model Have students turn to page 12. I read the label, but I'm still not sure what a bean pod is. I'll look in the Picture Glossary on page 16. Under *pod*, I see more clearly what a bean pod is.

Practice Have students turn to page 9 and choose one label to look up. Have students compare the picture on page 9 with the picture in the Picture Glossary.

Read the Book

As students read, invite them to share what they notice. Use some of the suggestions below to encourage and talk about the book.

Pages 2–3

Key Concept Words *seeds, soil*

Support Comprehension Ask students if they have seen any of these items and if so, where. Then ask what they think the boy will do with the items.

Pages 4–7

Key Concept Words *root, shoot*

Check Understanding We can see a root and a shoot. Where is the root? Where is the shoot? What is happening to them?

Pages 8–11

Key Concept Words *stem, leaves, flowers*

Support Comprehension Explain that on many plants, the fruit of the plant grows where the flowers once were.

Pages 12–15

Apply the Comprehension Strategy

Have students read pages 12–13. Encourage them to **Make a Prediction** about what they will read and see when they turn the pages.

I predict _____ because _____.

Have students turn to pages 14–15 to confirm their predictions.

Discuss the Book

Invite students to use the Word Bank to tell about the book and share what they have learned. Have them use the Picture Glossary to review what they saw in the book. Remind students to add words to their Vocabulary Logs.

Use *Learning Masters* page 13.

Reread for Fluency

Have students reread the entire book independently to build fluency. See *Customize the Reading.*

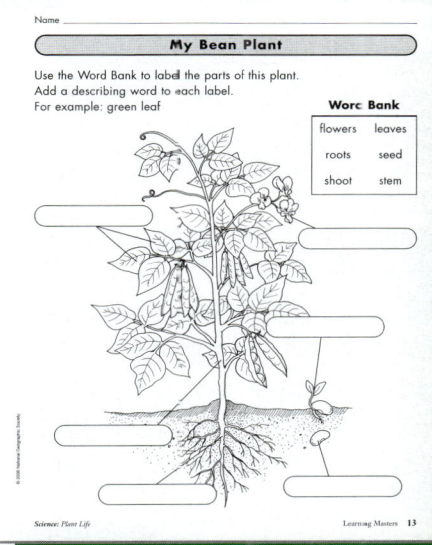
Customize the Reading

Students reread and talk about My Bean Plant *using one of the following options:*

- Look through the pages, summarizing the plant's sequence of growth steps.
- Reread the book while following along with the audiolesson.
- Read independently or aloud with a partner.

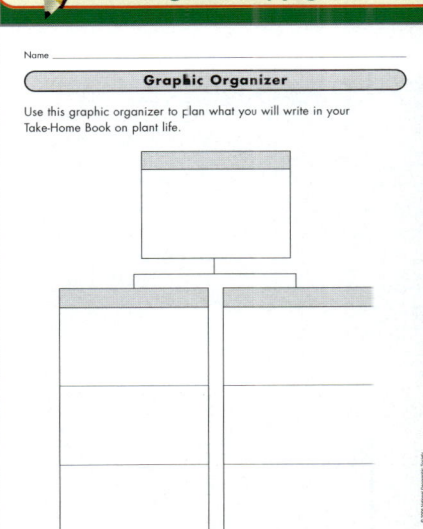

Guided Writing

Distribute copies of the **Take-Home Book Masters.** Read the title and page through the book. Explain that students will write books about the different parts of some plants. Work with students to:

- Complete the Contents page and the Picture Glossary.
- Label the parts of the plants.
- Share writing ideas for each set of pages.

Record students' writing ideas for the pages of their books on chart paper.

Have learning partners talk together to plan what they will write. Explain that each partner will complete a graphic organizer.

Students may add these headings to their graphic organizers: *Plants* (top), *Plant Parts and What They Do* (left column), *How People or Animals Use Parts* (right column).

Students could list in column one the plant parts shown in their Take-Home Books and tell what the plant parts do. In column two, students can tell how people or animals use the plant parts. Display the Word Bank and remind students to check their Vocabulary Logs as they begin to write.

Use *Learning Masters* page 14.

OBJECTIVES

- Use Key Concepts and Key Concept Words in writing
- Demonstrate oral language proficiency
- Demonstrate comprehension of theme selections
- Read related titles to reinforce Key Concepts and vocabulary

Materials

Take-Home Book Masters: *Plant Life*
Learning Masters pages 6–7, 15–16
Assessment Masters pages 179, 180, 185, 214, 215, 216, 228

Take-Home Book Masters

Plant Life

by _____

Rereading and Assessments

Allow time for students to independently reread the theme selections. Display the Word Bank for students' reference as they read.

As students reread, meet with individuals. Use the assessment tools listed on page 43 to evaluate students' progress and to update their records.

Guided Writing

Students continue writing the Take-Home Books they began in Lesson 4. Review the group list of writing ideas. Display the Word Bank.

Page through the theme books to review the text features, including the Picture Glossary and labels. Talk about text features students could add to their Take-Home Books. For example, they might add additional labels to the parts of plants featured in their books.

Point out that good writers:

- Make notes about what they want to include in their books. Students may add notes to their graphic organizers.

- Decide which information is most interesting and important. Students then focus on this information as they write.

- Add describing words and details to help the reader picture what is described.

Have students complete the Picture Glossary and About the Author last.

As students write, circulate to coach and support individuals.

Have partners exchange books and discuss what they like in each other's books. For example, a partner might like the words the other partner used to describe something. Have each writer decide what changes to make and then add any final touches.

Customize Instruction for ELLs

Newcomers/Beginning Have students add their own illustrations of plant parts that are not pictured, such as *roots* and *shoots*.

Developing Ask questions to prompt contributions to writing, such as: "How do flowers change on some plants?" *(Flowers become fruits or vegetables.)*

Expanding/Bridging Challenge students to vary sentence lengths. For example, they might want to have a long sentence followed by some short sentences.

Assessment Tools

Self-Assessment

Allow students to reflect and assess their own learning by completing *Learning Masters* pages 6–7.

- What I Learned, page 6
- How I Learned, page 7

Reading

The following assessment tools can help you evaluate and record students' progress in reading and understanding the theme books.

- Retelling Guide and Scoring Rubric, page 179
- Fluency Scoring Guide, page 180
- Oral Reading Record, page 185

Writing

Use the completed Take-Home Books and the following tools to assess students' development as writers.

- Writing Rubric, page 214
- Writing Traits Checklist, page 215

Content Assessment

Arrange a group walk. Have partners find two or three different plants and draw pictures and take notes about the plants. Have each pair make a poster with drawings of the plants they saw, with plant parts labeled. Have students list on the poster what plant parts do to help the plant (including parts that were hidden from view), and present their poster to other pairs.

Vocabulary and Oral Language

Use the following resources, in addition to the Think and Discuss scene on the *Theme Builder,* to assess oral language development.

- Content Vocabulary Checklist, page 216
- Oral Language Developmental Checklist, page 228

Learning Masters/pages 6–7

Optional Reading

Reading related titles allows students to explore concepts and vocabulary at different levels. It also allows them to use reading strategies in different types of texts. Encourage students to compare the theme books to the books in the next column.

Optional Titles

These related *Windows on Literacy* titles reinforce Key Concepts of the *Plant Life* theme.

Nonfiction Titles

Seeds Grow Into Plants Level 10

Plants on My Plate Level 10

Peanuts Level 17

Cactuses Level 18

Fiction Titles

A Tree of Her Own Level 13

The Mystery Seed Level 14

Related Fiction Titles

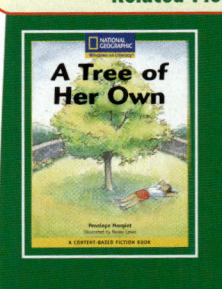 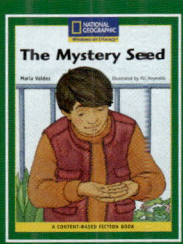

Learning Masters/pages 15–16

Home Connection

The Family Focus letters on *Learning Masters* pages 15–16 summarize key concepts about plant life.

In the Share and Learn activity, family members examine plants they have at home to find each of the plant parts.

Then and Now

ACADEMIC LANGUAGE/ELD

- Use academic vocabulary related to the study of the past and the present
- Use appropriate language forms to compare the past with the present and to make connections
- Develop fluency in reading, writing, listening to, and speaking English

SOCIAL STUDIES

- Learn about information sources to find out about the past
- Compare the past with the present to show how things have changed over time
- Describe how different technologies have improved and changed over time

READING/LANGUAGE ARTS

- Learn and apply the comprehension strategy: Making Connections
- Use the text features: Glossary and Highlighted Vocabulary
- Write about the past and the present
- Learn and use vocabulary related to the past and the present

Before Theme Assessment

To compare progress before and after teaching this theme, use one or more of the following informal assessment tools before beginning the theme.

- Oral Reading Record, page 187
- Fluency Scoring Guide, page 180
- Content Vocabulary Checklist, page 217
- Oral Language Developmental Checklist, page 228

Theme Materials

Concept Book

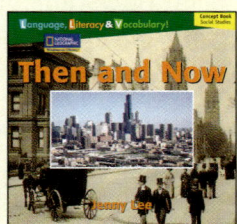

Nonfiction Books

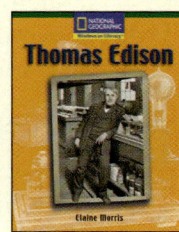

Level 14

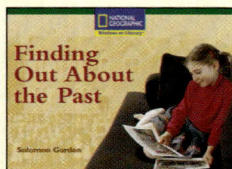

Level 14

Theme Builder

Learning Masters

Audiolesson on CD

Take-Home Book Masters

Optional Reading

Windows on Literacy Content-Based Fiction

Grandma's Attic Level 13

Driving Tin Lizzie Level 14

Windows on Literacy Nonfiction

School Today and Long Ago Level 11

Our Town Level 13

Henry Ford and the Car Level 19

Timelines 1900–2000 Level 20

Instructional Highlights

Key Concepts

- There are many information sources people can use to find out about the past.
- Comparing the past with the present shows how things have changed over time.
- Different kinds of technologies can be improved and changed over time.

Comprehension Strategy

Making Connections

Key Concept Words

change	machine
invent	the past
long ago	school

Text Features

Glossary

Highlighted Vocabulary

Theme Planner

Lesson 1*

Teacher's Guide
pp. 46–47

Read
Then and Now

- Introduce Concepts and Vocabulary
- Model and Share the Reading

* Before you begin Lesson 1, you may want to use the Before Theme Assessment tools listed on page 44.

Lesson 2

Teacher's Guide
pp. 48–49

Reread
Then and Now

- Develop Concepts and Vocabulary
- Introduce the Comprehension Strategy: Making Connections
- Small Group Reading
- Modeled Writing

Lesson 3

Teacher's Guide
pp. 50–51

Read
Thomas Edison

- Develop Concepts and Vocabulary
- Small Group Reading
- Practice the Comprehension Strategy: Making Connections
- Shared Writing

Lesson 4

Teacher's Guide
pp. 52–53

Read
Finding Out About the Past

- Review Concepts and Vocabulary
- Small Group Reading
- Apply the Comprehension Strategy: Making Connections
- Guided Writing

Lesson 5

Teacher's Guide
pp. 54–55

Assess and Extend

- Rereading and Assessments
- Guided Writing
- Assessment Tools
- Optional Reading
- Home Connection

Read *Then and Now*

Introduce Concepts and Vocabulary

OBJECTIVES

- Compare the past with the present to show how things have changed over time
- Learn and use vocabulary related to then and now
- Use photos to predict vocabulary
- Use text features, such as highlighted vocabulary, to learn new words

Materials

Photos: pictures of home and a classroom (preferably of your school) in the past

Theme Builder

Then and Now

Learning Masters page 17

Audiolesson 2

Theme Builder (Poem)

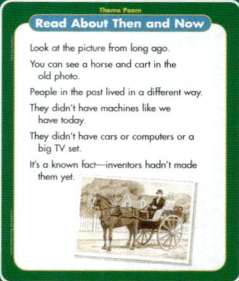

Theme Builder (Scene)

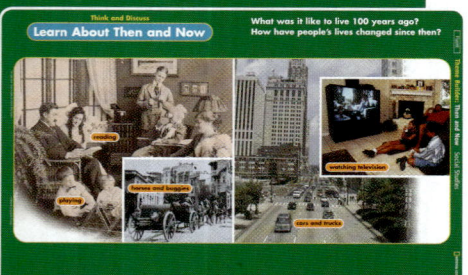

Introduce Theme Question

Ask students: What are some things that you use in school or at home that your grandparents didn't use when they were your age? Explain that students will learn about changes from the past to the present. They will also learn the language to use when comparing the past with the present.

Turn and Talk Have learning partners list some things that people didn't have in the past. Have pairs compare their lists.

Develop Oral Language

Display a classroom photo from the past. Model a sentence such as the following: In the past, students dipped their pens in inkwells before writing.

Then ask students what we use for writing today. Model a sentence such as the following: Today, we use a ballpoint pen for writing.

Tell students that they just compared a past way of writing with a present way. Explain that one way to find out about the past is to look at old photos.

Turn and Talk Have partners each compare something in the photo to something used today.

Introduce Theme Poem

Display the Theme Poem on the *Theme Builder.* Have students say the poem in unison. Have partners use *Learning Masters* page 17 to practice reading the Theme Poem.

Introduce Key Vocabulary

Use the Think and Discuss scene to teach Key Concept Words and model language forms.

Long ago, people used horses to get places. Today, people use cars to get places.

In the past, people didn't have TVs in their homes. Today, most people have TVs in their homes.

Over time, inventors made many machines. These machines have changed the way people live.

Continue to model sentences using the words listed below. As you introduce words, jot them down on chart paper. Display this Word Bank throughout the theme.

Turn and Talk Have students work with partners to practice using the words in sentences to compare things in the past with things now. For example: In the past, people _____. Today, people _____.

change	machine
invent	the past
long ago	school

Build Background

Display the Think and Discuss scene on the *Theme Builder* again. Ask students to describe the pictures.

Turn and Talk Have partners talk about what families did at home in the past and what they do today. Practice the language used for comparing. For example: In the past, families _____ at home. Today, families _____ at home.

Model and Share the Reading

Preview the Book

Distribute copies of *Then and Now*. Read aloud the title and the author's name. As you page through the book, point out:

- Most pages have pairs of pictures that compare things in the past with things today.
- Headings are important and tell about the main topic of each two pages. There is a Contents page.
- A Picture Glossary helps with remembering new words and phrases.

Predict Vocabulary

Encourage students to use pictures to predict vocabulary: Which words do you expect to see in this book?

Display pages 6–7 and cover the words: Which words do you expect to see on these pages?

Students may mention objects such as bikes, cars, and sewing machines. Have students talk with partners and name objects seen in the pictures. Continue the activity with other pages as time allows.

Model the Reading

Invite students to follow along as you read aloud pages 4–7 in *Then and Now*. Read fluently, modeling smooth, accurate reading with appropriate expression. Encourage students to ask questions and make observations.

Pages 4–5
Think Aloud This is like the Think and Discuss scene on the *Theme Builder.* I see that the pictures on page 4 show life in the past. They show a street and a home. I see that the pictures on page 5 show a street and a home as they are today. As I read the book, I will look for pairs of pictures—one that shows things in the past and one that shows things now.

Pages 6–7
Think Aloud As I look at the photos, I look for things as they were in the past. I ask myself, "How are things different today?" For example, people still use sewing machines, but now sewing machines use electricity. Today, cars are bigger, and they have doors.

Share the Reading

Now have partners complete the reading. Encourage them to stop after each pair of pages and have conversations about what they read. Ask them to share what they notice about how things in the past and things today are different.

Reread for Fluency

To have students practice fluent reading, read aloud pages 8–9. Have students echo-read each sentence after you finish, imitating your model. Then have students reread the entire book independently to build fluency. See *Customize the Reading.*

Customize the Reading

Students reread and talk about Then and Now *on their own to build fluency.*

- Students who are not yet able to read the book can say which pictures show "the past" and which show "today." They can also name any objects.
- Students who need extra support can reread the book while listening to the audiolesson.
- Students who can read the book might read independently or aloud with partners.

Customize Instruction for ELLs

Newcomers/Beginning During reading, ask students "before" questions such as, "What did people use for cooking before there were electric and gas stoves?" Have students point to the answer or answer with a word or two.

Developing During reading, ask students to complete "before" statements, such as, "Before there were electric stoves, _____."

Expanding/Bridging Encourage students to talk about two pictures using the language form: Before there were _____, there were _____.

Reread *Then and Now*

OBJECTIVES

- Compare the past with the present to understand how things change
- Use vocabulary to talk about how things in the past and the present are different
- Learn the comprehension strategy: Making Connections
- Read to gain fluency in oral and silent reading
- Write about how things in the past and present are different

Materials

Photos: Sets of photos showing similar places, things, or activities in the past and today

Theme Builder

Then and Now

Learning Masters pages 8, 18, 19

Audiolesson 2

Theme Builder (Graphic Organizer)

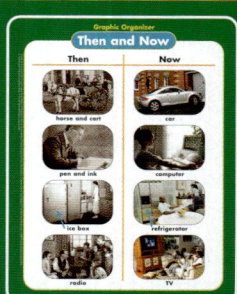

Develop Concepts and Vocabulary

Develop Oral Language

Display photos that show things from the past and similar things today. Ask students to compare things in the photos, using these language forms: In the past, _____. Today, _____.

Turn and Talk Encourage learning partners to talk about the pictures, making as many comparisons as they can, using the language forms.

Revisit the Theme Poem Display the Theme Poem on the Theme Builder. Have students read the poem in unison. Read the poem again, replacing *cars* and *computers* with two different modern items. Have students say the poem using the new items.

Build Background

Display the graphic organizer on the *Theme Builder* with only the headings and top photos uncovered. In the past, people used horses and buggies to get places. Today, they use cars. Uncover the next picture in the left column, and have students predict the item in the right column.

Turn and Talk Encourage partners to make oral sentences for each pair of items.

Begin Vocabulary Log As students read, encourage them to use sticky notes to tag words that they would like to save. After reading, students can record the words and their notes about them.

Use *Learning Masters* page 8.

Introduce the Comprehension Strategy

Introduce Making Connections

Students make connections to what they are reading by connecting a new concept to something they have already read, experienced, or know.

Think Aloud When I read a book, I look at the words and the pictures. Sometimes I can remember seeing the objects in real life. I connect what I have experienced and know already to what I am reading. When I do this, I am **making a connection.** This helps me better understand the book.

Model Making Connections

Turn to pages 8–9 and model the comprehension strategy and language forms for making connections.

I can connect to the pictures of things in the kitchen.

They remind me of my kitchen at home. I have seen my family members use a washing machine. I look in the refrigerator every day to get food. And I know what an electric stove is like because we have one in our kitchen.

This connection helps me understand how the machines of today work and what they do. This information helps me understand how the machines from the past may have worked and what they did.

For additional practice in making connections, have partners work on *Learning Masters* page 18.

Small Group Reading

As students read, invite them to share what they notice. Use some of the suggestions below to encourage observation and talk about the book.

Pages 4–13
Support Comprehension Guide students to connect to things in the past. *Do you see anything on these pages that reminds you of something you use at home?*

Pages 14–17
Check Understanding *Describe things that are the same and that are different in cities in the past and cities of today. (Both have buildings and roads. Modern cities have highways.)*

Pages 18–19
Check Understanding Have students use the Word Bank to describe how learning has changed through time. *Describe a school classroom in the past.*

Discuss the Book

Invite students to share what they learned. Have students describe how life was different long ago. Have them suggest ways that they can learn about the past. Encourage them to use the words in the Word Bank to discuss what they have read. Remind students to add words to their Vocabulary Logs.

Students can complete *Learning Masters* page 19.

Reread for Fluency

Have students follow along as you read pages 6–7 in a flat tone, without rising intonation for questions. Ask how you can improve your reading. *(Read with expression.)* Demonstrate reading the same text with expression and correct intonation. Have partners reread the book. Ask them to focus on improving the expression of their reading. Remind them to pay attention to ending punctuation. For other suggestions, see *Customize the Reading*

Learning Masters/pages 8, 18

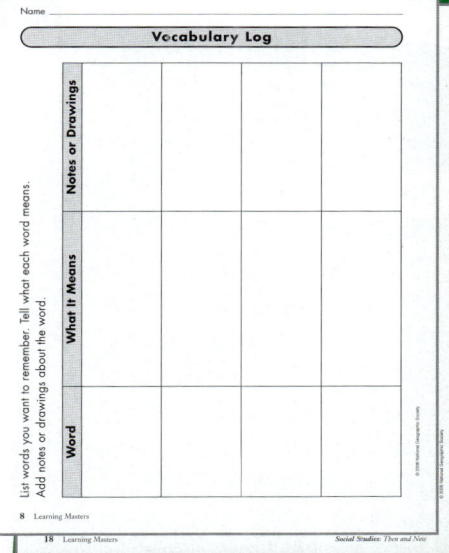

Customize the Reading

Students reread and talk about Then and Now *using one of the following options:*

- *Look through the pages, pointing to pictures and talking about life in the past.*
- *Reread the book while following along with the audiolesson.*
- *Read independently or read aloud with a partner.*

Modeled Writing

Use the graphic organizer on the *Theme Builder* to review some Key Concepts of the theme. Prepare to model writing using precise language to make comparisons clear.

Think Aloud I'm going to write to compare writing tools of the past with the tools of today. My audience is the students in this group. First, I'll write the main point I want to make.

Students of today still use ink. Students still use paper. But students use different writing tools in the classroom today than students used in the past.

Model developing this idea by contrasting pens and inkwells with writing implements of today.

Think Aloud I'll begin a new paragraph about what students in the past used for writing.

In the past, students dipped their pens in inkwells before writing their lessons on paper. The only color of ink was black.

Think Aloud Now, I'll write about what students today use for writing.

Today, students use pens, pencils, and markers. These writing tools come in different colors.

Learning Masters/page 19

Read *Thomas Edison*

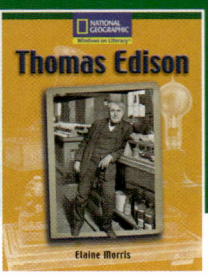

OBJECTIVES

- Read to gain fluency in oral and silent reading
- Practice the comprehension strategy: Making Connections
- Understand that inventions and technologies can be improved and changed over time
- Use a Glossary to comprehend text
- Use a photo to help find the meaning of a word

Materials

Theme Builder

Thomas Edison

Learning Masters pages 20

Audiolesson 2

Develop Concepts and Vocabulary

Develop Oral Language

Review the Key Concept Words *long ago, machine,* and *inventor.* What words mean the same as "long ago"? *(the past)* What are some machines we have in our classroom? *(computer, CD player)* What does a person do who thinks of and makes new machines? *(he or she invents)*

Turn and Talk Have learning partners discuss machines that people did not have in the past one hundred years. Tell students to think of what they learned from the book *Then and Now.*

Revisit the Theme Poem
Display the Theme Poem on the ***Theme Builder.*** Have students read the poem in unison. Replace "cars or computers" with "CDs or headphones" and read the poem together again.

Build Background

Distribute copies of *Thomas Edison.* Invite students to name some important machines in their lives. Indicate that the man in the picture was an inventor. He invented many inventions that are important to people today, including the electric lightbulb and the movie camera. Tell students that his name is Thomas Edison.

Small Group Reading

Get Ready to Read

Preview the Book Read aloud the title, the author's name, and the Think and Discuss question on the back cover: Do you use any of these things?

Page through the book and do the following:

- Point out how photos from the past are contrasted with photos from today.
- Invite students to name the objects they know or use.
- Ask students to predict what they will learn.

Predict Vocabulary Encourage students to use photos to predict vocabulary: Which words do you expect to see in this book?

Display a page and cover the words:

Which words do you expect to see on this page?

List the words students mention. Add Key Concept Words in the book that students do not mention.

Text Feature: Glossary

Introduce Display page 12. This is the Glossary. The boldfaced words are important words from *Thomas Edison.* The words are in alphabetical order. Next to each word, I see its definition.

Model Here's how to use the Glossary. On page 3, I read the word *inventor.* I'm not sure what an inventor is, so I turn to the Glossary. *Inventor* starts with an *i,* so I look for the *I's.* Then I read the definition.

Practice Have students find the boldfaced word on page 6 and check the definition of *lightbulb* in the Glossary.

Read the Book

As students read, invite them to share what they notice. Use some of the suggestions below to encourage observations and talk about the book.

Pages 2–3

Key Concept Word *invent*

Support Comprehension Ask students to find the highlighted word and say how it relates to the photo. (*Thomas Edison was an inventor. He created new machines.*)

Pages 4–5

Key Concept Words *change, machine*

Check Understanding Describe how the two machines in the pictures are the same and how they are different. (*They both play music. One is from the past, and the other is from today.*)

Page 8

Support Comprehension Point out the highlighted words *silent movies*. Explain that these are movies with no sound. Call on a volunteer to read the definition in the Glossary on page 12.

Pages 10–11

Practice the Comprehension Strategy

Encourage students to **Make Connections** to help them better understand pages 10–11.

Do you use any of these machines? Why do you use them? Do you know people who use them? Why do they use these machines?

Guide students to realize that their connection helps them understand what the objects are and helps them understand how the machines have changed from the past to now.

Discuss the Book

Invite students to use the Word Bank to tell about the book. What have they learned about inventors and machines? What have they learned about the past? Remind students to add words to their Vocabulary Logs.

Use *Learning Masters* page 20.

Reread for Fluency

Have students reread the entire book independently to build fluency. See *Customize the Reading*.

Customize the Reading

Students reread and talk about Thomas Edison *using one of the following options:*

- *Look through the pages, naming the inventions and pointing to those from the past and those from today.*
- *Reread the book while following along with the audiolesson.*
- *Read independently or aloud with a partner.*

Shared Writing

Review the paragraphs you modeled in Lesson 2. Invite students to help you begin a new piece of writing about a machine used in the home. Have volunteers suggest a machine, such as a refrigerator.

Review the information they learned about machines in the home. Help students frame sentences that show comparisons.

Customize Instruction for ELLs

Newcomers/Beginning Have students name the machines we have today and the machines people had in the past.

Developing Have students complete sentences, such as: "Today, we have electric and gas stoves to cook food. In the past, people had wood-burning stoves to cook food."

Expanding/Bridging Have students add other examples of machines they have in their kitchen that people in the past didn't have.

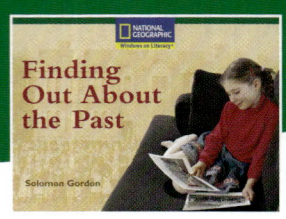

OBJECTIVES

- Read to gain fluency in oral and silent reading
- Apply the comprehension strategy: Making Connections
- Develop an understanding that there are many information sources that people can use to find out about the past
- Use Highlighted Vocabulary to comprehend text
- Use photos and text to summarize

Materials

Realia: photos, newspaper articles, and books about a school in the past

Theme Builder

Finding Out About the Past

Learning Masters pages 21, 22

Take-Home Book Masters: *Then and Now*

Audiolesson 2

Take-Home Book Masters

Then and Now

by _____

Review Concepts and Vocabulary

Develop Oral Language

Display a photo of a school in the past. Ask students to describe how schools in the past and today are alike and different. Invite them to use the following language forms: Today, we have _____. In the past, students didn't have _____.

Turn and Talk Have learning partners take turns contrasting what today's schools have with what schools in the past had. For example: Today, the teacher uses a marker to write on the board. In the past, the teacher used chalk to write on the board.

Revisit the Theme Poem Display the poem on the *Theme Builder*. Have students read the poem in unison. Have students make suggestions for different items for the second line. Read the poem again.

Build Background

Distribute copies of *Finding Out About the Past*. Review the ways to find out about the past that students learned in *Then and Now*. Display photos of your school or another school in the past. Ask students to make comparisons between the old photos and their school today.

Small Group Reading

Get Ready to Read

Preview the Book Read aloud the title, the author's name, and the Think and Discuss question on the back cover: How can I find out about the past?

Page through the book and do the following:

- Point out the two colors of type on some pages.
- Talk about what is shown by the use of two kinds of frames around the photos.
- Ask students to predict what they will learn.

Predict Vocabulary Encourage students to use photos to predict vocabulary: Which words do you expect to see in this book?

Display a page and cover the words: Which words do you expect to see on this page?

List the words that students mention. Add Key Concept Words in the book that students do not mention.

Text Feature: Highlighted Vocabulary

Introduce Authors highlight words so that the reader will notice them. As I look through the book, I see highlighted words at the bottoms of pages. These are questions. The author gives a question and then, on the next pages, he answers it.

Model Display page 3. I read the highlighted question: *How can I find out what my school was like in the past?* On pages 4 and 5, I find out the girl can read an old newspaper story to find out about the school.

Practice Have students read the question on page 5. Then have students read the answer on pages 6 and 7.

Read the Book

As students read, invite them to share what they notice. Use some of the suggestions below to encourage observations and talk about the book.

Pages 2–5

Key Concept Words *the past, school, long ago*

Support Comprehension Point out that page 2 shows a real school that was built many years ago, before the students were born. Talk about why the opening of a school would be in a newspaper article. Ask volunteers to tell about openings they have attended.

Pages 6–9

Apply the Comprehension Strategy

Encourage students to **Make Connections** and use these language forms:

I can connect to _____.

It reminds me of _____.

This connection helps me understand _____.

Pages 10–12

Check Understanding Ask a volunteer to tell the importance of the highlighted words.

Support Comprehension Tell students that page 12 is a summary page. What do you think the phrases under each picture refer to? Why are they highlighted? *(They answer the big question at the top of the page.)*

Discuss the Book

Invite students to use the Word Bank to discuss the book and to share what they learned. Ask them about the new ways they learned to find out about the past. Which way do they think would give them the most information? Have students add words to their Vocabulary Logs.

Use *Learning Masters* page 21.

Reread for Fluency

Have students reread the entire book independently to build fluency. See *Customize the Reading*.

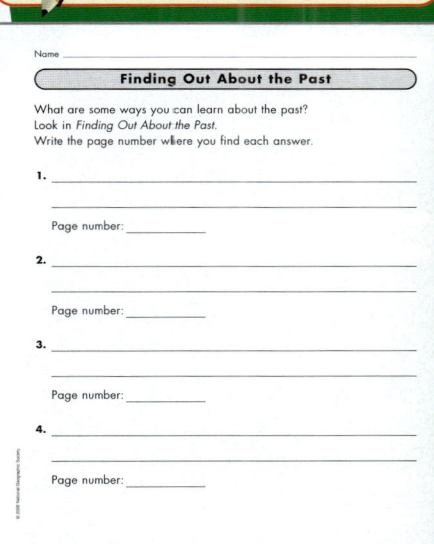

Learning Masters/page 21

Name _____

Finding Out About the Past

What are some ways you can learn about the past?
Look in *Finding Out About the Past*.
Write the page number where you find each answer.

1. _____

Page number: _____

2. _____

Page number: _____

3. _____

Page number: _____

4. _____

Page number: _____

Social Studies: Then and Now   Learning Masters   **21**

Customize the Reading

Students reread and talk about Finding Out About the Past *using one of the following options:*

- Look through the pages, looking at the pictures and naming ways to find out about the past.

- Reread the book while following along with the audiolesson.

- Read independently or aloud with a partner.

Guided Writing

Distribute copies of the ***Take-Home Book Masters***. Read the title and page through the book. Explain that they will write books about life today and in the past. Work with students to:

- Complete the Contents page.

- Describe the actions and objects shown in the book.

- Share writing ideas for each set of pages.

Record on chart paper students' writing ideas for the pages of their books. Have students suggest captions for the photos.

Have partners talk together to plan what to write. Ask each student to complete a graphic organizer to plan ideas to include with each photograph. Display the Word Bank and remind students to check their Vocabulary Logs as they begin to write.

Use *Learning Masters* page 22.

Learning Masters/page 22

Name _____

Graphic Organizer

Then	Now
Page 4	Page 4
Page 6	Page 6
Page 8	Page 8
Page 10	Page 10

22 Learning Masters   *Social Studies: Then and Now*

OBJECTIVES

- Use Key Concepts and Key Concept Words in writing
- Demonstrate oral language proficiency
- Demonstrate comprehension of theme selections
- Read related titles to reinforce Key Concepts and vocabulary

Materials

Take-Home Book Masters: *Then and Now*

Learning Masters pages 6–7, 23–24

Assessment Masters pages 179, 180, 187, 214, 215, 217, 228

Take-Home Book Masters

Rereading and Assessments

Allow time for students to independently reread the theme selections. Display the Word Bank for students' reference as they read.

As students reread, meet with individuals. Use the assessment tools listed on page 55 to evaluate students' progress and to update their records.

Guided Writing

Students continue writing the Take-Home Books they began in Lesson 4. Review the group list of writing ideas. Display the Word Bank.

Page through the theme books to review the text features, including highlighted words and Glossary. Talk about text features that students could add to their Take-Home Books. For example, they might highlight important words in their sentences. Point out that the last page is a Picture Glossary.

Point out that good writers:

- Plan writing. Have students use their completed graphic organizer to guide their writing.
- Use words such as *today*, *now*, *long ago*, and *in the past* to make clear the time they are writing about.

- Check verb tense. Remind students to use the past tense to write about life in the past and the present tense to talk about life today.

Have students complete the Picture Glossary and About the Author last.

As students write, circulate to coach and support individuals. If students need help, provide specific words to help them describe a picture. Guide them to add information or restate ideas.

Have partners exchange books and discuss what they like in each other's book. For example, a partner may like some interesting related information the writer added to what was learned in the theme.

Customize Instruction for ELLs

Newcomers/Beginning Have students complete the following language form for each page, using the pictures: Today, students _____. In the past, students _____.

Developing Have students vary the language they use to describe the time and the pictures. Have them look at *Then and Now*.

Expanding/Bridging Encourage students to write more than one sentence about each subject and time and to give personal reactions and information.

Assessment Tools

Self-Assessment

Allow students to reflect and assess their own learning by completing *Learning Masters* pages 6–7.

- What I Learned, page 6
- How I Learned, page 7

Reading

The following assessment tools can help you evaluate and record students' progress in reading and understanding the theme books.

- Retelling Guide and Scoring Rubric, page 179
- Fluency Scoring Guide, page 180
- Oral Reading Record, page 187

Writing

Use the completed Take-Home Books and the following tools to assess students' development as writers.

- Writing Rubric, page 214
- Writing Traits Checklist, page 215

Content Assessment

Working in groups, have students choose a place and make a "Then and Now" book about it. Places might be a kitchen, a classroom, a living room, or a street. Have students draw pictures that show old and new machines, transportation, and so on. Have them write at least two sentences under each picture to describe the place. Have each group present its book. Ask them to tell what sources they used to learn about the past.

Vocabulary and Oral Language

Use the following resources, in addition to the Think and Discuss scene on the *Theme Builder,* to assess oral language development.

- Content Vocabulary Checklist, page 217
- Oral Language Developmental Checklist, page 228

Optional Reading

Reading related titles allows students to explore concepts and vocabulary at different levels. It also allows them to use reading strategies in different types of texts. Encourage students to compare the theme books to the books in the next column.

Optional Titles

These related *Windows on Literacy* titles reinforce Key Concepts of the *Then and Now* theme.

Nonfiction Titles

School Today and Long Ago
Level 11

Our Town Level 13

Henry Ford and the Car Level 19

Timelines 1900–2000 Level 20

Fiction Titles

Grandma's Attic Level 13

Driving Tin Lizzie Level 14

Home Connection

The Family Focus letters on *Learning Masters* pages 23–24 summarize key concepts about life in the past and finding out about it.

In the Share and Learn activity, family members share experiences about school days—in the past and today.

Learning Masters/pages 6–7

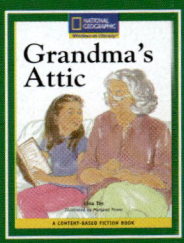
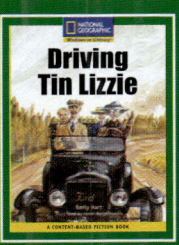

Related Fiction Titles

Learning Masters/pages 23–24

Overview

Providing Goods

STANDARDS

ACADEMIC LANGUAGE/ELD
- Use academic vocabulary related to the study of providing goods
- Use appropriate language forms to ask informational questions and to make inferences
- Develop fluency in reading, writing, listening to, and speaking English

SOCIAL STUDIES
- Describe how people make and grow goods that other people want
- Understand that the distribution of goods involves a sequence of steps
- Discuss how the distribution of goods involves different forms of transportation

READING/LANGUAGE ARTS
- Learn and apply the comprehension strategy: Making Inferences
- Use the text features: Special Page Features and Labels
- Write about providing goods
- Learn and use vocabulary related to providing goods

Before Theme Assessment

To compare progress before and after teaching this theme, use one or more of the following informal assessment tools before beginning the theme.
- Oral Reading Record, page 189
- Fluency Scoring Guide, page 180
- Content Vocabulary Checklist, page 218
- Oral Language Developmental Checklist, page 228

Theme Materials

Concept Book

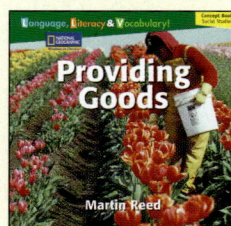

Nonfiction Books

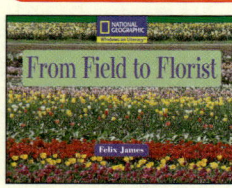

Level 14

Level 14

Theme Builder

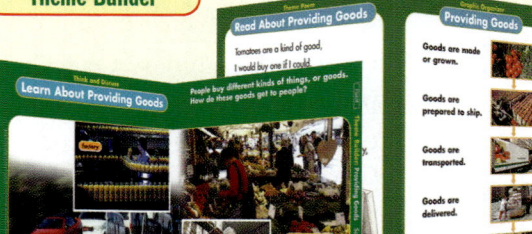

Learning Masters

Audiolesson on CD

Take-Home Book Masters

Optional Reading

Windows on Literacy Content-Based Fiction

Grandpa's Castanets Level 13

Peggy's Pickles Level 14

Windows on Literacy Nonfiction

Loading the Airplane Level 10

What's on the Ships? Level 12

Jack's Boat Level 15

From Hive to Home Level 16

Instructional Highlights

Key Concepts

- People grow and make products that other people want.
- The distribution of goods involves a sequence of steps.
- The distribution of goods involves different forms of transportation.

Comprehension Strategy

Making Inferences

Key Concept Words

buy	stores
goods	transport
move	truck
sell	warehouse

Text Features

Special Page Features

Labels

Theme Planner

Lesson 1*

Teacher's Guide
pp. 58–59

Read
Providing Goods

- Introduce Concepts and Vocabulary

- Model and Share the Reading

* Before you begin Lesson 1, you may want to use the Before Theme Assessment tools listed on page 56.

Lesson 2

Teacher's Guide
pp. 60–61

Reread
Providing Goods

- Develop Concepts and Vocabulary

- Introduce the Comprehension Strategy: Making Inferences

- Small Group Reading

- Modeled Writing

Lesson 3

Teacher's Guide
pp. 62–63

Read
From Field to Florist

- Develop Concepts and Vocabulary

- Small Group Reading

- Practice the Comprehension Strategy: Making Inferences

- Shared Writing

Lesson 4

Teacher's Guide
pp. 64–65

Read
What's on the Truck?

- Review Concepts and Vocabulary

- Small Group Reading

- Apply the Comprehension Strategy: Making Inferences

- Guided Writing

Lesson 5

Teacher's Guide
pp. 66–67

Assess
and Extend

- Rereading and Assessments

- Guided Writing

- Assessment Tools

- Optional Reading

- Home Connection

Read *Providing Goods*

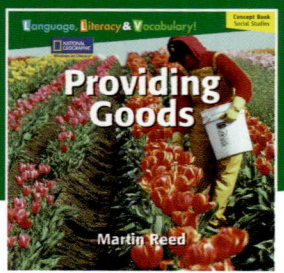

Language, Literacy & Vocabulary!
Concept Book
Social Studies

Providing Goods

Martin Reed

- Understand that people grow and make goods that people want
- Learn and use vocabulary related to providing goods
- Use photos to predict vocabulary
- Use text features, such as labels, to learn new words

Materials

Realia: fresh produce, any manufactured items such as food, school supplies, DVDs, and CDs

Theme Builder

Providing Goods

Learning Masters page 25

Audiolesson 3

Theme Builder (Poem)

Theme Poem
Read About Providing Goods

Tomatoes are a kind of good,
I would buy one if I could.
Tomatoes need to be sold,
Load them up before they're old!
Put them on a truck so fast,
At the store, they won't last!
Now tomatoes are ready for people to buy,
Once they're sold,
    say good-bye!

Sunshine Tomatoes

Theme Builder (Scene)

Think and Discuss
Learn About Providing Goods

People buy different kinds of things, or goods. How do these goods get to people?

factory
farmers' market
truck
warehouse

Introduce Concepts and Vocabulary

Introduce Theme Question

Ask students: In what kinds of stores does your family shop? For what kinds of things does your family shop? Explain that students will learn about providing goods. They will also learn the language to use when discussing the goods that people buy and how people provide these goods.

Turn and Talk Provide conversation partners with several examples of goods. Have students decide where the items might have come from and how they got to the store.

Develop Oral Language

Show students a piece of produce. Ask them to tell where it would likely come from. This food came from a grower. The grower might be in the United States, or in another country.

Then ask students to tell how the produce might have been delivered to the store. If the food was grown in our country, it probably came to the store on a truck. If it came from another country, it may have traveled by boat, and then by train or truck.

Point out that goods are the things that someone grows or makes that other people buy.

Turn and Talk Ask partners to name some goods that they have already used today. Then challenge the partners to name objects that they have used that were not goods.

Introduce Theme Poem

Display the Theme Poem on the *Theme Builder*. Have students say the poem in unison. Have learning partners use *Learning Masters* page 25 to practice reading the poem.

Introduce Key Vocabulary

Use the Think and Discuss scene to teach Key Concept Words and model language forms.

How do goods get to the store?

The goods might travel on boat, truck, or train to the store.

Continue to model sentences using the words listed below. As you introduce words, jot them down on chart paper. Display this Word Bank throughout the theme.

Turn and Talk Have partners practice using the words to discuss how goods get from the place they are made to the stores where they are sold. For example: This _____ came from _____. It was carried to the store by _____.

buy	sell	truck
goods	stores	warehouse
move	transport	

Build Background

Display the Think and Discuss scene on the *Theme Builder* again. Ask students to tell how each picture relates to providing goods.

Turn and Talk Have partners use the pictures to describe the sequence of how goods get to the people who want to buy them. For example: The cars are made in the (*factory*). They are then loaded on a (*truck*). They are moved to the car lot.

Model and Share the Reading

Preview the Book

Distribute copies of *Providing Goods*. Read aloud the title and the author's name. As you page through the book, point out:

- The headings in colored bars are questions.
- The boldfaced words are vocabulary words.
- The photos have captions to help explain the pictures.

Predict Vocabulary

Encourage students to use pictures to predict vocabulary: Which words do you expect to see in this book?

Display pages 6–7 and cover the words: Which words do you expect to see on these pages?

Students may mention the food, clothing, and flowers shown in the pictures. Add these words to the Word Bank. Have students talk with partners and use *goods*, *food*, *shoes*, and *flowers* to describe the types of goods. Continue the activity with other pages as time allows.

Model the Reading

Invite students to follow along as you read aloud pages 4–7 in *Providing Goods*. Read fluently, modeling smooth, accurate reading with appropriate expression. After reading each pair of pages, pause to think aloud. Also, encourage students to ask questions and make observations.

Pages 4–5
Think Aloud This is like the Think and Discuss scene on the **Theme Builder.** The labels give you names of places and things that make goods, transport goods, or sell goods.

Pages 6–7
Think Aloud Goods are things that people need and want to buy. People would buy the food in the first picture at a grocery store or a restaurant. People buy flowers at a florist.

Share the Reading

Now have partners complete the reading. Ask students to pause after reading one or two pages and discuss what they have read. Ask them to share the details that the pictures added to the text.

Reread for Fluency

To have students practice fluent reading, read aloud page 12 of *Providing Goods* with clear pronunciation. Have students in unison echo-read each sentence as you finish, imitating your model. Then have students reread the entire book independently to build fluency. See *Customize the Reading*.

Learning Masters/page 25

Name _____

Theme Poem

Tomatoes are a kind of good,
I would buy one if I could.
Tomatoes need to be sold,
Load them up before they're old!
Put them on a truck so fast,
At the store, they won't last!
Now tomatoes are ready for people to buy,
Once they're sold,
    say good-bye!

Sunshine Tomatoes

Social Studies: Providing Goods   Learning Masters 25

Customize the Reading

Students reread and talk about Providing Goods *on their own to build fluency.*

- *Students who are not yet able to read the book can look at examples in the photos and describe what they see.*
- *Students who need extra support can reread the book while listening to the audiolesson.*
- *Students who can read the book might read independently or aloud with partners.*

Customize Instruction for ELLs

Newcomers/Beginning As you read aloud, have students point to the pictures as you describe them or read their corresponding captions.

Developing Point to classroom objects such as textbooks or school supplies. Ask questions such as, "Where did this come from?" Lead students to respond with statements such as, "The _____ was made at _____."

Expanding/Bridging Have students look at the pages in *Providing Goods* and give the sequence of how goods come to stores for people to buy.

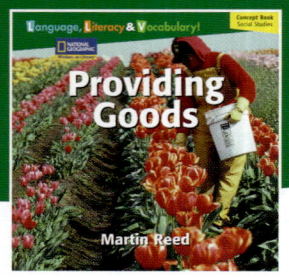

Language, Literacy & Vocabulary!

Providing Goods

Martin Reed

OBJECTIVES

- Understand that goods are transported from where they are made to where they are sold
- Use vocabulary to describe the sequence of making and selling goods
- Learn the comprehension strategy: Making Inferences
- Read to gain fluency in oral and silent reading
- Write a description of how a good is made and prepared to sell

Materials

Realia: large map of the United States; models of cars, trains, planes, and buildings

Theme Builder

Providing Goods

Learning Masters pages 8, 26, 27

Audiolesson 3

Theme Builder (Graphic Organizer)

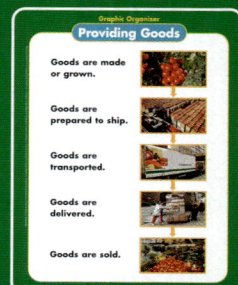

Graphic Organizer

Providing Goods

Goods are made or grown.

Goods are prepared to ship.

Goods are transported.

Goods are delivered.

Goods are sold.

Develop Concepts and Vocabulary

Develop Oral Language

To start the discussion, ask students: What are some goods that you used today? Write the responses on the board. Then have students answer informational questions such as: How were they made?

Turn and Talk Have partners ask similar informational questions and provide possible answers for other goods listed on the board.

Revisit the Theme Poem Display the Theme Poem on the *Theme Builder*. Say the poem again. This time, let students suggest a new good to replace tomatoes.

Build Background

Display the graphic organizer on the *Theme Builder* with only the first box of the flowchart visible.

Uncover the sentence, read it, and invite students to predict what step comes next. Uncover the next step and talk about it. Continue in this manner.

Turn and Talk Encourage partners to ask and answer an informational question using *who, what, where, when, why,* or *how* for each box of the flowchart.

Begin Vocabulary Log As students read, encourage them to use sticky notes to tag words that they would like to save. After reading, students can record the words and their notes about them.

Use *Learning Masters* page 8.

Introduce the Comprehension Strategy

Introduce Making Inferences

When students make inferences, they are filling in the missing information that the writer has not stated in the text. Students combine information from the text with things they already know to infer meaning.

Think Aloud When I read a book, the author doesn't tell me everything I need to know. I have to think about what I'm reading and put that together with things I already know. That's called **making inferences.**

Model Making Inferences

Turn to pages 14–15 and model the comprehension strategy and the language forms for making inferences.

The words tell me that some goods come from across the oceans. **The pictures show me** that the goods can travel on ships to shipping docks.

I know that trucks bring the goods to stores around the country. **I infer that** trucks get goods from shipping docks **because** that is where the ships bring them.

For additional practice in making inferences, have partners work on *Learning Masters* page 26.

Small Group Reading

As students read, invite them to share what they notice. Use some of the suggestions below to encourage observations and talk about the book.

Pages 4–7
Support Comprehension Guide students to think of goods that would go to a store and goods that would go to a warehouse.

Pages 8–11
Check Understanding Describe how transporting goods from a farm might be different from transporting goods made in a factory. (*Goods from a farm will spoil and need to get to stores quickly. Things such as cars or tools can be transported much more slowly.*)

Pages 12–17
Support Comprehension Ask a volunteer to summarize these pages. (*Companies use many different types of transportation to move goods and many different kinds of stores to sell them.*)

Pages 18–19
Check Understanding Have students use the Word Bank to tell how goods are provided to the people who need them.

Discuss the Book
Invite students to share what they learned. Ask them to name some goods that they read about in the book and describe how the goods get to a store for people to buy. Encourage students to use the words in the Word Bank to discuss what they have read. Remind students to add words to their Vocabulary Logs.

Students can complete *Learning Masters* page 27.

Reread for Fluency
Have students follow along as you read page 16 as fast as you can. Ask students why it might have been difficult to understand you. (*You read too fast.*) Point out that reading too fast makes it hard for the audience to hear you. Ask a volunteer to read the sentence slowly and clearly. Have partners choose four consecutive pages and practice the correct speed of their reading. For other suggestions, see *Customize the Reading.*

Learning Masters/pages 8, 26

Vocabulary Log

Notes or Drawings

What It Means

Word

List words you want to remember. Tell what each word means. Add notes or drawings about the word.

8 Learning Masters

26 Learning Masters   *Social Studies: Providing Goods*

Customize the Reading

Students reread and talk about Providing Goods *using one of the following options:*

- Look through the pages for different goods, transportation, and stores.
- Reread the book while following along with the audiolesson.
- Read independently or read aloud with a partner.

Modeled Writing

Use the graphic organizer on the *Theme Builder* to review some Key Concepts of the theme. Prepare to model writing using precise language to tell an order of steps.

Think Aloud I'm going to write about getting goods to the stores. My goal is to tell the steps in this process. My audience is the students in this group. My first sentences should show an interesting beginning.

A big, soft, red chair is in the store window. The chair was made at a factory. How did the chair get from the factory to the store?

Discuss the steps in the process of moving goods from a factory to a store. Have students suggest words that will help you tell the order in which things happen, such as *next, then,* and *finally.*

Think Aloud I'll start at the factory. I'll use the word *then* to show that one thing happened after the other.

At the factory, the workers finished making many chairs. A truck arrives. It will take the chairs to the city. The red chair is loaded on a truck with many other chairs. Then the truck driver drives away.

Learning Masters/page 27

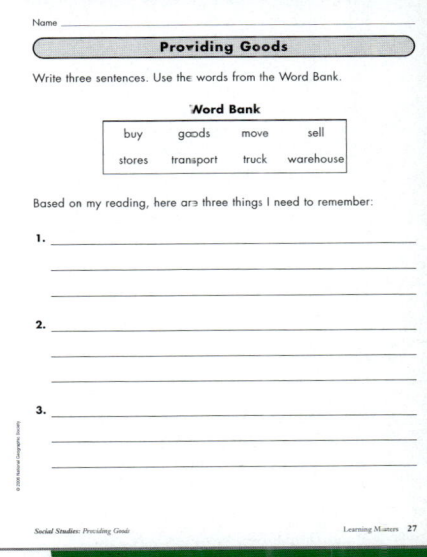

Name

Providing Goods

Write three sentences. Use the words from the Word Bank.

Word Bank

| buy | goods | move | sell |
| stores | transport | truck | warehouse |

Based on my reading, here are three things I need to remember:

1. _____
2. _____
3. _____

Social Studies: Providing Goods   Learning Masters **27**

Read *From Field to Florist*

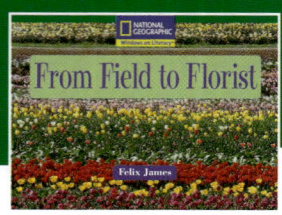

OBJECTIVES

- Read to gain fluency in oral and silent reading
- Practice the comprehension strategy: Making Inferences
- Understand that the distribution of goods involves a sequence of steps
- Use Special Page Features to help comprehend text
- Use context clues to find the meaning of words

Materials

Theme Builder

From Field to Florist

Learning Masters page 28

Audiolesson 3

Develop Concepts and Vocabulary

Develop Oral Language

Model the Key Concept Words *stores*, *sell*, *truck*, and *buy*. For example, students can make up riddles that have a Key Concept Word as an answer, such as:

Where can you go when you need a new pencil for school? *(a store)*

Turn and Talk Have conversation partners role-play working in a store to practice using the Key Concept Words in a realistic situation.

Revisit the Theme Poem Display the poem on the *Theme Builder*. This time, have students suggest another new good to replace the previous one.

Build Background

Distribute copies of *From Field to Florist*. Invite students to give examples of flowers they have seen for sale at florists and grocery stores. Help students understand that greenhouses help businesses by growing flowers. Ask students to describe two ways that growers can provide flowers. Then have students share ideas on how the flowers are cared for.

Some flowers are grown in fields.

Some flowers are grown in greenhouses.

Small Group Reading

Get Ready to Read

Preview the Book Read aloud the title, the author's name, and the Think and Discuss question on the back cover: How do flowers get to a flower store?

Page through the book and do the following:

- Point out that inset photos focus on an important idea on the page.
- Point out that other photos will help clarify new words.
- Ask students to predict what they will learn.

Predict Vocabulary Encourage students to use photos to predict vocabulary: Which words do you expect to see in this book?

Display a page and cover the words: Which words do you expect to see on this page?

List the words students mention. Add Key Concept Words in the book that students do not mention.

Text Feature: Special Page Features

Introduce Display the flowchart on page 12. This is a flowchart. It tells you the steps in getting flowers from the grower into the hands of someone buying them.

Model I see that flowers are grown first. Then they are brought to a flower market. Next, the flowers are brought to a flower shop. Finally, someone buys the flowers.

Practice Have students take turns reading the chart aloud to each other.

Read the Book

As students read, invite them to share what they notice. Use some of the suggestions below to encourage observations and talk about the book.

Pages 2–3

Key Concept Words *store, sell*

Support Comprehension Explain to students that sometimes the person selling flowers at a flower shop is called a *florist*. Ask a volunteer to point to a person who is a florist.

Pages 6–9

Key Concept Word *truck*

Check Understanding How are flowers sent to market? (*The flowers are picked and then put in trucks.*)

Help students understand that florists buy flowers at a market at a low price, then sell them at their stores for a higher price.

Pages 10–11

Practice the Comprehension Strategy

Encourage students to **Make Inferences** to help them better understand pages 10–11.

What grouping of flowers would customers want to buy? What does the text tell you about the flowers that helps you figure out what the customers want? How does the picture help you?

Guide students to realize that customers may want flowers that are already arranged in bunches. The picture shows a happy customer with bunches of flowers.

Discuss the Book

Invite students to use the Word Bank to tell about the book. Ask students to use these words to describe what they learned in *From Field to Florist* and *Providing Goods*. Have them point out parts of each book that are similar. Remind students to add words to their Vocabulary Logs.

Use *Learning Masters* page 28.

Reread for Fluency

Have students reread the entire book independently to build fluency. See *Customize the Reading*.

Customize the Reading

Students reread and talk about From Field to Florist *using one of the following options:*

- *Look through the pages, describing the scenes shown in the pictures.*
- *Reread the book while following along with the audiolesson.*
- *Read independently or aloud with a partner.*

Shared Writing

Review the writing you modeled in Lesson 2. Ask volunteers to offer details to make the writing more interesting and specific. Invite students to participate as you continue writing. Guide them to add more steps, such as taking goods to a warehouse before they are brought to stores.

Customize Instruction for ELLs

Newcomers/Beginning Have students look through books and magazines for a possible product to suggest as goods.

Developing Provide students with sentence frames such as: Workers in factories build *(DVD players)*. People use them to *(watch movies)*.

Expanding/Bridging Have students describe the kinds of stores in which specific products might be sold.

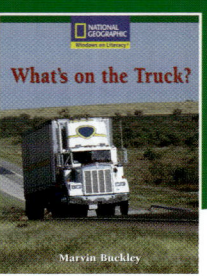

Lesson 4

Read *What's on the Truck*

OBJECTIVES

- Read to gain fluency in oral and silent reading
- Apply the comprehension strategy: Making Inferences
- Develop an understanding that the distribution of goods involves different forms of transportation
- Use Labels to comprehend text
- Make comparisons among different uses for trucks

Materials

Photos: various kinds of delivery and transport trucks

Theme Builder

What's on the Truck?

Learning Masters pages 29, 30

Take-Home Book Masters: *Providing Goods*

Audiolesson 3

Take-Home Book Masters

Providing Goods

by _____

Review Concepts and Vocabulary

Develop Oral Language

Model the Key Concept Words *truck, move, stores,* and *buy.* Encourage students to use the words in describing their own knowledge of types of trucks that transport goods from place to place. What trucks do you see on the road? What do they seem to be carrying? What kinds of businesses would use trucks to bring them goods?

Turn and Talk Have conversation partners take turns asking and answering questions about goods that are moved on a truck. For example: Where would a truck carrying lettuce be going? A truck carrying lettuce would be going to a grocery store or a restaurant. Encourage students to follow your model to ask and answer questions about goods.

Revisit the Theme Poem Display the poem on the *Theme Builder.* This time, assign eight students to each read a line of the poem aloud.

Build Background

Distribute copies of *What's on the Truck?* Display the various photos of delivery and transport trucks. Invite students to speculate what each truck is carrying based on any signs on the truck and its size. What could this truck carry? How do you know?

Small Group Reading

Get Ready to Read

Preview the Book Read aloud the title, the author's name, and the Think and Discuss question on the back cover: What do trucks carry?

Page through the book and do the following:

- Point out the captions and labels below the inset photos.
- Talk about the highlighted question that repeats throughout the book: "What's on the truck?"
- Ask students to predict what they will learn.

Predict Vocabulary Encourage students to use photos to predict vocabulary: Which words do you expect to see in this book?

Display a page and cover the words: Which words do you expect to see on this page?

List the words that students mention. Add Key Concept Words in the book that students do not mention.

Text Feature: Labels

Introduce Point out the small inset photo and label on page 5. Under this photo is a label. The label tells what the photo shows.

Model Point to the photo of the factory. This page talks about a factory. The label helps me understand what the author means by a factory.

Practice Students can find more labels in the book. Encourage them to find information in the text on the page that tells more about each label.

Read the Book

As students read, invite them to share what they notice. Use some of the suggestions below to encourage observations and talk about the book.

Pages 2–3

Key Concept Words *move, truck*

Support Comprehension Point out that the inset photo shows what the inside of the truck might look like. Ask students to find the label.

Pages 4–5

Apply the Comprehension Strategy

Encourage students to **Make Inferences** and use these language forms.

I infer _____ because _____.

Ask students to explain how they used information from the text and pictures as well as their own experiences to help them understand things not stated in the text.

Pages 6–9

Key Concept Words *stores, buy*

Check Understanding What is the difference between how the trucks are used on pages 6 and 8? (*The truck on page 6 is delivering goods to a store to be sold. The truck on page 8 is delivering to homes things that were already sold.*)

Pages 10–11

Support Comprehension Explain to students that people often call trucking companies that take items from one home to another *movers*.

Page 12

Support Comprehension Ask a volunteer to explain what it means to move to a new home.

Discuss the Book

Invite students to use the Word Bank to discuss the book and to share what they learned. Ask them to describe what they found unusual about the book. Ask students to tell about experiences they may have had in moving from one home to another. Have students add words to their Vocabulary Logs.

Use *Learning Masters* page 29.

Reread for Fluency

Have students reread the entire book independently to build fluency. See *Customize the Reading*.

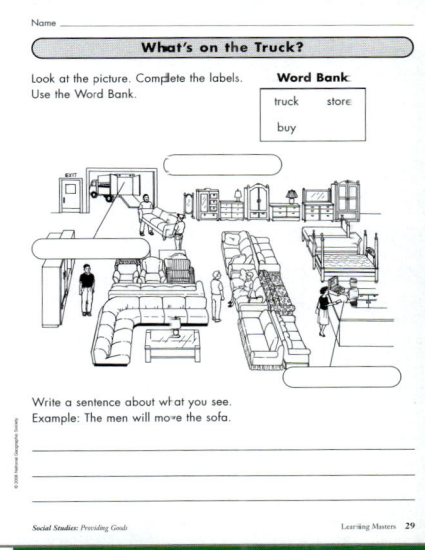

Customize the Reading

Students reread and talk about What's on the Truck? *using one of the following options:*

- *Look through the pages, pointing to each truck and naming what it is carrying and where it is going.*
- *Reread the book while following along with the audiolesson.*
- *Read independently or aloud with a partner.*

Guided Writing

Distribute copies of the *Take-Home Book Masters*. Read the title and page through the book. Explain that students will write books about goods being transported to a store for people to buy. Work with students to:

- Discuss the photos.
- Describe the sequence of making the goods, transporting them, and selling them in a store.
- Share writing ideas for each pair of pages.

Record students' writing ideas for the pages of their books on chart paper. Have them suggest labels for the photos.

Have partners work together to plan what to write. Ask each student to complete a graphic organizer to plan the book. Remind students that they can include inset drawings to help clarify what the book is describing.

Display the Word Bank and remind students to check their Vocabulary Logs as they begin to write.

Use *Learning Masters* page 30.

OBJECTIVES

- Use Key Concepts and Key Concept Words in writing
- Demonstrate oral language proficiency
- Demonstrate comprehension of theme selections
- Read related titles to reinforce Key Concepts and vocabulary

Materials

Take-Home Book Masters:
Providing Goods

Learning Masters pages 6–7, 31–32

Assessment Masters pages 179, 180, 189, 214, 215, 218, 228

Take-Home Book Masters

Providing Goods

by _____

Rereading and Assessments

Allow time for students to independently reread the theme selections. Display the Word Bank for students' reference as they read.

As students reread, meet with individuals. Use the assessment tools listed on page 67 to evaluate students' progress and to update their records.

Guided Writing

Students continue writing the Take-Home Books they began in Lesson 4. Review the group list of writing ideas. Display the Word Bank.

Page through the theme books to review the text features, including special page features and labels. Talk about text features that students could add to their Take-Home Books. For example, they might draw illustrations or find photos in magazines that can be placed in the text and labeled.

Point out that good writers:

- Organize their ideas before writing. Students plan what they will write.
- Use precise words. Students may use Key Concept Words as well as other words that describe the pictures and ideas.

- Reread. Students should reread their books after the books are complete to be sure that the words have the meanings that students intended.

Have students complete the Picture Glossary and About the Author last.

As students write, circulate to coach and support individuals. If students need help, try reading back to them what they have written and asking guiding questions.

Have partners exchange books and discuss what they like in each other's book. Partners can also offer suggestions on ways to improve the books, such as telling where additional illustrations would be helpful. Each writer decides what changes to make and adds any final touches.

Customize Instruction for ELLs

Newcomers/Beginning Ask students questions with "embedded" answers based on their illustrations to help find the words to write.

Developing Have students read phrases or sentences aloud to a partner.

Expanding/Bridging Have students read the entire text for correct capitalization. Point out that special names of businesses, such as Anna's Grocery, should be capitalized.

Assessment Tools

Self-Assessment

Allow students to reflect and assess their own learning by completing *Learning Masters* pages 6–7.

- What I Learned, page 6
- How I Learned, page 7

Reading

The following assessment tools can help you evaluate and record students' progress in reading and understanding the theme books.

- Retelling Guide and Scoring Rubric, page 179
- Fluency Scoring Guide, page 180
- Oral Reading Record, page 189

Writing

Use the completed Take-Home Books and the following tools to assess students' development as writers.

- Writing Rubric, page 214
- Writing Traits Checklist, page 215

Content Assessment

Have students use magazines and catalogues to find pictures of *goods*, *transportation*, and *stores*. Have students glue the pictures they find to a brochure with the three interior pages labeled *Goods*, *Transportation*, and *Stores*. Have students describe each picture and explain how they decided on which page to place it.

Vocabulary and Oral Language

Use the following resources, in addition to the Think and Discuss scene on the *Theme Builder*, to assess oral language development.

- Content Vocabulary Checklist, page 218
- Oral Language Developmental Checklist, page 228

Optional Reading

Reading related titles allows students to explore concepts and vocabulary at different levels. It also allows them to use reading strategies in different types of texts. Encourage students to compare the theme books to the books in the next column.

Optional Titles

These related *Windows on Literacy* titles reinforce Key Concepts of the *Providing Goods* theme.

Nonfiction Titles

Loading the Airplane Level 10

What's on the Ships? Level 12

Jack's Boat Level 15

From Hive to Home Level 16

Fiction Titles

Grandpa's Castanets Level 13

Peggy's Pickles Level 14

Home Connection

The Family Focus letters on *Learning Masters* pages 31–32 summarize key concepts about providing goods. In the Share and Learn activity, family members talk about goods that they buy, the stores at which they shop, and how they think the goods got to the stores.

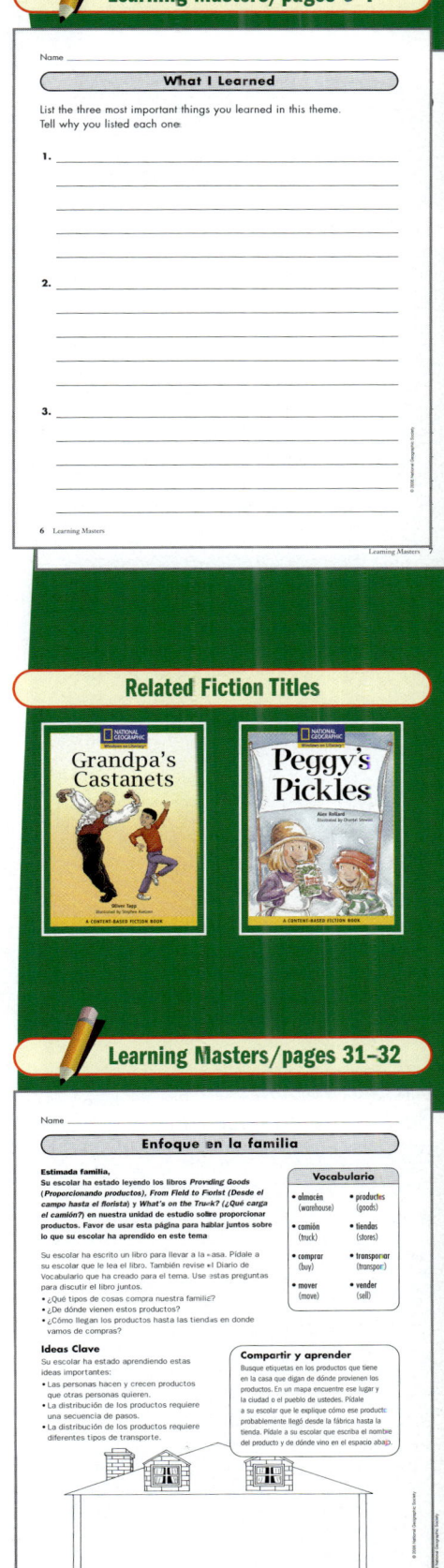

Learning Masters/pages 6–7

Related Fiction Titles

Learning Masters/pages 31–32

Measurement

STANDARDS

ACADEMIC LANGUAGE/ELD

- Use academic vocabulary related to the study of measurement
- Use appropriate language forms to explain measurement and to ask questions
- Develop fluency in reading, writing, listening to, and speaking English

MATH

- Use measurement in daily life
- Estimate and measure length, height, weight, and volume
- Measure the sizes, weights, and volumes of things, using nonstandard, U.S. customary, and metric units

READING/LANGUAGE ARTS

- Learn and apply the comprehension strategy: Asking Questions
- Use the text features: Contents and Headings and Inset Art
- Write about measurement
- Learn and use vocabulary related to measurement

Before Theme Assessment

To compare progress before and after teaching this theme, use one or more of the following informal assessment tools before beginning the theme.

- Oral Reading Record, page 191
- Fluency Scoring Guide, page 180
- Content Vocabulary Checklist, page 219
- Oral Language Developmental Checklist, page 228

Theme Materials

Concept Book

Measurement
Tessa Patel

Nonfiction Books

Measurement Tools
Level 14

Gingerbread
Level 14

Theme Builder

Learning Masters

Audiolesson on CD

Take-Home Book Masters

Measurement

by _____

Optional Reading

Windows on Literacy
Content-Based Fiction

How Much Bigger? Level 13

Neighborhood Soup Level 14

Windows on Literacy
Nonfiction

How Many Are in the Crowd? Level 14

Antlers Level 16

Giraffes Level 17

Numbers and You Level 21

Instructional Highlights

Key Concepts

- People use measurement in daily life.
- Length, height, weight, and volume can be estimated and measured.
- People can measure the sizes, weights, and volumes of things, using nonstandard, U.S. customary, and metric units.

Comprehension Strategy

Asking Questions

Key Concept Words

centimeter	meter
cup	ounce
feet/foot	pint
gallon	pound
gram	quart
inch	tablespoon
kilogram	teaspoon
liter	

Text Features

Contents/Headings

Inset Art

Theme Planner

Lesson 1*	Lesson 2	Lesson 3	Lesson 4	Lesson 5
Teacher's Guide pp. 70–71	Teacher's Guide pp. 72–73	Teacher's Guide pp. 74–75	Teacher's Guide pp. 76–77	Teacher's Guide pp. 78–79
Read *Measurement*	**Reread** *Measurement*	**Read** *Measurement Tools*	**Read** *Gingerbread*	**Assess and Extend**
• Introduce Concepts and Vocabulary	• Develop Concepts and Vocabulary	• Develop Concepts and Vocabulary	• Review Concepts and Vocabulary	• Rereading and Assessments
• Model and Share the Reading	• Introduce the Comprehension Strategy: Asking Questions	• Small Group Reading	• Small Group Reading	• Guided Writing
* Before you begin Lesson 1, you may want to use the Before Theme Assessment tools listed on page 68.	• Small Group Reading	• Practice the Comprehension Strategy: Asking Questions	• Apply the Comprehension Strategy: Asking Questions	• Assessment Tools
	• Modeled Writing	• Shared Writing	• Guided Writing	• Optional Reading
				• Home Connection

Lesson 1

Read *Measurement*

Measurement

Tessa Patel

OBJECTIVES

- Estimate and measure length, height, weight, and volume, using standard and nonstandard units
- Learn and use vocabulary related to measurement
- Use photos to predict vocabulary
- Use text features, such as inset art, to learn new words

Materials

Realia: rulers, measuring cup

Theme Builder

Measurement

Learning Masters page 33

 Audiolesson 4

Theme Builder (Response)

Theme Builder (Scene)

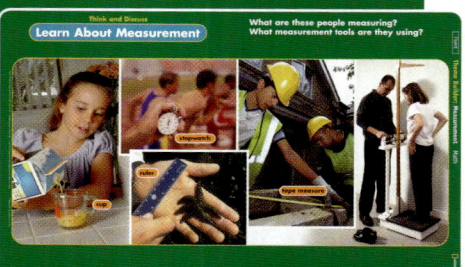

Introduce Concepts and Vocabulary

Introduce Theme Question

Ask students: How do you use measurement? Explain that they will learn about measurement. They will also learn the language to use when describing different types of measurements.

Turn and Talk Provide learning partners with several objects of varying lengths from the classroom. Have students estimate the length of each in inches. Then have them measure the length of each object in finger lengths, in inches, and in centimeters. Have students talk together about their measurements.

Develop Oral Language

Display a ruler. Model a sentence describing a ruler. A ruler is a tool that is used to measure length.

Next, display a measuring cup. Ask students to give some suggestions of things that are measured in this cup. Model a sentence about measuring liquids. I can use this measuring cup to measure one cup of water.

Turn and Talk Have partners talk about which tool would be best to measure different objects in the classroom, a ruler or a measuring cup.

Introduce Theme Response

Display the Theme Response on the *Theme Builder*. Have students say each response after you say the leader's part. Have learning partners use *Learning Masters* page 33 to practice reading the Theme Response.

Introduce Key Vocabulary

Use the Think and Discuss scene to teach Key Concept Words and model language forms.

Sometimes we want to find out how heavy something is. So we measure its weight. We measure pounds.

Continue to model sentences to identify objects in the scene and possible measurement units. As you introduce words, jot them down on chart paper. Display this Word Bank throughout the theme.

Turn and Talk Have students work with partners to practice using the words for measurement and language forms for explaining.

inch	pound	cup
feet/foot	gram	pint
centimeter	kilogram	quart
meter	teaspoon	gallon
ounce	tablespoon	liter

Build Background

Display the Think and Discuss scene on the *Theme Builder* again. Ask students to explain what is being measured and how it is measured.

Turn and Talk Have partners talk about how the girl is measuring the orange juice and practice using language forms for explaining. For example: Sometimes we want to find out how much liquid there is. So we measure the volume. We use (cups).

Model and Share the Reading

Preview the Book

Distribute copies of *Measurement*. Read aloud the title and the author's name. As you page through the book, point out:

- Most pages talk about one type of measurement, such as weight, volume, temperature, and time.
- The boldfaced words are vocabulary words.
- Inset art is used to show some measuring tools.

Predict Vocabulary

Encourage students to use pictures to predict vocabulary: Which words do you expect to see in this book?

Display pages 6–7 and cover the words: Which words do you expect to see on these pages?

Students may mention the objects on the pages, such as measuring tools and yarn. Add these words to the Word Bank. Have students talk with partners to describe the units of measurement they think are being used. Continue the activity with other pages as time allows.

Model the Reading

Invite students to follow along as you read aloud pages 4–7 in *Measurement*. Read fluently, modeling smooth, accurate reading with appropriate expression. After reading each pair of pages, pause to think aloud. Also, encourage students to ask questions and make observations.

Pages 4–5
Think Aloud This is like the Think and Discuss scene on the *Theme Builder*. I see all kinds of tools used for measuring.

Pages 6–7
Think Aloud The heading on this page is "Length, Width, and Height." I see measuring tools that must be used for measuring length, width, and height.

Share the Reading

Now have partners complete the reading. Encourage them to pause after reading one or two pages and have a discussion about what they read. Ask them to share the questions they have about the pages.

Reread for Fluency

To have students practice fluent reading, read aloud pages 6–7 of *Measurement*, sentence by sentence. Have students echo-read each sentence as you finish it. Then have students reread the entire book independently to build fluency. See *Customize the Reading*.

Customize the Reading

Students read and talk about Measurement *on their own to build fluency.*

- *Students who are not yet able to read the book can make comparisons between measurement types.*
- *Students who need extra support can reread the book while listening to the audiolesson.*
- *Students who can read the book might read independently or aloud with partners.*

Customize Instruction for ELLs

Newcomers/Beginning During reading, have students point to objects in the classroom. Use prompts such as, "Point to something we can measure with a measuring tape."

Developing Point to an object in the classroom and ask questions such as, "What would you use to measure this?" Have students answer in phrases or sentences.

Expanding/Bridging Ask students to find two objects in the classroom they would measure with a yardstick and explain their choices.

Lesson 2

Reread *Measurement*

Language, Literacy & Vocabulary!
Concept Book Math

Measurement

Tessa Patel

OBJECTIVES

- Understand that length, height, weight and volume can be estimated and measured, using nonstandard, U.S. customary and metric units
- Use vocabulary to explain how to measure objects
- Learn the comprehension strategy: Asking Questions
- Write an explanation of how to measure

Materials

Realia: ball, pencil, envelope, eraser, pen

Theme Builder

Measurement

Learning Masters pages 8, 34, 35

Audiolesson 4

Theme Builder (Graphic Organizer)

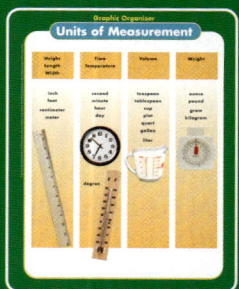

Develop Concepts and Vocabulary

Develop Oral Language

Display several objects, such as a ball, a pencil, an envelope, an eraser, and a pen. Ask students to think about how to measure these objects. Next, ask questions such as: What unit can I use to measure the length of the pen?

Turn and Talk Encourage learning partners to talk about the different units that can be used to measure each object.

Revisit the Theme Response Display the Theme Response on the *Theme Builder*. Begin the response again, replacing *inches* with *centimeters*, *pounds* with *ounces*, *minutes* with *seconds*, and *cups* with *teaspoons*. Read the revised response as a group.

Build Background

Display the graphic organizer on the *Theme Builder* with the unit and photos covered. Read the top left box, and have students predict some of the units for measuring height, length, and width. Then uncover the bottom left box and read the units aloud.

Turn and Talk Encourage partners to talk together about items that could be measured by using each unit.

Begin Vocabulary Log As students read, encourage them to use sticky notes to tag words that they would like to save. After reading, students can record the words and their notes about them.

Use *Learning Masters* page 8.

Introduce the Comprehension Strategy

Introduce Asking Questions

When students ask questions, they generate questions as they read, look for answers that may or may not be in the text, and self-monitor their comprehension.

When I read a book, I often wonder about the things I am reading and seeing in the pictures. That's called **asking questions.** I ask myself questions about what the words mean, how well I understand the information, and other things I want to learn. I look for answers to my questions in the text and make sure I understand before I continue reading.

Model Asking Questions

Turn to pages 8–9 and model the comprehension strategy and language forms for asking questions.

Think Aloud Before I read, I wondered what the people were using to measure.

While I read, I wondered why the people were using different units to measure certain things.

After I read, I wondered what other types of measurement people use every day.

For additional practice in asking questions, have partners work on *Learning Masters* page 34.

Small Group Reading

As students read, invite them to share what they notice. Use some of the suggestions below to encourage observations and talk about the book.

Pages 4–9
Support Comprehension Guide students to think about how length, width, and height are measured. Encourage them to use these language forms: We want to find out _____. So we _____. We use a _____.

Pages 10–13
Check Understanding Explain the difference between measuring weight and measuring volume. (*Measuring weight is measuring how heavy an object is. Measuring volume is measuring the amount of space something takes up.*)

Pages 14–17
Support Comprehension Ask a volunteer to summarize the information on these pages. (*A thermometer is used to measure temperature. Time is measured in minutes, hours, days, weeks, months, and years.*)

Pages 18–19
Check Understanding Using the Word Bank, tell how each unit listed is used in measurement. (*Inches and feet, and centimeters and meters, measure length, width, and height. Ounces and pounds, and grams and kilograms, measure weight. Teaspoons, tablespoons, cups, pints, quarts and gallons, and liters measure volume.*)

Discuss the Book
Invite students to share what they learned. Ask students to tell what they know about measuring objects. Encourage them to use the words in the Word Bank to discuss what they have read. Remind students to add words to their Vocabulary Logs.

Students can complete *Learning Masters* page 35.

Reread for Fluency
Have students follow along as you reread two sentences from page 14 in one breath. Ask students why it may have been difficult to understand you. (*You didn't pause. You ran everything together.*) Demonstrate how to read the sentences including pauses in the appropriate places. Have partners reread pages 14–15 for fluency. Ask them to focus on improving using appropriate pauses in their reading. For other suggestions, see *Customize the Reading.*

Learning Masters/pages 8, 34

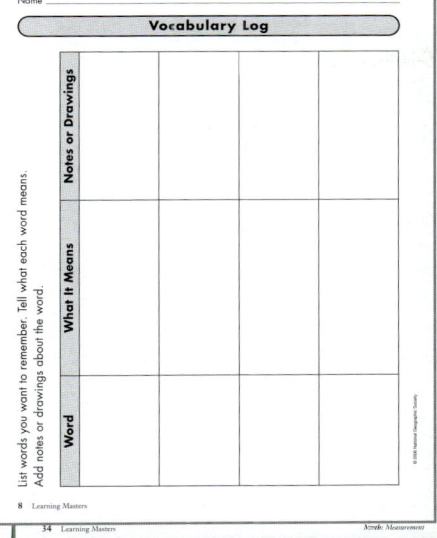

Customize the Reading
Students reread and talk about Measurement *using one of the following options:*

- *Look through the pages, hunting for tools used for measuring.*
- *Reread the book while following along with the audiolesson.*
- *Read independently or read aloud with a partner.*

Learning Masters/page 35

Modeled Writing

Use the graphic organizer on the *Theme Builder* to review some Key Concepts of the theme. Prepare to model writing using precise language to tell an order of steps.

Think Aloud I'm going to write about measuring our classroom. My goal is to tell the steps in this process. My audience is the students in this group.

Our classroom is wide and long. There are six sets of windows on one wall. There is enough room for everyone to line up by another wall.

We can guess how big our classroom is. But to be sure, we will measure it.

Think Aloud I'll tell how we measure the room and use words that show order, like *first* and *then.*

First, we measure the room's length. One person holds the measuring tape at one end of the room, and we pull the tape straight. Then we mark with a paperclip where the tape ends and move the tape to measure again.

OBJECTIVES

- Read to gain fluency in oral and silent reading
- Practice the comprehension strategy: Asking Questions
- Develop an understanding that people can measure the sizes, weights, and volumes of things, using nonstandard, U.S. customary, and metric units
- Use the Contents and Headings to find information
- Make a connection during reading

Materials

Realia: rulers; measuring cup, pint and quart containers; tablespoon, teaspoon, measuring tape, scale

Theme Builder

Measurement Tools

Learning Masters page 36

Audiolesson 4

Develop Concepts and Vocabulary

Develop Oral Language

Model the Key Concept Words *foot, cup, tablespoon, teaspoon, pint,* and *quart.* Display a ruler, a measuring cup, a tablespoon, and a teaspoon. These objects are all tools used for measurement. This measuring cup can measure cups, and can fill pints and quarts with liquid. The ruler can measure length, height, and width.

Turn and Talk Have learning partners measure different objects with a ruler. Have students talk about the measurements. I can measure my pencil with the ruler. My pencil is six inches long.

Revisit the Theme Response Display the response on the *Theme Builder.* Replace *inches, pounds, minutes,* and *cups* with *centimeters, grams, hours,* and *tablespoons.* Have students point to objects that can be measured in centimeters as you say that word.

Build Background

Distribute copies of *Measurement Tools.* Display a measuring cup, a ruler, a measuring tape, and a scale. Have students talk about how they can use each measurement tool in their everyday lives. What is each tool commonly used for?

Small Group Reading

Get Ready to Read

Preview the Book Read aloud the title, the author's name, and the Think and Discuss question on the back cover: What would you use to weigh a baby?

Page through the book and do the following:

- Point out the colored bars with the statements in them.
- Talk about how the Index page helps the reader find information.
- Ask students to predict what they will learn.

Predict Vocabulary Encourage students to use photos to predict vocabulary: Which words do you expect to see in this book?

Display a page and cover the words: Which words do you expect to see on this page?

List the words that students mention. Add Key Concept Words in the book that students do not mention.

Text Feature: Contents

Introduce Have students look at the Contents on page 2. The Contents tells what information is in this book.

Model I want to find information about cups and spoons. I see the listing here for cups and spoons, and a page number—page 10. When I turn to page 10, I see the heading matches the listing in the Contents.

Practice Have students name the listing they would choose in the Contents to find information about different kinds of tools. (*Many Kinds of Tools*)

Read the Book

As students read, invite them to share what they notice. Use some of the suggestions below to encourage observations and talk about the book.

Pages 3–5

Key Concept Words *cup, tablespoon, teaspoon*

Practice the Comprehension Strategy

Guide students to see that asking questions will help them remember and understand what they read.

What is bigger? A teaspoon or a tablespoon?

Pages 6–9

Key Concept Word *foot*

Support Comprehension Point out that the people in these photos are using measurement as part of their everyday lives. Ask students to think of other uses around home or work for the measurement tools shown.

Pages 14–16

Support Comprehension Ask students what listing they would find in the Contents for page 14. *(Scales)* Then have students explain how the scales on pages 14–15 are being used. Have students share how they use scales in their homes.

Discuss the Book

Invite students to use the Word Bank to discuss the book and to share what they learned. Ask students how what they learned in this book is related to what they learned in the book *Measurement. (Both books talk about how to measure things such as height, weight, and volume. Both books talk about units of measurement and how to use different measuring tools.)* Have students add words to their Vocabulary Logs.

Use *Learning Masters* page 36.

Reread for Fluency

Have students reread the entire book independently to build fluency. See *Customize the Reading.*

Learning Masters/page 36

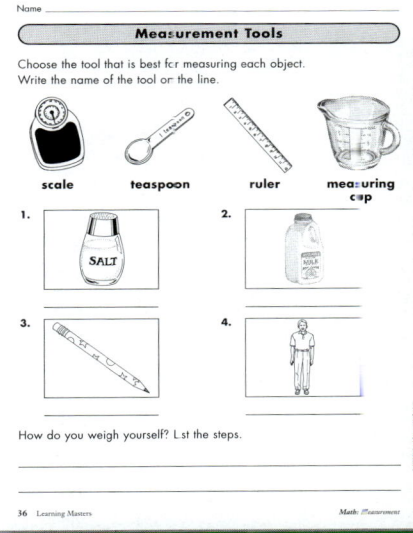

Customize the Reading

Students reread and talk about Measurement Tools using one of the following options:

- Look through the pages and name the different tools used for measurement.
- Reread the book while following along with the audiolesson.
- Read independently or aloud with a partner.

Shared Writing

Review the writing you modeled in Lesson 2. Invite students to participate as you continue writing. Explain that you want to write a paragraph about measuring volume and weight. Guide students to frame sentences that describe different ways to measure the weight of an object. Then guide students to frame sentences that describe different ways to measure volume. As students continue, encourage them to put the steps they include for measuring weight and volume in the correct order.

Customize Instruction for ELLs

Newcomers/Beginning Have students point to objects in the book that are used for measuring volume and name them.

Developing Encourage students to finish sentences such as, "We use a *(scale)* to measure *(weight)*."

Expanding/Bridging Have students list their own examples of measuring weight and volume.

OBJECTIVES

- Read to gain fluency in oral and silent reading
- Apply the comprehension strategy: Asking Questions
- Understand that people use measurement in daily life
- Use inset art to comprehend text
- Understand that measurements are highlighted in the text

Materials

Realia: measuring cup, water, teaspoon, sugar, tablespoon, flour

Theme Builder

Gingerbread

Learning Masters pages 37, 38

Take-Home Book Masters: *Measurement*

 Audiolesson 4

 **Take-Home Book Masters**

Measurement

by _____

Review Concepts and Vocabulary

Develop Oral Language

Model the Key Concept Words *cup*, *tablespoon*, and *teaspoon*. Have students complete sentences using the words. For example, show students a measuring cup filled with water, a teaspoon filled with sugar, and a tablespoon filled with flour.

The _____ is full of water.

The _____ is full of sugar.

The _____ is full of flour.

Turn and Talk Have students talk with a learning partner about times when they have used a measuring cup, tablespoon, and teaspoon.

Revisit the Theme Response Display the response on the *Theme Builder*. This time, replace *inches*, *pounds*, *minutes*, and *cups* with *feet*, *ounces*, *seconds*, and *teaspoons*. Invite students to hold up a 12-inch ruler while saying *feet*.

Build Background

Distribute copies of *Gingerbread*. Invite students to share their experiences with baking. Ask them to talk about the different measurements they used in recipes. Encourage them to use the language forms for explaining:

We wanted to _____. So we _____.
We used a _____.

Small Group Reading

Get Ready to Read

Preview the Book Read aloud the title, the author's name, and the Think and Discuss question on the back cover: Do you know how to make gingerbread?

Page through the book and do the following:

- Point out the inset art on the pages.
- Invite students to find some of the objects that are in the Picture Glossary.
- Ask students to predict what they will learn.

Predict Vocabulary Encourage students to use photos to predict vocabulary: Which words do you expect to see in this book?

Display a page and cover the words: Which words do you expect to see on this page?

List the words students mention. Add Key Concept Words in the book that students do not mention.

Text Feature: Inset Art

Introduce Display pages 4–5. On this page, there is one big photo and a small picture of a measuring cup. This small picture is called inset art. It focuses attention on the measuring cup and shows the correct measurement.

Model The first thing that I notice on page 5 is the inset art of the measuring cup. This tells me that the measuring cup is used on this page and shows how much sugar is measured.

Practice Ask students what the inset art on page 9 tells them.

Read the Book

As students read, invite them to share what they notice. Use some of the suggestions below to encourage observations and talk about the book.

Pages 2–5

Key Concept Word *cup*

Support Comprehension Ask students to summarize what has happened in the book so far. *(The people are making gingerbread. They have measured the butter and sugar.)*

Pages 6–9

Apply the Comprehension Strategy

Encourage students to **Ask Questions** to help them better understand pages 6–9.

Before I read, I wondered _____.

While I read, I wondered _____.

After I read, I wondered _____.

Pages 10–13

Support Comprehension Ask students to describe what Mom did after she used butter to grease the baking pan.

Pages 14–16

Check Understanding What ingredients were used to make the gingerbread? *(butter, sugar, molasses, eggs, flour, ginger, baking soda)*

Discuss the Book

Invite students to use the Word Bank to tell about the book. What have they learned about measurement from both theme books? How do people use measurement in their everyday lives? Remind students to add words to their Vocabulary Logs.

Use *Learning Masters* page 37.

Reread for Fluency

Have students reread the entire book independently to build fluency. See *Customize the Reading.*

Learning Masters/page 37

Gingerbread

Draw a picture of a measuring cup.
Draw a picture of a teaspoon.
Draw a picture of a tablespoon.

Describe what they all have in common.

Write a sentence about each tool. Tell what you would measure with it.

Math: Measurement   *Learning Masters* 37

Customize the Reading

Students reread and talk about Gingerbread *using one of the following options:*

- *Look through the pages and name the ingredients used throughout the book.*
- *Reread the book while following along with the audiolesson.*
- *Read independently or aloud with a partner.*

Learning Masters/page 38

Graphic Organizer

Use this graphic organizer to plan what you will write in your Take-Home Book on measurement.

Length	Time	Volume	Weight

38 Learning Masters   *Math: Measurement*

Guided Writing

Distribute copies of the *Take-Home Book Masters.* Read the title and page through the book. Explain that students will write books about measuring. Work with students to:

- Describe the photos.
- Describe what is being measured and how the measurement is made.
- Share writing ideas for each set of pages.

Record students' writing ideas for the pages of their books on chart paper.

Have partners talk together to plan what to write. Then have each student complete a graphic organizer. In each column, have students list a few notes about what they would like to include. They may also want to write words to use for each section of their books. Display the Word Bank and remind students to check their Vocabulary Logs as they plan and then begin to write.

Use *Learning Masters* page 38.

OBJECTIVES

- Use Key Concepts and Key Concept Words in writing
- Demonstrate oral language proficiency
- Demonstrate comprehension of theme selections
- Read related titles to reinforce Key Concepts and vocabulary

Materials

Take-Home Book Masters: *Measurement*

Learning Masters pages 6–7, 39–40

Assessment Masters pages 179, 180, 191, 214, 215, 219, 228

Take-Home Book Masters

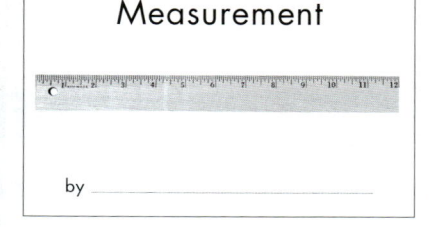

Measurement

by _____

Rereading and Assessments

Allow time for students to independently reread the theme selections. Display the Word Bank for students' reference as they read.

As students reread, meet with individuals. Use the assessment tools listed on page 79 to evaluate students' progress and to update their records.

Guided Writing

Students continue writing the Take-Home Books they began in Lesson 4. Review the group list of writing ideas. Display the Word Bank.

Page through the theme books to review the text features, including inset art and the contents and headings. Talk about text features that students could add to their Take-Home Books. For example, they might draw inset art to emphasize an idea shown in some photos in their books.

Point out that good writers:

- Plan their writing. Students can use their completed graphic organizer as a springboard for writing.
- Vary their sentences. Students may include compound sentences.

- Revise their work. Have students check that each paragraph has a main idea and that each sentence supports that main idea.

Have students complete the Picture Glossary and About the Author last.

As students write, circulate to coach and support individuals. If students need help, try asking what they might add to help the reader understand their idea. Guide them to add information.

Have partners exchange books and discuss what they like in each other's book. Partners can offer suggestions for improvement, such as reorganizing a confusing sentence. Each writer decides what changes to make.

Customize Instruction for ELLs

Newcomers/Beginning Provide sentence frames such as the following: We want to find out _____ . So we _____ . We use a _____ .

Developing Provide sentence stems and have students suggest words to complete the sentences. Have students read their completed sentences to a partner.

Expanding/Bridging Have partners suggest complete sentences or ways to phrase an idea. Encourage students to use compound sentences.

Assessment Tools

Self-Assessment

Allow students to reflect and assess their own learning by completing *Learning Masters* pages 6–7.

- What I Learned, page 6
- How I Learned, page 7

Reading

The following assessment tools can help you evaluate and record students' progress in reading and understanding the theme books.

- Retelling Guide and Scoring Rubric, page 179
- Fluency Scoring Guide, page 180
- Oral Reading Record, page 191

Writing

Use the completed Take-Home Books and the following tools to assess students' development as writers.

- Writing Rubric, page 214
- Writing Traits Checklist, page 215

Content Assessment

Have students create a poster that includes the various units of measurement they have learned. Students can draw pictures to represent each unit and group the units according to what they measure (such as length, time, or volume). Have groups measure a few items in U.S. customary, metric, and nonstandard units and compare the measurements. Have them present their findings to another group.

Vocabulary and Oral Language

Use the following resources, in addition to the Think and Discuss scene on the *Theme Builder,* to assess oral language development.

- Content Vocabulary Checklist, page 219
- Oral Language Developmental Checklist, page 228

Learning Masters/pages 6–7

Optional Reading

Reading related titles allows students to explore concepts and vocabulary at different levels. It also allows them to use reading strategies in different types of texts. Encourage children to compare the theme books to the books in the next column.

Optional Titles

These related *Windows on Literacy* titles reinforce Key Concepts of the *Measurement* theme.

Nonfiction Titles

How Many Are in the Crowd? Level 14

Antlers Level 16

Giraffes Level 17

Numbers and You Level 21

Fiction Titles

How Much Bigger? Level 13

Neighborhood Soup Level 14

Related Fiction Titles

Learning Masters/pages 39–40

Home Connection

The Family Focus letters on *Learning Masters* pages 39–40 summarize key concepts about measurement.

In the Share and Learn activity, family members will work together to measure ingredients and make a favorite family recipe.

79

Overview

Wind, Water, and Sunlight

STANDARDS

ACADEMIC LANGUAGE/ELD
- Use academic vocabulary related to the study of wind, water, and sunlight
- Use appropriate language forms to visualize and to explain the forces of wind, water, and sunlight
- Develop fluency in reading, writing, listening to, and speaking English

SCIENCE
- Recognize that wind, water, and sunlight are powerful forces
- Describe how wind, water, and sunlight can change nonliving things
- Identify the ways people and other living things use wind, water, and sunlight

READING/LANGUAGE ARTS
- Learn and apply the comprehension strategy: Visualizing
- Use the text features: Highlighted Vocabulary and Special Page Features
- Write about wind, water, and sunlight
- Learn and use vocabulary related to wind, water, and sunlight

Before Theme Assessment

To compare progress before and after teaching this theme, use one or more of the following informal assessment tools before beginning the theme.

- Oral Reading Record, pages 193
- Fluency Scoring Guide, page 180
- Content Vocabulary Checklist, page 220
- Oral Language Developmental Checklist, page 228

Theme Materials

Concept Book

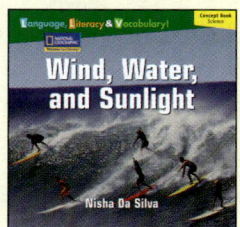

Nonfiction Books

Level 15

Level 16

Theme Builder

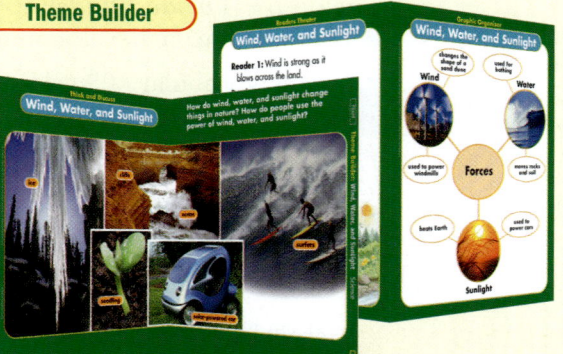

Learning Masters

Audiolesson on CD

Take-Home Book Masters

Optional Reading

Windows on Literacy
Content-Based Fiction

Sailing with Sam Level 15

Too Close to the Sun: A Play Based on the Ancient Myth of Icarus Level 16

Windows on Literacy
Nonfiction

Water Power Level 15

When a Storm Comes Level 15

Light Level 22

The Sun Level 22

Instructional Highlights

Key Concepts

- Wind, water, and sunlight are powerful forces.
- Wind, water, and sunlight can change nonliving things.
- People and other living things use wind, water, and sunlight.

Comprehension Strategy

Visualizing

Key Concept Words

heat	sunlight
melts	water
power	wind

Text Features

Highlighted Vocabulary

Special Page Features

Theme Planner

Lesson 1*	Lesson 2	Lesson 3	Lesson 4	Lesson 5
Teacher's Guide pp. 82–83	Teacher's Guide pp. 84–85	Teacher's Guide pp. 86–87	Teacher's Guide pp. 88–89	Teacher's Guide pp. 90–91
Read *Wind, Water, and Sunlight*	**Reread** *Wind, Water, and Sunlight*	**Read** *Sun Power*	**Read** *Wind Power*	**Assess and Extend**
• Introduce Concepts and Vocabulary	• Develop Concepts and Vocabulary	• Develop Concepts and Vocabulary	• Review Concepts and Vocabulary	• Rereading and Assessments
• Model and Share the Reading	• Introduce the Comprehension Strategy: Visualizing	• Small Group Reading	• Small Group Reading	• Guided Writing
* Before you begin Lesson 1, you may want to use the Before Theme Assessment tools listed on page 80.	• Small Group Reading	• Practice the Comprehension Strategy: Visualizing	• Apply the Comprehension Strategy: Visualizing	• Assessment Tools
	• Modeled Writing	• Shared Writing	• Guided Writing	• Optional Reading
				• Home Connection

Read *Wind, Water, and Sunlight*

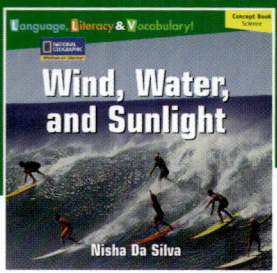

Language, Literacy & Vocabulary!
NATIONAL GEOGRAPHIC
Wind, Water, and Sunlight
Nisha Da Silva

OBJECTIVES

- Recognize the power of wind, water, and sunlight
- Learn and use vocabulary related to wind, water, and sunlight
- Use photos to predict vocabulary
- Use text features, such as sidebars, to learn more about a concept

Materials

Realia: cup of water

Photos: hurricane destruction, sunlight on snow

Theme Builder

Wind, Water, and Sunlight

Learning Masters page 41

Audiolesson 5

Theme Builder (Readers Theater)

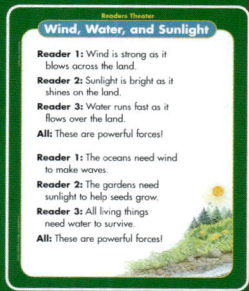

Theme Builder (Scene)

Introduce Concepts and Vocabulary

Introduce Theme Question

Ask students: What are all the different ways you have used water today? Explain that students will learn about wind, water, and sunlight. Tell them they will also learn the language to use when explaining about wind, water, and sunlight.

Turn and Talk Have learning partners make a three-column chart labeled *Wind*, *Water*, and *Sunlight*. Ask students to fill in the columns with what they know about each one.

Develop Oral Language

Display a cup of water. Pour the water over a small object so that the object moves. Model a sentence that includes the words *water* and *makes*: Water makes the pencil move.

Show a photo of destruction from a hurricane. Model a sentence that includes the words *wind* and *make*: A strong wind can make windows break.

Show a photo of sunlight shining on snow. Model a sentence that includes the words *sunlight* and *make*: Sunlight can make snow melt.

Turn and Talk Have partners discuss powerful actions caused by water, wind, and sunlight.

Introduce Readers Theater

Display the Readers Theater selection on the *Theme Builder*. Ask three students to read the parts. Tell them to read the "All" part together. Have partners use *Learning Masters* page 41 to discuss what each natural force does.

Introduce Key Vocabulary

Use the Think and Discuss scene to teach Key Concept Words and model language forms.

People use sunlight to drive solar-powered cars.

The power of water makes rocks change shape.

Continue to model sentences, using the words listed below to help explain the concepts in the scene. As you introduce words, jot them down on chart paper. Display this Word Bank throughout the theme.

Turn and Talk Have partners work together to create sentences. Tell them to use the vocabulary words and a language form such as the following:

People use _____ to _____.

heat	sunlight
melts	water
power	wind

Build Background

Display the Think and Discuss scene on the *Theme Builder* again. Ask students to explain whether each photo shows the power of wind, water, or sunlight.

Turn and Talk Have partners practice explaining to each other how the forces of wind, water, and sunlight each affect the seedling. For example: Sunlight makes *(the seedling grow)*.

Model and Share the Reading

Learning Masters/page 41

Preview the Book

Distribute copies of *Wind, Water, and Sunlight*. Read aloud the title and the author's name. As you page through the book, point out:

- Headings tell about the concepts introduced on the pages.
- Some pages include "Did You Know?" sidebars that provide more information.
- The Picture Glossary shows the meanings of important words.

Predict Vocabulary

Encourage students to use pictures to predict vocabulary: Which words do you expect to see in this book?

Display pages 6–7 and cover the words: Which words do you expect to see on these pages?

Students may mention *sand dunes*, *blows*, and *plants*. Add these words to the Word Bank. Have students talk with partners as they use the words *wind* and *makes* to explain each photo. Continue the activity as time allows.

Model the Reading

Invite students to follow along as you read aloud pages 4–7 in *Wind, Water, and Sunlight*. Read fluently, modeling smooth, accurate reading with appropriate expression. After reading each pair of pages, pause to think aloud. Also, encourage students to ask questions and make observations.

Pages 4–5
Think Aloud These pages are like the Think and Discuss pictures we talked about earlier. Each photo shows the power of wind, water, or sunlight.

Pages 6–7
Think Aloud The heading tells me these pages are about the power of wind. I can see examples of this power in each photo. The highlighted words are vocabulary words.

Share the Reading

Now have partners complete the reading. Encourage them to pause after reading one or two pages and have conversations about what they have read. Ask them to share their questions.

Reread for Fluency

Model fluency as you emphasize pace while reading aloud pages 8–9 in *Wind, Water, and Sunlight*. Have students echo-read each sentence as you finish, imitating your model. Then have them read the entire book independently to build fluency. See *Customize the Reading*.

Readers Theater

Reader 1: Wind is strong as it blows across the land.

Reader 2: Sunlight is bright as it shines on the land.

Reader 3: Water runs fast as it flows over the land.

All: These are powerful forces!

Reader 1: The oceans need wind to make waves.

Reader 2: The gardens need sunlight to help seeds grow.

Reader 3: All living things need water to survive.

All: These are powerful forces!

Science: Wind, Water, and Sunlight — Learning Masters **41**

Customize the Reading

Students reread and talk about Wind, Water, and Sunlight *on their own to build fluency.*

- *Students who are not yet able to read the book can look for examples of people using wind, water, and sunlight.*
- *Students who need extra support can reread the book while listening to the audiolesson.*
- *Students who can read the book might read independently or aloud with partners.*

Customize Instruction for ELLs

Newcomers/Beginning During reading, have students draw examples to show ways people use wind, water, and sunlight.

Developing Ask students to make statements explaining how people use wind, water, and sunlight. Encourage them to use this language form: People use ＿＿＿ to ＿＿＿.

Expanding/Bridging Ask students to use Key Concept Words as they answer the questions on pages 8, 12, and 16 of *Wind, Water, and Sunlight*.

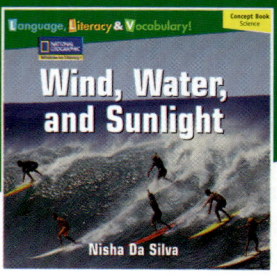

OBJECTIVES

- Understand that people and other living things use wind, water, and sunlight and that these powerful forces can change nonliving things
- Use vocabulary to name the powerful forces and explain what they can do
- Learn the comprehension strategy: Visualizing
- Read to gain fluency in oral and silent reading
- Write to explain the power of wind, water, and sunlight

Materials

Theme Builder

Wind, Water, and Sunlight

Learning Masters pages 8, 42, 43

Audiolesson 5

Theme Builder (Graphic Organizer)

Develop Concepts and Vocabulary

Develop Oral Language

Have students try to blow a pencil across their desks. Ask them to name the force that they are imitating. Explain how you know wind is a powerful force.

Turn and Talk Have conversation partners discuss examples of the power of wind and of sunlight and water. Have them use this language form: The power of (*wind*) makes (*trees bend*).

Revisit Readers Theater Display the Readers Theater selection on the *Theme Builder.* Invite three pairs to read the parts. After each line, have all students repeat, in unison, which force each pair of readers is presenting.

Build Background

Display the graphic organizer on the *Theme Builder* with only the center oval showing. Ask students to name the three forces this book is about. Then uncover the ovals that name and show the forces. Have students discuss examples of how each force can affect the land and how people use each resource.

Turn and Talk Encourage partners to use the examples of each force in sentences that connect back to the center oval.

Begin Vocabulary Log As students read, encourage them to use sticky notes to tag words they would like to save. After reading, students can record the words and their notes about them.

Use *Learning Masters* page 8.

Introduce the Comprehension Strategy

Introduce Visualizing

When students visualize, they create mental images to guide them in understanding what they are reading. By combining information they already know with descriptive words in the text, students can develop mental pictures to help them understand the text.

Think Aloud When I read a book, words and phrases can help me make a picture in my mind of what I'm reading. I combine things that I already know with new information from the reading to help me picture what is happening in the book. When I do this, I am **visualizing.** This helps me better understand the book.

Model Visualizing

Turn to pages 8–9, and model the comprehension strategy and language forms for visualizing.

In my mind, I can picture clothes hanging on a line in a backyard. The wind makes these clothes move and flap. They snap in the wind.

I know that the clothes are wet when they are first put on the line. The wind blows on them throughout the day and helps them dry.

The picture in my mind helps me understand the power of the wind.

For additional practice in visualizing, have partners work on *Learning Masters* page 42.

Small Group Reading

As students read, invite them to share what they notice. Use some of the suggestions below to encourage observations and talk about the book.

Pages 4–9
Support Comprehension Guide students in visualizing additional examples of the power of wind. Encourage them to picture a kite flying on a windy day. What keeps the kite in the sky? How does the kite move? What causes these actions?

Pages 10–17
Support Comprehension Ask a volunteer to summarize the pages about water and another to summarize the pages about sunlight.

Pages 18–19
Check Understanding Have students use the Word Bank to help them describe and explain what they see in each photo. What are the forces affecting the things in each photo?

Discuss the Book

Invite students to share what they have learned. Have them compare the many ways people use wind, water, and sunlight. Encourage them to use the words in the Word Bank to discuss what they have read. Remind students to add words to their Vocabulary Logs.

Students can complete *Learning Masters* page 43.

Reread for Fluency

At a rate that is much too slow, read aloud the sidebar on page 13. Then ask students how you might make your reading smoother, clearer, and more interesting. *(Read faster.)* Point out that it is important to use a speed that makes sense, based on what they are reading. Demonstrate reading this sidebar again, with attention to pace. Then have partners reread pages 6–13. Ask them to focus on improving the pace of their reading. For other suggestions, see *Customize the Reading.*

Learning Masters/pages 3, 42

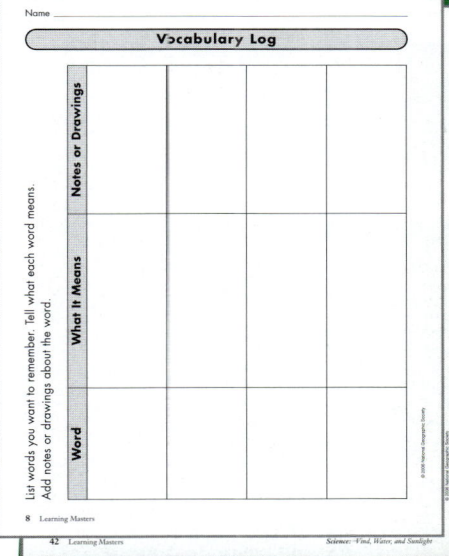

Customize the Reading

Students reread and talk about Wind, Water, and Sunlight, *using one of the following options:*

- Look through the pages and find the photos of places where someone might feel heat from sunlight.
- Reread the book while following along with the audiolesson.
- Read independently or read aloud with a partner.

Modeled Writing

Use the graphic organizer on the *Theme Builder* to review some Key Concepts of the theme. Prepare to model writing, including how to use active verbs.

Think Aloud I know that the wind is a powerful force. I'll write about something that shows the wind's force—the waves of the ocean. I'll begin by picturing the ocean with tall waves. Some words to describe the waves are *mighty, tall, strong,* and *rushing.* Some words to describe the actions of the waves are *crash, roll, boom,* and *race.* I'm going to describe a scene. My purpose is to show the wind's force. My audience is the students in this group.

Tall waves crash against the sand. They boom and roll into shore. First one wave comes, and then another wave follows. The waves are racing each other.

Think Aloud Now I want to tell that the wind is causing the tall waves. I'll begin a new paragraph.

The wind whistles. It blows and shakes the trees on shore. The wind pushes against the ocean water. It makes the ocean's waves high and strong.

Learning Masters/page 43

Lesson 3

Read *Sun Power*

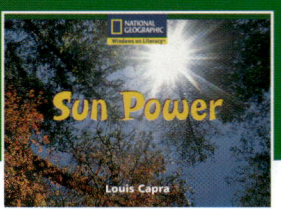

OBJECTIVES

- Read to gain fluency in oral and silent reading
- Practice the comprehension strategy: Visualizing
- Understand that sunlight is a powerful force
- Use Highlighted Vocabulary to comprehend text
- Analyze a compound word

Materials

Theme Builder

Sun Power

Learning Masters page 44

Audiolesson 5

Develop Concepts and Vocabulary

Develop Oral Language

Model a sentence, using the following language form for explaining, as well as the Key Concept Words *heat*, *melts*, and *power*.

Sun power melts snow.

Sun power can heat a home.

Turn and Talk Have learning partners challenge each other with riddles. Provide the following example:

Because of this power, my car does not need gasoline. I can use sunlight. (*Answer: Sun power; sun power makes solar-powered cars run.*)

Revisit Readers Theater Display the Readers Theater selection on the *Theme Builder*. Have students suggest a new line for wind, sunlight, or water. Then read the Readers Theater selection again with the new line.

Build Background

Distribute copies of *Sun Power*. Ask students to remember how it feels to stand in sunlight. Have them describe the warmth and brightness of sunlight. Then explain that, because the sun is so far away, its power must be very strong to reach Earth.

Small Group Reading

Get Ready to Read

Preview the Book Read aloud the title, the author's name, and the Think and Discuss question on the back cover: What makes this car go?

Page through the book, and do the following:

- Point out the questions.
- Point out the heading *Sun power!* on each partial page.
- Ask students to predict what they will learn.

Predict Vocabulary Encourage students to use photos to predict vocabulary: Which words do you expect to see in this book?

Display a page and cover the words: Which words do you expect to see on this page?

List the words students mention. Add Key Concept Words in the book that students do not mention.

Text Feature: Highlighted Vocabulary

Introduce Direct students' attention to the phrase *sun power* on page 4. These words are a different color and style than the words below them. This tells us the words are important.

Model Point out and read aloud the question on page 2. I think I know the answer. When I turn the page, the highlighted words on page 4 answer the question. Highlighting is used to show answers. Highlighting also emphasizes the answer.

Practice Have partners look through the book to read the questions and say in unison the answer that is highlighted.

Read the Book

As students read, invite them to share what they notice. Use some of the suggestions below to encourage observations and talk about the book.

Pages 2–5

Key Concept Words *power, sunlight*

Support Comprehension After students turn the partial page, point out the word *sun*. Point out how the word *sun* is part of the compound vocabulary word *sunlight*. Knowing the word *sun* helps them know the meaning of *sunlight*—light directly from the sun.

Pages 6–9

Key Concept Words *melts, heat*

Practice the Comprehension Strategy

Use questions to help students **Visualize** the information on pages 6–9.

Can you picture in your mind what it's like to be near this ice? Can you picture how the ice begins to melt and crack apart in sunlight? How does the ice sound? How does it look? How would it feel beneath your feet?

Pages 10–17

Support Comprehension Make sure students understand that they are looking at a solar-powered car and solar panels. Explain that the panels collect and store the power from sunlight.

Pages 19–23

Check Understanding What warms you and helps dry clothes outside? (*The heat from the sun warms both people and clothes and helps clothes dry.*)

Discuss the Book

Invite students to use the Word Bank to discuss the book and share what they learned. Have them discuss what they found most interesting in the book. Then ask what else helps dry clothes. Remind students that they read about it in *Wind, Water, and Sunlight. (Wind helps dry clothes.)* Have students add words to their Vocabulary Logs.

Use *Learning Masters* page 44.

Reread for Fluency

Have students reread the entire book independently to build fluency. See *Customize the Reading.*

Learning Masters/page 44

Name _____

Sun Power

Write two more questions for a test about sun power.
Give your questions to a partner.
Answer your partner's questions.
Talk to your partner about the answers.

1. How does the sun help plants? _____

Answer: Sunlight helps plants grow.

2. _____

Answer: _____

3. _____

Answer: _____

44   Learning Masters   Science: *Wind, Water, and Sunlight*

Customize the Reading

Students reread and talk about Sun Power, *using one of the following options:*

- *Look through the pages, explaining how sun power affects each item.*
- *Reread the book while following along with the audiolesson.*
- *Read independently or aloud with a partner.*

Shared Writing

Review the paragraphs you modeled in Lesson 2. Tell students you want to write about how wind changes other nonliving things. Have volunteers provide examples of changes made by the force of the wind. Help students write a sentence to tell the main idea of the paragraph. Ask them to suggest describing words and phrases that help explain how the changes happen.

Customize Instruction for ELLs

Newcomers/Beginning Have students point out and name what is shown in the photo segments that remain visible after a partial page is turned.

Developing Ask students to use the word *power* to explain something other than wind and give examples of it.

Expanding/Bridging Have students share how they visualize the wind blowing or other forces at work, using vivid describing words.

Lesson 4   Read *Wind Power*

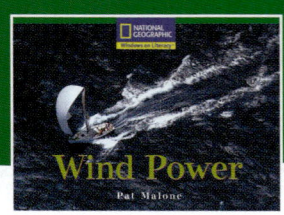

OBJECTIVES

- Read to gain fluency in oral and silent reading
- Apply the comprehension strategy: Visualizing
- Understand that wind is a powerful force
- Use Special Page Features to answer questions
- Check predictions during reading

Materials

Photos: hurricane destruction of buildings

Theme Builder

Wind Power

Learning Masters pages 45, 46

Take-Home Book Masters: *Wind, Water, and Sunlight*

Audiolesson 5

Take-Home Book Masters

Wind, Water, and Sunlight

by _____

Review Concepts and Vocabulary

Develop Oral Language

Display the photos of hurricane destruction. Ask students to think about the force needed to do this damage. Then model using Key Concept Words: The power of wind has enough force to break windows.

Encourage students to share experiences they have had with the power of wind. Have them use the Key Concept Words *power* and *wind*.

Turn and Talk Have conversation partners share additional wind-related experiences. Tell them to take turns completing this language form:

Wind power can make (*a kite fly*).

Revisit Readers Theater
Display the Readers Theater selection on the *Theme Builder*. Organize students into three groups. Have each group read a part aloud. Some students can pantomime with the reading.

Build Background

Distribute copies of *Wind Power*. Remind students that even though wind cannot be seen, the effects of the wind can be seen. Ask students to tell about some things that show the wind's power. Encourage them to use this language form for explaining:

The wind's power can make _____.

Small Group Reading

Get Ready to Read

Preview the Book Read aloud the title, the author's name, and the Think and Discuss question on the back cover: What helps this kite fly?

Page through the book and do the following:

- Point out the Index at the end of the book.
- Encourage students to run their fingers across pages to find partial pages.
- Ask students to predict what they will learn.

Predict Vocabulary Encourage students to use photos to predict vocabulary: Which words do you expect to see in this book?

Display a page, and cover the words: Which words do you expect to see on this page?

List the words students mention. Add Key Concept Words in the book that students do not mention.

Text Feature: Special Page Features

Introduce Display pages 2 and 3 in *Wind Power*. Read the question and then turn the half-page. The half-page is a special feature. It gives an answer and a picture.

Model On pages 6 and 7, I read, "What makes trees grow bent over?" I think it's the wind. When I turn the half-page, I see "Wind power!" I see a picture of a tree blown sideways.

Practice Have partners work together to read the question on page 10, suggest an answer, and then turn the half-page to see what the answer tells them.

Read the Book

As students read, invite them to share what they notice. Use some of the suggestions below to encourage observations and talk about the book.

Pages 2–9

Key Concept Words *wind, power*

Support Comprehension Point out the partial pages. Have students try to predict answers before turning each partial page.

Pages 10–13

Apply the Comprehension Strategy

Encourage students to **Visualize** to help them understand pages 10–13.

In my mind, I can picture _____.

I know that _____.

The picture in my mind helps me understand _____.

Guide students in understanding that their visualizations can help them make pictures in their minds of wind sending the seeds far away and then floating to the ground to take root.

Pages 14–17

Check Understanding Tell how sand dunes move to new places. (*Wind power blows sand to new places.*)

Pages 18–23

Support Comprehension Ask partners to explain to each other how a windmill works.

Discuss the Book

Invite students to share what they learned about wind power. Have them use the Word Bank to compare what they learned in this book to what they learned about wind in *Wind, Water, and Sunlight*. Remind students to add words to their Vocabulary Logs.

Use *Learning Masters* page 45.

Reread for Fluency

Have students reread the entire book independently to build fluency. See *Customize the Reading*.

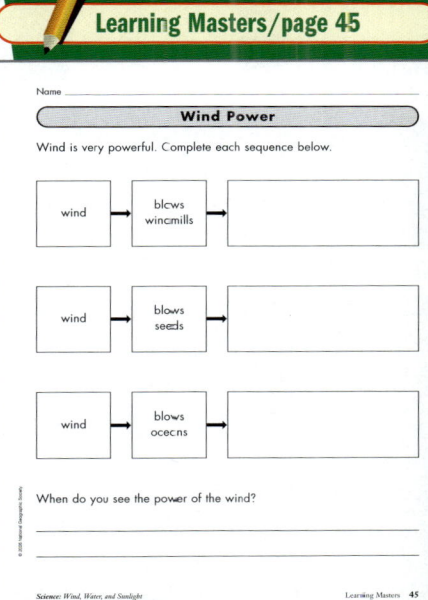

Learning Masters/page 45

Customize the Reading

Students reread and talk about Wind Power, using one of the following options:

- *Look through the pages and find the nonliving things.*
- *Reread the book while following along with the audiolesson.*
- *Read independently or aloud with a partner.*

Guided Writing

Distribute copies of the **Take-Home Book Masters**. Read the title and page through the book. Explain that students will write books about wind, water, and sunlight. Work with students to:

- Complete the Contents page.
- Explain how people use each powerful force.
- Share writing ideas for each pair of pages.

Record students' writing ideas for the pages of their books on chart paper. Have them suggest ways to explain how people use each of the forces.

Tell partners that they will plan what to write. Explain that each partner will complete a web graphic organizer. Guide students to write two examples for each force on their webs. Have them add describing words in the circle beneath each force name. Display the Word Bank, and remind students to check their Vocabulary Logs as they begin to write.

Use *Learning Masters* page 46.

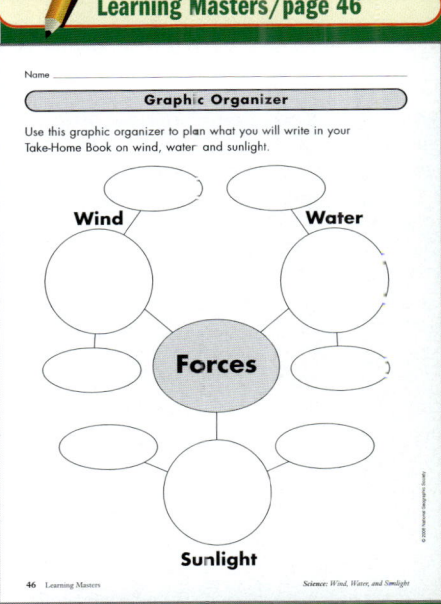

Learning Masters/page 46

OBJECTIVES

- Use Key Concepts and Key Concept Words in writing
- Demonstrate oral language proficiency
- Demonstrate comprehension of theme selections
- Read related titles to reinforce Key Concepts and vocabulary

Materials

Take-Home Book Masters:
Wind, Water, and Sunlight

Learning Masters pages 6–7, 47–48

Assessment Masters pages 179, 180, 193, 214, 215, 220, 228

Take-Home Book Masters

Wind, Water, and Sunlight

by _____

Rereading and Assessments

Allow time for students to independently reread the theme selections. Display the Word Bank for students' reference as they read.

As students reread, meet with individuals. Use the assessment tools listed on page 91 to evaluate students' progress and to update their records.

Guided Writing

Students continue writing the Take-Home Books they began in Lesson 4. Review the group list of writing ideas. Display the Word Bank.

Page through the theme books to review the text features, including the special page features of sidebars and partial pages, as well as highlighted vocabulary. Talk about text features that students could add to their Take-Home Books. For example, they might highlight important words in their own sentences or in the sentences provided on the pages.

Point out that good writers:

- Plan their writing. Have students use their completed graphic organizers to guide their writing.

- May show cause and effect. Remind students to use words such as *because* and *so* when they want to tell why something happened.

- Revise their work. After writing, have students check that the correct verb tense is used.

Have students complete the Picture Glossary and About the Author last.

As students write, circulate to coach and support individuals. If students need help, suggest the use of a language form.

Have partners exchange books and discuss what they like in each other's books. Each writer decides which changes to make and adds any final touches.

Customize Instruction for ELLs

Newcomers/Beginning Have students provide drawings of people using wind, water, and sunlight.

Developing Have students write the answers to the following questions: "How do people use wind? "Why do plants need sunlight?"

Expanding/Bridging Encourage students to read the entire text to check for sense. Ask them to make sure they have explained how wind, water, and sunlight are used and how they affect nonliving things.

Assessment Tools

Self-Assessment

Allow students to reflect and assess their own learning by completing *Learning Masters* pages 6–7.

- What I Learned, page 6
- How I Learned, page 7

Reading

The following assessment tools can help you evaluate and record students' progress in reading and understanding the theme books.

- Retelling Guide and Scoring Rubric, page 179
- Fluency Scoring Guide, page 180
- Oral Reading Record, page 193

Writing

Use the completed Take-Home Books and the following tools to assess students' development as writers.

- Writing Rubric, page 214
- Writing Traits Checklist, page 215

Content Assessment

Have partners create a new three-column chart like the one they did in Lesson 1. Have students use the following column headings: *Powerful Force, A Nonliving Thing It Can Change, How People or Living Things Use It.* Tell students they can use words or drawings to fill in the chart. Have partners present their chart to another pair of students.

Vocabulary and Oral Language

Use the following resources, in addition to the Think and Discuss scene on the *Theme Builder,* to assess oral language development.

- Content Vocabulary Checklist, page 220
- Oral Language Developmental Checklist, page 228

Optional Reading

Reading related titles allows students to explore concepts and vocabulary at different levels. It also allows them to use reading strategies in different types of texts. Encourage students to compare the theme books to the books in the next column.

Optional Titles

These related *Windows on Literacy* titles reinforce Key Concepts of the *Wind, Water, and Sunlight* theme.

Nonfiction Titles

Water Power Level 15

When a Storm Comes Level 15

Light Level 22

The Sun Level 22

Fiction Titles

Sailing with Sam Level 15

Too Close to the Sun: A Play Based on the Ancient Myth of Icarus Level 16

Home Connection

The Family Focus letters on *Learning Masters* pages 47–48 summarize key concepts about wind, water, and sunlight.

In the Share and Learn activity, family members discuss what might make the ice of a glacier, and snow on the ground, melt.

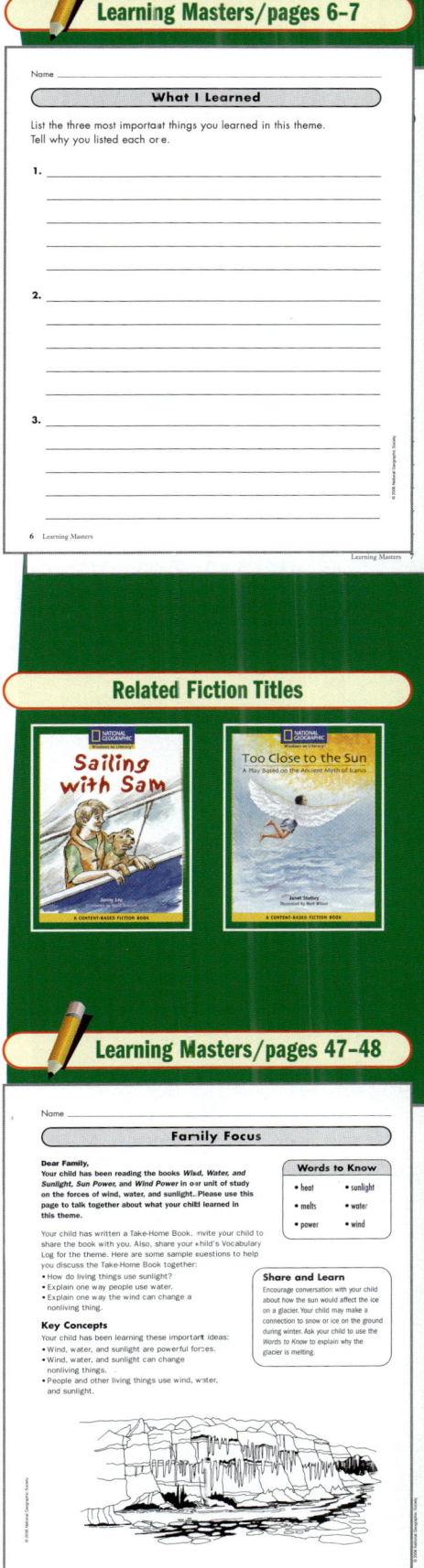

Overview

Prehistoric Life

STANDARDS

ACADEMIC LANGUAGE/ELD

- Use academic vocabulary related to the study of prehistoric life
- Use appropriate language forms to define and to ask questions
- Develop fluency in reading, writing, listening to, and speaking English

SCIENCE

- Recognize that scientists study fossils to learn about plants and animals from the prehistoric past
- Understand that many plants and animals that lived long ago are now extinct
- Explain how fossils are formed over a long period of time

READING/LANGUAGE ARTS

- Learn and apply the comprehension strategy: Asking Questions
- Use the text features: Contents/Headings and Captions
- Write about prehistoric life
- Learn and use vocabulary related to prehistoric life

Before Theme Assessment

To compare progress before and after teaching this theme, use one or more of the following informal assessment tools before beginning the theme.

- Oral Reading Record, page 195
- Fluency Scoring Guide, page 180
- Content Vocabulary Checklist, page 221
- Oral Language Developmental Checklist, page 228

Theme Materials

Concept Book

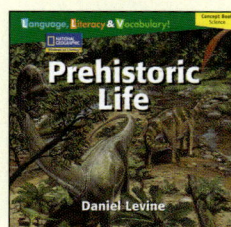

Nonfiction Books

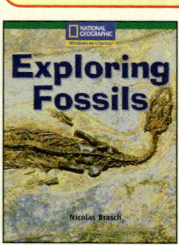

Level 16

Level 16

Theme Builder

Learning Masters

Audiolesson on CD

Take-Home Book Masters

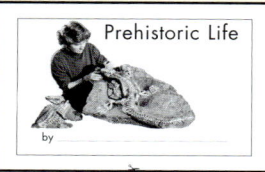

Optional Reading

Windows on Literacy Content-Based Fiction

Jada's Adventure Level 15

Dinosaur Dig Level 16

Windows on Literacy Nonfiction

SuperCroc Level 24

Dinosaur Detectives Level 24

Instructional Highlights

Key Concepts

- Scientists study fossils to learn about plants and animals from the prehistoric past.
- Many plants and animals that lived long ago are now extinct.
- Fossils are formed over a long period of time.

Comprehension Strategy

Asking Questions

Key Concept Words

dinosaur   prehistoric

extinct   remains

fossil   skeleton

paleontologist

Text Features

Contents/Headings

Captions

Theme Planner

Lesson 1*

Teacher's Guide pp. 94–95

Read
Prehistoric Life

- Introduce Concepts and Vocabulary

- Model and Share the Reading

* Before you begin Lesson 1, you may want to use the Before Theme Assessment tools listed on page 92.

Lesson 2

Teacher's Guide pp. 96–97

Reread
Prehistoric Life

- Develop Concepts and Vocabulary

- Introduce the Comprehension Strategy: Asking Questions

- Small Group Reading

- Modeled Writing

Lesson 3

Teacher's Guide pp. 98–99

Read
Exploring Fossils

- Develop Concepts and Vocabulary

- Small Group Reading

- Practice the Comprehension Strategy: Asking Questions

- Shared Writing

Lesson 4

Teacher's Guide pp. 100–101

Read
Dinosaur Extremes

- Review Concepts and Vocabulary

- Small Group Reading

- Apply the Comprehension Strategy: Asking Questions

- Guided Writing

Lesson 5

Teacher's Guide pp. 102–103

Assess
and Extend

- Rereading and Assessments

- Guided Writing

- Assessment Tools

- Optional Reading

- Home Connection

Lesson 1

Read *Prehistoric Life*

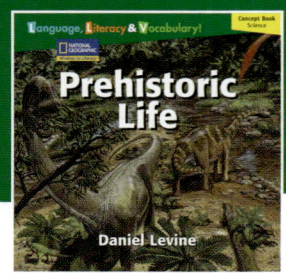

Prehistoric Life
Daniel Levine

OBJECTIVES

- Understand that scientists study fossils of plants and animals
- Learn and use vocabulary related to prehistoric life
- Use photos to predict vocabulary
- Use text features, such as Contents and Headings, to learn how a book is organized

Materials

Realia: fossils or photos of fossils, including animal skeleton and plant fossils; handprint made in clay

Theme Builder

Prehistoric Life

Learning Masters page 49

Audiolesson 6

Theme Builder (Chant)

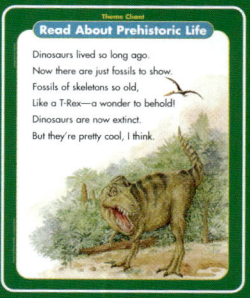

Theme Chant
Read About Prehistoric Life
Dinosaurs lived so long ago.
Now there are just fossils to show.
Fossils of skeletons so old,
Like a T-Rex—a wonder to behold!
Dinosaurs are now extinct.
But they're pretty cool, I think.

Theme Builder (Scene)

Think and Discuss
Learn About Prehistoric Life
What do you know about prehistoric life?
How do we learn about prehistoric life?

Introduce Concepts and Vocabulary

Introduce Theme Question

Ask students: What would you like to learn about dinosaurs? How would you go about learning about them? Where does information about dinosaurs come from? Explain that they will learn about prehistoric life. They will also learn the language to use when defining.

Turn and Talk Ask learning partners to tell what they think a fossil is and how they think it was made.

Develop Oral Language

Hold up the clay handprint. Explain to students that just as a hand has made an imprint in the clay, animals and plants that lived long ago have made imprints. Explain that after thousands of years, some imprints become like rock and are called *fossils*. Hold up a photo of a plant fossil. Model a sentence using *fossils* and *remains:* Fossils are the remains of animals and plants that lived a long time ago.

Now hold up a photo of a fossil of an animal. Model a sentence using *extinct* and *skeleton:* This fossil is the skeleton of an extinct animal.

Turn and Talk Have partners name objects that can become fossils.

Introduce Theme Chant

Display the Theme Chant on the *Theme Builder.* Have students say the chant in unison and then to a partner. Have learning partners use *Learning Masters* page 49 to practice reading the Theme Chant.

Introduce Key Vocabulary

Use the Think and Discuss scene to teach Key Concept Words and model language forms.

Scientists called paleontologists study prehistoric life.

The skeleton of a dinosaur is a type of remain called a fossil.

Continue to model sentences using the words listed below to help identify objects in the scene. As you introduce words, jot them down on chart paper. Display this Word Bank throughout the theme.

Turn and Talk Have students work with partners to practice using the words and the language forms for defining objects and concepts. For example: The _____ is/are _____ and is/are called _____.

dinosaur	prehistoric
extinct	remains
fossil	skeleton
paleontologist	

Build Background

Display the Think and Discuss scene on the *Theme Builder* again. Ask students to describe what they see.

Turn and Talk Have partners talk about each picture by using the language forms for defining. A microscope is a tool used to study fossils.

Model and Share the Reading

Preview the Book

Distribute copies of *Prehistoric Life*. Read aloud the title and the author's name. As you page through the book, point out:

- The highlighted words are vocabulary words.
- The headings match the listings on the Contents page.
- Captions provide information about the photos.

Predict Vocabulary

Encourage students to use pictures to predict vocabulary: Which words do you expect to see in this book?

Display pages 6–7 and cover the words: Which words do you expect to see on these pages?

Students may mention the objects on the pages, such as *dinosaurs*, *plants*, *fossils*, and *mammoths*. Add these words to the Word Bank. Have students talk with partners and use the words in sentences. Continue the activity with other pages as time allows.

Model the Reading

Invite students to follow along as you read aloud pages 4–7 in *Prehistoric Life*. Read fluently, modeling smooth, accurate reading with appropriate expression. After reading each pair of pages, pause to think aloud. Also, encourage students to ask questions and make observations.

Pages 4–5
Think Aloud This is like the Think and Discuss scene on the *Theme Builder*. It shows animals from prehistoric times and how we study them.

Pages 6–7
Think Aloud The boldfaced words are vocabulary words. They must be important words to understand. When I look at the pictures, I see that two of them are drawings, not photos. This is because these animals were extinct by the time people lived on Earth.

Share the Reading

Now have partners complete the reading. Encourage them to pause after reading one or two pages and have conversations about what they read. Ask them to share what they might ask a paleontologist if they could.

Reread for Fluency

Model reading the paragraph on page 6, paying attention to punctuation as you read. Then have students read the paragraph in unison, imitating your model. Have students reread the entire book independently to build fluency. See *Customize the Reading*.

Learning Masters/page 49

Theme Chant

Dinosaurs lived so long ago.
Now there are just fossils to show.
Fossils of skeletons so old,
Like a T-Rex—a wonder to behold!
Dinosaurs are now extinct.
But they're pretty cool, I think.

Science: Prehistoric Life   Learning Masters **49**

Customize the Reading

Students reread and talk about Prehistoric Life *on their own to build fluency.*

- *Students who are not yet able to read the book can point to and name items in pictures.*
- *Students who need extra support can reread the book while listening to the audiolesson.*
- *Students who can read the book might read independently or aloud with partners.*

Customize Instruction for ELLs

Newcomers/Beginning As you read aloud, have students point to objects on the page that no longer exist.

Developing Have students read pages aloud with a partner.

Expanding/Bridging Have students write captions for several of the pictures in the book.

Reread *Prehistoric Life*

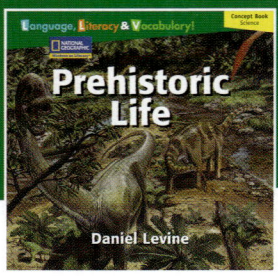

OBJECTIVES

- Understand that scientists study fossils to learn about plants and animals from the prehistoric past
- Use vocabulary to talk about prehistoric life
- Learn the comprehension strategy: Asking Questions
- Read to gain fluency in oral and silent reading
- Write about prehistoric life

Materials

Theme Builder

Prehistoric Life

Learning Masters pages 8, 50, 51

Audiolesson 6

Theme Builder (Graphic Organizer)

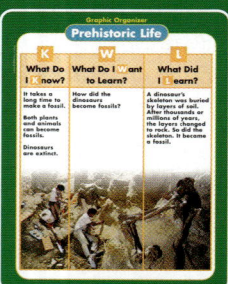

Develop Concepts and Vocabulary

Develop Oral Language

Display the *Theme Builder* and ask students how scientists learn about prehistoric life. Then have students turn to pages 10–11 in *Prehistoric Life*. Model sentences using *paleontologist, fossil, remains, dinosaur,* and *skeleton* to describe what is shown on these pages.

Turn and Talk Have learning partners role-play using the tools shown on page 11 of *Prehistoric Life*. Ask them to describe what they find out as they use the tools.

Revisit the Theme Chant Display the Theme Chant on the *Theme Builder*. Ask students which words rhyme. Have them practice reading the chant with the correct rhythm.

Build Background

Display the graphic organizer on the *Theme Builder* and read the information in the columns. Tell students that fossils are formed over a long period of time. Now go through the columns again and have volunteers suggest information or questions to add to each column. Add students' ideas to the chart with sticky notes. At the end of the theme, check the chart to answer the questions and see what students learned.

Turn and Talk Ask partners to talk about what they would like to learn about prehistoric life.

Begin Vocabulary Log As students read, encourage them to use sticky notes to tag words that they would like to save. After reading, students can record the words and their notes about them.

Use *Learning Masters* page 8.

Introduce the Comprehension Strategy

Introduce Asking Questions

When students ask questions, they look for answers that may or may not be in the text.

Think Aloud When I read a book, I often wonder about things I am reading and seeing in the pictures. That's called **asking questions.**

Model Asking Questions

Turn to page 10 and model the comprehension strategy and language forms for asking questions.

Before I read, I wondered how people find out about dinosaurs. I see they look at fossils.

While I read, I wondered what *remains* are. I see that fossils and skeletons are remains.

After I read, I wondered how the paleontologist knew it was a dinosaur skeleton.

For additional practice in asking questions, have partners work on *Learning Masters* page 50.

Small Group Reading

As students read, invite them to share what they notice. Use some of the suggestions below to encourage observations and talk about the book.

Pages 6–11

Support Comprehension Guide students to ask questions as they read the text. Model:

Do I understand the meaning of the boldfaced words?

Do I know why there are two pictures of a plant and two of a crocodile?

How do you become a paleontologist?

Pages 12–15

Check Understanding Explain what kind of information the captions on these pages provide. (*The captions tell about specific examples of fossilized plants and animals.*)

Pages 16–17

Support Comprehension Ask a volunteer to summarize these pages. (*We can build models of prehistoric animals from seeing their skeletons.*)

Pages 18–19

Check Understanding Have students use the Word Bank to help them describe what they see.

Discuss the Book

Invite students to share what they learned. Ask them to talk about the fossils they have seen. Encourage them to use the words in the Word Bank to discuss what they have read. Remind students to add words to their Vocabulary Logs.

Students can complete *Learning Masters* page 51.

Reread for Fluency

Read the sentences on page 12 in a flat tone, and ask students what is wrong with how you read. (*You should read with expression.*) Then read the sentences again, using expression. Ask partners to read the sentences to each other, using fluent, expressive voices. Then ask partners to offer each other helpful suggestions on how to improve their reading before trying again. For other suggestions, see *Customize the Reading*.

Learning Masters/pages 8, 50

Name

Vocabulary Log

8 Learning Masters

50 Learning Masters — Science: Prehistoric Life

Customize the Reading

Students reread and talk about *Prehistoric Life* using one of the following options:

- Look through the pages, naming the kinds of fossils they see.
- Reread the book while following along with the audiolesson.
- Read independently or read aloud with a partner.

Modeled Writing

Use the graphic organizer on the *Theme Builder* to review some Key Concepts of the theme. Prepare to model writing a clear main idea.

Think Aloud Remember that we already know some things about fossils. I'm going to write about how fossils are made. That's my main idea. My audience is the students in this group.

It takes thousands and millions of years for plant and animal remains to become fossils.

Think Aloud Now that I've introduced fossils, I will get to my main idea.

Over time, the dirt surrounding the remains of a plant or animal may turn to rock.

Think Aloud A clear main idea tells the audience what the rest of the writing is going to be about.

Paleontologists have to break through the rock to find the remains, which have hardened into a fossil.

Learning Masters/page 51

Name

Prehistoric Life

Read pages 12–16 in *Prehistoric Life*. Write a fact or an example of a fossil in each circle of the web. Then write about one of your ideas.

fossils

One important idea about fossils is

Science: Prehistoric Life — Learning Masters 51

Lesson 3

Read *Exploring Fossils*

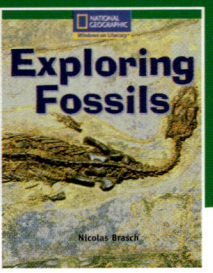

OBJECTIVES

- Read to gain fluency in oral and silent reading
- Practice the comprehension strategy: Asking Questions
- Understand that fossils are formed over a long period of time
- Use Contents and Headings to find information
- Use pictures to help support and confirm text meaning

Materials

Theme Builder

Exploring Fossils

Learning Masters page 52

Audiolesson 6

Develop Concepts and Vocabulary

Develop Oral Language

Model the Key Concept Words *remains*, *fossils*, *skeleton*, and *prehistoric*.

I have seen a collection of fossils.

The only remains of the animal was its skeleton.

Turn and Talk Have learning partners make up fill-in-the-blank sentences that use the Key Concept Words and exchange papers with another pair.

These dinosaur eggs are _____.

Revisit the Theme Chant

Display the chant on the *Theme Builder*. Assign a line of the chant to each student in the group. Have students read the chant aloud, standing when it is their turn to read.

Build Background

Distribute copies of *Exploring Fossils*. Invite students to share when and where they may have seen or found a fossil. Have students describe the fossil.

Small Group Reading

Get Ready to Read

Preview the Book Read aloud the title, the author's name, and the Think and Discuss question on the back cover: What is a fossil?

Page through the book and do the following:

- Point out the headings on the Contents page and the headings on the pages.
- Point out how the photos show real fossils.
- Ask students to predict what they will learn.

Predict Vocabulary Encourage students to use photos to predict vocabulary: Which words do you expect to see in this book?

Display a page and cover the words: Which words do you expect to see on this page?

List the words students mention. Add Key Concept Words in the book that students do not mention.

Text Feature: Contents/Headings

Introduce Display the Contents on page 2. This is the Contents page. It lists all the sections of the book and tells what pages they are on.

Model I see that *How Was This Plant Fossil Formed?* is on page 6. I turn to page 6 and see the same heading. I also see plant fossils in a photo.

Practice Have students turn to the Contents. Ask which page will tell about animal fossils. *(page 8)* Ask what the heading is on that page.

Read the Book

As students read, invite them to share what they notice. Use some of the suggestions below to encourage observations and talk about the book.

Pages 3–5

Key Concept Words *fossils, remains*

Check Understanding Ask students to answer the questions on page 3. Make sure they understand that the top photo is a leaf and the bottom photo is a fish.

Pages 6–9

Key Concept Word *skeleton*

Support Comprehension Ask students to match the heading on page 8 to the section in the Contents. Then have them describe what they see and answer the question on the page.

Pages 10–13

Check Understanding Ask students who the people are on pages 10–13.

What do you call scientists who study fossils? (*paleontologists*)

Page 16

Key Concept Word *prehistoric*

Practice the Comprehension Strategy

Encourage students to **Ask Questions** to help them better understand page 16.

What is the girl holding? What else do I see in the picture? Does the author mean that I might find a fossil someday?

Guide students to understand how just a small piece of a rock can tell us much about life long ago.

Discuss the Book

Invite students to use the Word Bank to tell about the book. What have they learned about fossils? Can they say how fossils tell us about the past? Remind students to add new words to their Vocabulary Logs.

Use *Learning Masters* page 52.

Reread for Fluency

Have students reread the entire book independently to build fluency. See *Customize the Reading*.

Learning Masters/page 52

Name _____

Exploring Fossils

Complete the following sentence:

Based on my reading, here are two important ideas to remember:

1. _____

2. _____

Draw a picture of a fossil. Tell what the picture shows.

_____

52   Learning Masters   *Science: Prehistoric Life*

Customize the Reading

Students reread and talk about Exploring Fossils *using one of the following options:*

- Look through the pages, naming what they see.
- Reread the book while following along with the audiolesson.
- Read independently or aloud with a partner.

Shared Writing

Review the paragraph you modeled in Lesson 2. Give the paragraph a heading such as those in *Prehistoric Life* and *Exploring Fossils*. For example: *What Are Fossils?* Invite students to help you write a second paragraph about people who study fossils. The new paragraph can come under the heading *Who Studies Fossils?* Help students frame sentences stating the new paragraph's main idea. Ask them to think about what information they would like to include.

Customize Instruction for ELLs

Newcomers/Beginning Have students act out a paleontologist digging for a fossil and finding one. Have them describe their actions.

Developing Ask students to list words that tell some of the things that a paleontologist does. (*digs, brushes, discovers, studies, researches*) Use some of the words in the writing.

Expanding/Bridging Ask students to suggest sentences telling what paleontologists do, how they do it, and the tools they use while doing their job.

Read *Dinosaur Extremes*

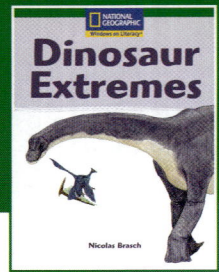

Dinosaur Extremes

Nicolas Brasch

OBJECTIVES

- Read to gain fluency in oral and silent reading
- Apply the comprehension strategy: Asking Questions
- Develop an understanding that many plants and animals that lived long ago are now extinct
- Use the captions to comprehend text
- Compare and contrast the sizes and characteristics of the dinosaurs in the book

Materials

Realia: plastic dinosaurs

Theme Builder

Dinosaur Extremes

Learning Masters pages 53, 54

Take-Home Book Masters: *Prehistoric Life*

Audiolesson 6

Take-Home Book Masters

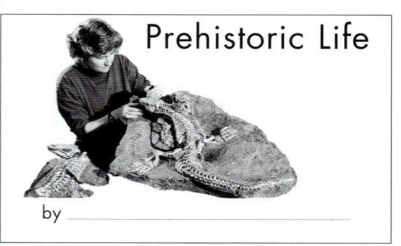

Prehistoric Life

by _____

Review Concepts and Vocabulary

Develop Oral Language

Pass out one plastic dinosaur to each student. Have students talk about the characteristics of the dinosaurs they have. Then put students in pairs and have them compare their dinosaurs. They can use the following language form. My dinosaur is _____, but your dinosaur is _____.

Turn and Talk Let pairs continue to compare their dinosaurs using the language form. Ask students to think about the size and shape of the dinosaurs.

Revisit the Theme Chant Display the chant on the *Theme Builder*. Ask volunteers to read it aloud. The volunteers can replace *T-Rex* with another dinosaur they've read about.

Build Background

Distribute copies of *Dinosaur Extremes*. Talk about what "extreme" means with students. Ask them what they think is the world's fastest animal. Ask them what they think is the largest animal. Can they think of extremes in their own lives?

Small Group Reading

Get Ready to Read

Preview the Book Read aloud the title, the author's name, and the Think and Discuss question on the back cover: Which dinosaur was the slowest dinosaur?

Page through the book and do the following:

- Point out the small boxes and the comparisons in them.
- Point out the pronunciation guide on each page of the book.
- Ask students to predict what they will learn.

Predict Vocabulary Encourage students to use the pictures to predict vocabulary: Which words do you expect to see in this book?

Display a page and cover the words: Which words do you expect to see on this page?

List the words students mention. Add Key Concept Words in the book that students do not mention.

Text Feature: Captions

Introduce Have students look at the caption on page 6. A caption gives brief information about the picture near it.

Model This caption helps the reader understand what the picture shows. A bird and ruler are shown together to show the bird's size.

Practice Have students point out the pictures and captions and tell what the captions tell them about the pictures.

Read the Book

As students read, invite them to share what they notice. Use some of the suggestions below to encourage observations and talk about the book.

Pages 4–7

Key Concept Word *dinosaur*

Apply the Comprehension Strategy

Encourage students to **Ask Questions** as they read:

Before I read, I wondered _____ .

While I read, I wondered _____ .

After I read, I wondered _____ .

Pages 8–11

Support Comprehension Point out that the word *Argentinosaurus* might give a clue about where this dinosaur was found. Read the small boxes. Talk about the measuring tools. Have students suggest other things to compare to each dinosaur to show its weight and height.

Pages 12–15

Support Comprehension Ask students what the caption on page 12 is about. *(speed)*

Check Understanding What characteristics of dinosaurs have we read about? *(their size and speed)*

Discuss the Book

Invite students to use the Word Bank to discuss the book and to share what they learned. Ask them what they learned that they didn't know before. Have students add words to their Vocabulary Logs.

Use *Learning Masters* page 53.

Reread for Fluency

Have students reread the entire book independently to build fluency. See *Customize the Reading.*

Guided Writing

Distribute copies of the *Take-Home Book Masters.* Read the title and page through the book. Explain that they will write books about prehistoric life. Work with students to:

- Complete the Contents page.
- Answer the questions and tell about the pictures.
- Share writing ideas for each pair of pages.

Record students' writing ideas for the pages of their books on chart paper. Have them suggest labels they might like to add to the pictures.

Have partners talk together to plan what to write. Have each student complete a graphic organizer. Students might label the columns *Fossils, Paleontologists, Dinosaurs.* Have students write a few notes in each column as they look through the Take-Home Books. They may want to include these ideas as they write their Take-Home Book pages.

Display the Word Bank and remind students to check their Vocabulary Logs as they begin to write.

Use *Learning Masters* page 54 to help students organize their ideas.

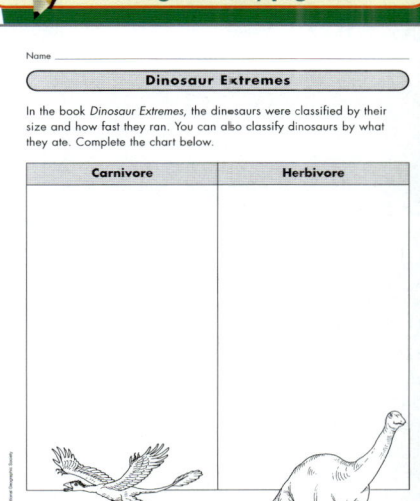

Learning Masters/page 53

Name _____

Dinosaur Extremes

In the book *Dinosaur Extremes*, the dinosaurs were classified by their size and how fast they ran. You can also classify dinosaurs by what they ate. Complete the chart below.

Carnivore	Herbivore

Science: Prehistoric Life   Learning Masters **53**

Customize the Reading

Students reread and talk about Dinosaur Extremes *using one of the following options:*

- *Look through the pages, naming two characteristics of each dinosaur.*
- *Reread the book while following along with the audiolesson.*
- *Read independently or aloud with a partner.*

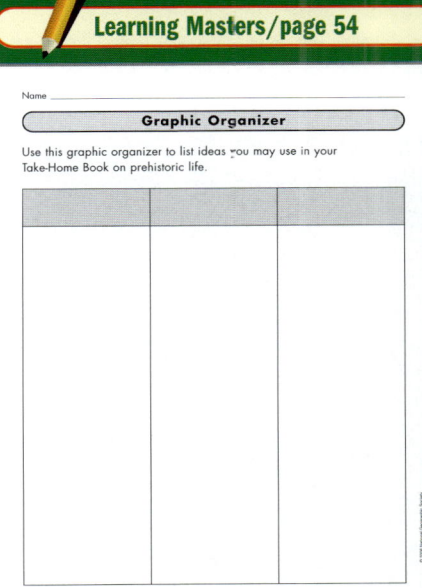

Learning Masters/page 54

Name _____

Graphic Organizer

Use this graphic organizer to list ideas you may use in your Take-Home Book on prehistoric life.

54 Learning Masters   *Science: Prehistoric Life*

OBJECTIVES

- Use Key Concepts and Key Concept Words in writing
- Demonstrate oral language proficiency
- Demonstrate comprehension of theme selections
- Read related titles to reinforce Key Concepts and vocabulary

Materials

Take-Home Book Masters:
Prehistoric Life

Learning Masters pages 6–7, 55–56

Assessment Masters pages 179, 180, 195, 214, 215, 221, 228

Take-Home Book Masters

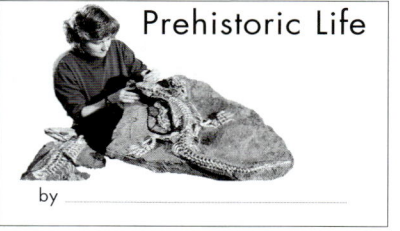

Prehistoric Life

by _____

Rereading and Assessments

Allow time for students to independently reread the theme selections. Display the Word Bank for students' reference as they read.

As students reread, meet with individuals. Use the assessment tools listed on page 103 to evaluate students' progress and to update their records.

Guided Writing

Students continue writing the Take-Home Books they began in Lesson 4. Review the group list of writing ideas. Display the Word Bank.

Page through the theme books to review the text features, including the Contents page and captions. Talk about text features that students could add to their Take-Home Books. For example, they might add captions to provide extra information. Students might also add comparison boxes like those shown in *Dinosaur Extremes*.

Point out that good writers:

- Vary their sentences by sometimes using compound sentences.
- Check verb tense. After writing, have students check that the correct verb tense is used throughout.

- Edit their work. Ask students to cut out or restate any repeated thoughts.

Have students complete the Picture Glossary and About the Author last.

As students write, circulate to coach and support individuals. If students need help, ask them to reread each sentence and check to see if it says what they intended it to say.

Have partners exchange books and discuss what they like in each other's book. For example, a partner might like the way the sentences were varied. Partners can also offer suggestions on ways to improve the books, such as giving more detail. Each writer decides what changes to make and adds any final touches.

Customize Instruction for ELLs

Newcomers/Beginning Have students work with a bridging partner to write text, create drawings, and add labels or captions.

Developing Have students write simple sentences and ask a partner to check whether their sentences make sense.

Expanding/Bridging Have students write statements that include definitions and comparisons: "A paleontologist studies prehistoric life." "A microraptor was the smallest meat-eater."

Assessment Tools

Self-Assessment

Allow students to reflect and assess their own learning by completing *Learning Masters* pages 6–7.

- What I Learned, page 6
- How I Learned, page 7

Reading

The following assessment tools can help you evaluate and record students' progress in reading and understanding the theme books.

- Retelling Guide and Scoring Rubric, page 179
- Fluency Scoring Guide, page 180
- Oral Reading Record, page 195

Writing

Use the completed Take-Home Books and the following tools to assess students' development as writers.

- Writing Rubric, page 214
- Writing Traits Checklist, page 215

Content Assessment

Have students work together in small groups to make a bulletin board display that shows how a fossil is made, from when an animal or a plant was alive to someone finding its fossil. The steps should be accompanied by sentences that explain what is happening.

Vocabulary and Oral Language

Use the following resources, in addition to the Think and Discuss scene on the *Theme Builder*, to assess oral language development.

- Content Vocabulary Checklist, page 221
- Oral Language Developmental Checklist, page 228

Optional Reading

Reading related titles allows students to explore concepts and vocabulary at different levels. It also allows them to use reading strategies in different types of texts. Encourage students to compare the theme books to the books in the next column.

Optional Titles

These related *Windows on Literacy* titles reinforce Key Concepts of the *Prehistoric Life* theme.

Nonfiction Titles

SuperCroc Level 24

Dinosaur Detectives Level 24

Fiction Titles

Jada's Adventure Level 15

Dinosaur Dig Level 16

Home Connection

The Family Focus letters on *Learning Masters* pages 55–56 summarize key concepts about prehistoric life.

In the Share and Learn activity, family members discuss what it might have been like in the time of dinosaurs.

Learning Masters/pages 6–7

What I Learned

List the three most important things you learned in this theme. Tell why you listed each one.

1. _____
2. _____
3. _____

6 Learning Masters

Learning Masters 7

Related Fiction Titles

Jada's Adventure

Dinosaur Dig

Learning Masters/pages 55–56

Family Focus

Dear Family,
Your child has been reading the books *Prehistoric Life, Exploring Fossils,* and *Dinosaur Extremes* in our unit of study on prehistoric life. Please use this page to talk together about what your child learned in this theme.

Your child has written a Take-Home Book. Invite your child to share the book with you. Also, share your child's Vocabulary Log for the theme. Here are some sample questions to help you discuss the book together:
- What are fossils made of?
- Who studies fossils?
- Who studies dinosaurs?
- What are the names of some dinosaurs?

Words to Know
- dinosaur
- prehistoric
- extinct
- remains
- fossil
- skeleton
- paleontologist

Key Concepts
Your child has been learning these important ideas:
- Scientists study fossils to learn about plants and animals from the prehistoric past.
- Many plants and animals that lived long ago are now extinct.
- Fossils are formed over a long period of time.

Share and Learn
Encourage conversation with your child about prehistoric life. Discuss what plants and animals may have looked like, including dinosaurs. Ask your child to use the *Words to Know* in your discussion.

Science: Prehistoric Life

Learning Masters 55

56 Learning Masters

Science: Prehistoric Life

Overview

Maps

STANDARDS

ACADEMIC LANGUAGE/ELD
- Use academic vocabulary related to the study of maps
- Use appropriate language forms to ask informational questions and to determine importance
- Develop fluency in reading, writing, listening to, and speaking English

SOCIAL STUDIES
- Understand that maps represent landforms, bodies of water, and places
- Identify and locate continents, oceans, lakes, rivers, mountains, countries, cities, roads, and buildings on maps
- Understand that maps can show the same place in different ways and for different purposes

READING/LANGUAGE ARTS
- Learn and apply the comprehension strategy: Determining Importance
- Use the text features: Maps and Graphic Symbols
- Write about maps
- Learn and use vocabulary related to maps

Before Theme Assessment

To compare progress before and after teaching this theme, use one or more of the following informal assessment tools before beginning the theme.
- Oral Reading Record, page 198
- Fluency Scoring Guide, page 180
- Content Vocabulary Checklist, page 222
- Oral Language Developmental Checklist, page 228

Theme Materials

Concept Book

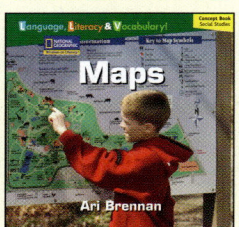

Maps
Ari Brennan

Nonfiction Books

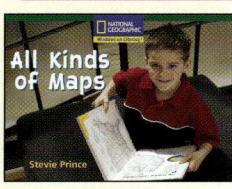

All Kinds of Maps
Stevie Prince
Level 15

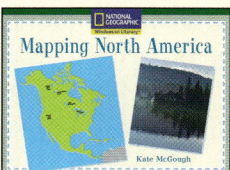

Mapping North America
Kate McGough
Level 16

Theme Builder

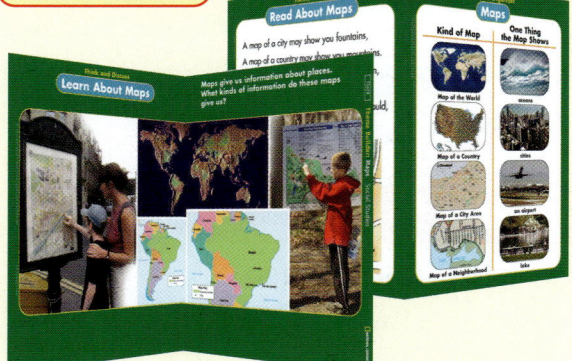

Learning Masters

Language, Literacy & Vocabulary!
Learning Masters
Fluent

Audiolesson on CD

Take-Home Book Masters

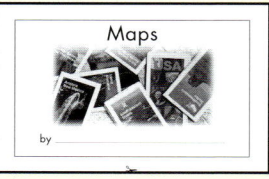

Maps
by _____

Optional Reading

**Windows on Literacy
Content-Based Fiction**

The Treasure Map: A Play
Level 15

The Bike Trail Level 16

**Windows on Literacy
Nonfiction**

Zoo Map Level 10

On a Treasure Hunt Level 16

The Key to Maps Level 17

Places to Visit Level 17

More Places to Visit Level 18

Instructional Highlights

Key Concepts

- Maps represent landforms, bodies of water, and places.

- People can use maps and their symbols to identify and locate continents, oceans, lakes, rivers, mountains, countries, cities, roads, and buildings.

- Maps that show the same place in different ways can be used for different purposes.

Comprehension Strategy

Determining Importance

Key Concept Words

border	landforms
continent	mountain
country	ocean
highway	river
lake	road

Text Features

Maps

Graphic Symbols

Theme Planner

Lesson 1*

Teacher's Guide pp. 106–107

Read
Maps

- Introduce Concepts and Vocabulary

- Model and Share the Reading

* Before you begin Lesson 1, you may want to use the Before Theme Assessment tools listed on page 104.

Lesson 2

Teacher's Guide pp. 108–109

Reread
Maps

- Develop Concepts and Vocabulary

- Introduce the Comprehension Strategy: Determining Importance

- Small Group Reading

- Modeled Writing

Lesson 3

Teacher's Guide pp. 110–111

Read
All Kinds of Maps

- Develop Concepts and Vocabulary

- Small Group Reading

- Practice the Comprehension Strategy: Determining Importance

- Shared Writing

Lesson 4

Teacher's Guide pp. 112–113

Read
Mapping North America

- Review Concepts and Vocabulary

- Small Group Reading

- Apply the Comprehension Strategy: Determining Importance

- Guided Writing

Lesson 5

Teacher's Guide pp. 114–115

Assess
and Extend

- Rereading and Assessments

- Guided Writing

- Assessment Tools

- Optional Reading

- Home Connection

Lesson 1

Read *Maps*

Language, Literacy & Vocabulary!
NATIONAL GEOGRAPHIC
Maps
Ari Brennan
Concept Book
Social Studies

Theme Builder (Poem)

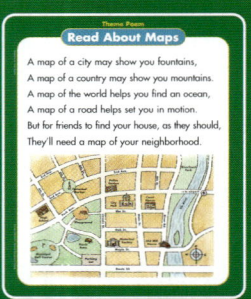

Theme Builder (Scene)

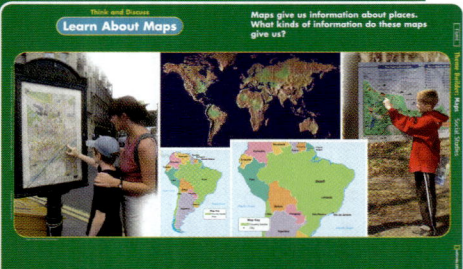

Introduce Concepts and Vocabulary

Introduce Theme Question

Ask students: If you wanted to tell a friend how to get from school to your home, could you draw a map? What would you put on the map to help the friend find his or her way? Explain that they will learn about maps. They will also learn the language to use when working with maps and asking questions about them.

Turn and Talk Have learning partners talk together and create a simple map from their seats in the classroom to a nearby destination, such as the school playground or gym.

Develop Oral Language

Display a map of the local area. Point to the school and ask: What is this building?

Choose an easily identifiable landmark, such as a lake, park or river, and ask: Where is the (lake)?

Provide basic facts about the map (area depicted, distance scale, cardinal directions).

Turn and Talk Have learning partners take turns asking each other informational questions about the map, using the language forms: Where is the (park)? Which direction is (east)? How do you get from the school to the (park)?

Introduce Theme Poem

Display the Theme Poem on the ***Theme Builder***. Have students recite the poem in unison. Have learning partners use Learning Masters page 57 to practice reading the Theme Poem.

Introduce Key Vocabulary

Use the Think and Discuss scene to teach Key Concept Words and model language forms.

Which maps show landforms, such as mountains? Which map shows a country's borders? How many maps show oceans?

Continue to model questions using the words listed below to help identify what maps can tell us. As you introduce words, jot them down on chart paper. Display this Word Bank throughout the theme.

Turn and Talk Have students work with partners to practice using the words and the language forms for asking informational questions. For example: What is a _____?

border	lake	ocean
continent	landforms	river
country	mountain	road
highway		

Build Background

Display the Think and Discuss scene on the ***Theme Builder*** again. Have students ask any questions they have about the maps.

Turn and Talk Have partners use the language forms to ask each other informational questions about the maps. For example: Where is an ocean? What is its name?

Model and Share the Reading

Preview the Book

Distribute copies of *Maps*. Read aloud the title and the author's name. As you page through the book, point out:

- Some maps have call-outs to highlight information.
- Maps include map keys that include graphic symbols.
- Most photos and some maps have captions.

Predict Vocabulary

Encourage students to use pictures to predict vocabulary: Which words do you expect to see in this book?

Display pages 6–7 and cover the words: Which words do you expect to see on these pages?

Students may mention *world*, *map*, or *water*. Add these words to the Word Bank. Have students read the call-outs and discuss the definitions. Continue the activity with other pages as time allows.

Model the Reading

Invite students to follow along as you read aloud pages 4–7 in *Maps*. Read fluently, modeling smooth, accurate reading with appropriate expression. After reading each pair of pages, pause to think aloud. Also, encourage students to ask questions and make observations.

Pages 4–5
Think Aloud This is like the Think and Discuss scene on the **Theme Builder**. In the photos, people are pointing to maps that show a small area. The other maps show large areas.

Pages 6–7
Think Aloud I see that the continents are different colors on the map. That helps me remember what the continents are and where the continents are located. I know that some scientists count Europe and Asia as one continent. That's because Europe and Asia share one land mass.

Share the Reading

Now have partners complete the reading. Encourage them to pause after reading one or two pages to have conversations about what they have read. Ask them to talk about the kinds of maps they have seen or used.

Reread for Fluency

To have students practice fluent reading, read the sidebars on pages 7, 13, 15, and 17 aloud with appropriate pace and expression. Have students echo-read each sentence as you finish, imitating your model. Then have students reread the entire book independently to build fluency. See *Customize the Reading*.

Learning Masters/page 57

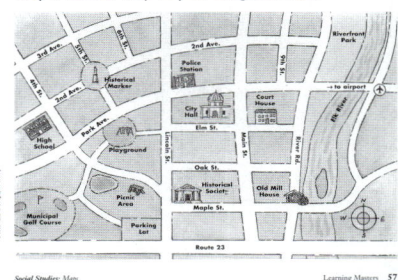

Customize the Reading

Students reread and talk about Maps on their own to build fluency.

- *Students who are not yet able to read the book can point to continents to the north, south, east, or west of a continent you name.*
- *Students who need extra support can reread the book while listening to the audiolesson.*
- *Students who can read the book might read independently or aloud with partners.*

Customize Instruction for ELLs

Newcomers/Beginning Have students name countries important to their heritage. Help them locate the continent each country is in on the world map. Have them compare how far different continents may be from the continent of North America.

Developing When reading "Four Directions" on page 7, have students stand up and face north. Have them point to the north and south when reading the last two sentences of the text.

Expanding/Bridging Ask students to use complete sentences to tell which continents are near each ocean. Help with pronunciation as necessary.

Lesson 2

Reread *Maps*

Language, Literacy & Vocabulary!
Maps
Ari Brennan

OBJECTIVES

- Understand that maps can be used to locate land, water, roads, and other features, and that they sometimes show the same area in different ways
- Use vocabulary to describe information shown on maps
- Learn the comprehension strategy: Determining Importance
- Read to gain fluency in oral and silent reading
- Write about using a map

Materials

Realia: map of North America

Theme Builder

Maps

Learning Masters pages 8, 58, 59

Audiolesson 7

Theme Builder (Graphic Organizer)

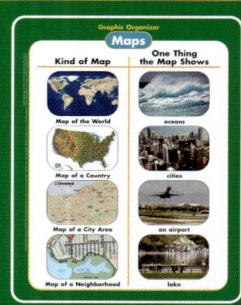

Develop Concepts and Vocabulary

Develop Oral Language

Display a map that includes physical features of North America. Point to oceans, lakes, the U.S. borders with Canada and Mexico, rivers, and mountains. Then trace the outline of the entire continent. For each item, ask questions such as: What is this called? Where is it located?

Turn and Talk Have learning partners ask each other to define or describe the map's features, using these language forms: What is a(n) *(ocean)*? An ocean is large body of salt water.

Revisit the Theme Poem Display the theme poem on the *Theme Builder*. Reread the poem. Then assign pairs of students to read each beginning phrase naming a type of map. Have the whole group read the rest of each line and the last two lines in the poem.

Build Background

Display the graphic organizer on the *Theme Builder* with the right column covered except for the row heading. For each entry under "Kind of Map," have students name some things that the kind of map could show. Then uncover the second row so students can see one possible answer.

Turn and Talk Have learning partners ask each other questions using the language form: What kind of map shows *(roads)*?

Begin Vocabulary Log As students read, encourage them to use sticky notes to tag words that they would like to save. After reading, students can record the words and their notes about them.

Use *Learning Masters* page 8.

Introduce the Comprehension Strategy

Introduce Determining Importance

When students determine importance, they sort interesting details from stated and unstated main ideas in the text to identify the most important information.

Think Aloud When I read a book, I know that some of the information is really important. Some of the information is very interesting, but it is not as important as the big ideas. When I look for the important ideas, that's called **determining importance.**

Model Determining Importance

Turn to pages 8–9 to model the comprehension strategy.

When I read these pages, I notice that the pictures and captions are connected to important parts of the map.

The pictures show waterfalls and a ruin in the mountains. Interesting!

The important idea on these pages, though, is that a map of a continent may show things such as country borders.

For additional practice in determining importance, have partners work on *Learning Masters* page 58.

Small Group Reading

As students read, invite them to share what they notice. Use some of the suggestions below to encourage observations and talk about the book.

Pages 6–11
Support Comprehension Ask a volunteer to summarize these pages. (*Different kinds of maps show different information.*)

Pages 12–13
Support Comprehension Guide students to determine what is important information on these pages. (*Maps often contain symbols that stand for real things. These symbols are explained on a map key.*)

Pages 14–17
Check Understanding Tell how you could use a map of a neighborhood. (*It could show the best route to get some place.*)

Pages 18–19
Check Understanding Have students use the Word Bank to help them as they describe the maps in the scene. Which map shows roads and highways? Which maps show oceans?

Discuss the Book

Invite students to share what they learned. Ask them to talk about the kinds of maps they learned about and what information they contain. Encourage them to use the words in the Word Bank to discuss what they have read. Remind students to add words to their Vocabulary Logs.

Students can complete *Learning Masters* page 59.

Reread for Fluency

Have students follow along as you quietly read page 15 with your face partially blocked by the book. Ask how you can improve your reading. (*Read louder and more clearly.*) Demonstrate reading louder and more clearly, holding the book away from your face, and projecting your voice outward. To build fluency, have partners practice rereading in a clear voice pages 6–9. For other suggestions, see *Customize the Reading*.

Learning Masters/pages 8, 58

Vocabulary Log

List words you want to remember. Tell what each word means. Add notes or drawings about the word.

Word	What It Means	Notes or Drawings

8 Learning Masters

58 Learning Masters   *Social Studies: Maps*

Customize the Reading

Students reread and talk about Maps *using one of the following options:*

- *Look through the pages to find all of the symbols used in the map keys included in different maps.*
- *Reread the book while following along with the audiolesson.*
- *Read independently or read aloud with a partner.*

Modeled Writing

Use the graphic organizer on the *Theme Builder* to review some Key Concepts of the theme. Prepare to model writing, including presenting a clear main idea.

Think Aloud I'm going to write about using maps on a road trip. I'll use the pronouns *I* and *we* to tell about my experiences. My purpose is to tell about an experience with reading maps. My audience is the students in this group. First, I'll tell the main point I want to make.

Last summer, my family and I visited a national park. We used a road map to find the best route to the park.

Think Aloud The road map shows all of the roads and highways across several states. By studying the map I knew what highways to take to get to the park. I'll write about that.

We drove along Route 1 to get to the national park. I saw the symbol for a river on the map. Later, we crossed the river. I saw cities on the map. We drove near the cities.

Learning Masters/page 59

Maps

Read the paragraphs on this page.
Underline or highlight important words or information.
Write about the text you highlighted or underlined.

A map of the world shows oceans and continents. There are seven continents. Five continents are next to the Atlantic Ocean.

Maps can be large or small. Some maps are colorful. Some maps show landforms. Others show country borders. Different kinds of maps show different information.

Often you will find a map key. A map key shows the symbols that are on the map. A symbol is a small drawing that stands for a real thing. A picture of an airplane stands for an airport.

This text is important because

Social Studies: Maps   Learning Masters 59

Lesson 3

Read *All Kinds of Maps*

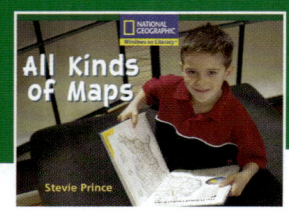

OBJECTIVES

- Read to gain fluency in oral and silent reading
- Practice the comprehension strategy: Determining Importance
- Understand that different maps can show the same place in different ways
- Use maps to comprehend text
- Understand information given in map keys

Materials

Theme Builder

All Kinds of Maps

Learning Masters pages 60

Audiolesson 7

Develop Concepts and Vocabulary

Develop Oral Language

Write the following Key Concept Words on the board: *country, highway, mountain, river,* and *road.* Ask students informational questions, using the Key Concept Words. For example:

What countries have you visited?

What highway is near our school?

Turn and Talk Have learning partners ask each other questions using the Key Concept Words. Encourage them to follow your model.

What is the name of the road that our school is on?

Revisit the Theme Poem

Display the poem on the *Theme Builder.* Invite volunteers to name examples of Key Concept Words as they are read in the poem.

Build Background

Distribute copies of *All Kinds of Maps.* Tell students that this book shows a country, the United States, divided into states. Ask students to name other states they have visited. Explain that they are in the same country, even when traveling from state to state.

Small Group Reading

Get Ready to Read

Preview the Book Read aloud the title, the author's name, and the Think and Discuss question on the back cover: What does a population map show?

Page through the book and do the following:

- Point out that most of the maps have keys that explain the information found on them.
- Show students that the labeled photos help to explain the map keys.
- Ask students to predict what they will learn.

Predict Vocabulary Encourage students to use photos to predict vocabulary: Which words do you expect to see in this book?

Display a page and cover the words. Which words do you expect to see on this page?

List the words that students mention. Add Key Concept Words in the book that students do not mention.

Text Feature: Maps

Introduce Display the political map on pages 4–5 and point to your state. This map shows the 50 states that make up the country called the United States of America. The state we live in is right here.

Model Display the physical map on pages 6–7. This map is a physical map. Its map key shows how to find mountains, deserts, lakes, and rivers.

Practice Have students look at other maps in the book. Ask them what information is shown.

Read the Book

As students read, invite them to share what they notice. Use some of the suggestions below to encourage observations and talk about the book.

Pages 4–7

Key Concept Words *mountain, river*

Support Comprehension Have students look carefully at the map key on page 7. Tell them that the map key uses different colors and textures to indicate the types of landforms found in the country.

Pages 8–9

Key Concept Word *country*

Practice the Comprehension Strategy

Encourage students to **Determine Importance.**

What do you notice about the map on this page? What do the three colors represent? What is the most important idea to remember?

Pages 10–11

Support Comprehension Have students compare this map to the physical map on pages 6–7. Point out that much of the *dry* climate area is labeled *desert* on the physical map. On page 10, have students describe physical features for an area that would be very cold.

Pages 12–15

Key Concept Words *road, highway*

Check Understanding Ask questions such as: What part of the country has the most farmland? *(the middle of the country)*

Discuss the Book

Invite students to use the Word Bank to discuss the book and to share what they learned. Ask them what kinds of maps in this book were also presented in *Maps.* *(physical map, political map, road map)* Have students add words to their Vocabulary Logs.

Use *Learning Masters* page 60.

Reread for Fluency

Have students reread the entire book independently to build fluency. See *Customize the Reading.*

Learning Masters/page 60

Name _____

All Kinds of Maps

Use the Word Bank to complete the sentences. Then draw a map of your classroom in the box.

Word Bank
lake   road
borders   continent
landforms

1. A physical map shows you _____, such as mountains or lakes.

2. A large mass of land is a _____.

3. People traveling by car use a _____ map to help them find their way.

4. A political map shows _____ between countries.

5. A body of water surrounded by land is called a _____.

60   Learning Masters   *Social Studies: Maps*

Customize the Reading

Students reread and talk about All Kinds of Maps using one of the following options:

- *Look through the pages and find a place in the United States where lots of people live.*
- *Reread the book while following along with the audiolesson.*
- *Read independently or aloud with a partner.*

Shared Writing

Review the writing you modeled in Lesson 2. Invite students to help you write a new paragraph about the road trip to a national park. Have volunteers suggest what other maps you may have used on the trip. For example, you may have used a trail map when hiking in the mountains. Help students frame a sentence stating the main idea. Have them use their Vocabulary Logs to add details.

Customize Instruction for ELLs

Newcomers/Beginning Have students suggest landforms that might be seen at or on the way to a national park.

Developing Have students finish sentences such as: "From the highway, we could see _____."

Expanding/Bridging Have students describe what they might see on a trail map at a national park, such as symbols for lakes, mountains, or rivers.

Read *Mapping North America*

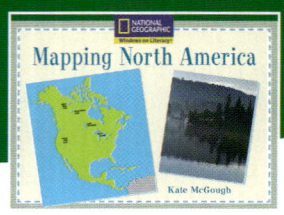

OBJECTIVES

- Read to gain fluency in oral and silent reading
- Apply the comprehension strategy: Determining Importance
- Understand that people can use maps and graphic symbols to locate continents, lakes, rivers, mountains, countries, cities, roads, and buildings
- Use graphic symbols to comprehend information on maps
- Use labels to interpret maps

Materials

Theme Builder

Mapping North America

Learning Masters pages 61, 62

Take-Home Book Masters: *Maps*

Audiolesson 7

Take-Home Book Masters

Maps

by _____

Review Concepts and Vocabulary

Develop Oral Language

Write the following Key Concept Words on the board: *border, continent, country, lake, mountain,* and *river.* Model asking informational questions, using the words.

What is a *(continent)*?

A continent is a main land area of Earth.

Turn and Talk Have learning partners take turns asking informational questions. Encourage students to follow your model. For example:

What country do we live in?
We live in the United States of America.

Revisit the Theme Poem Display

the poem on the *Theme Builder.* Have students read the poem in unison or with parts assigned to volunteers.

Build Background

Distribute copies of *Mapping North America.* Ask students if they know the names of countries in North America as well as lakes, mountains, or rivers that can be found on the continent. Provide at least one example of each. Encourage students to frame questions using the language form: Where is _____?

Small Group Reading

Get Ready to Read

Preview the Book Read aloud the title, the author's name, and the Think and Discuss question on the back cover: Which city do you live near?

Page through the book and do the following:

- Point out that every map in the book shows the same area, but each has different information.
- Turn to the Index and have students identify words with which they are already familiar.
- Ask students to predict what they will learn.

Predict Vocabulary Encourage students to use photos to predict vocabulary: Which words do you expect to see in this book?

Display a page and cover the words: Which words do you expect to see on this page?

List the words students mention. Add Key Concept Words in the book that students do not mention.

Text Feature: Graphic Symbols

Introduce Display the map of mountain ranges on page 9. Look at the little picture near the top. This is a symbol for a mountain range. A *symbol* is a picture that stands for a real thing.

Model The mountain range symbol shows me three mountain ranges in North America.

Practice Have students turn to page 13. Ask what symbol is used for a city and have students find and name cities.

Read the Book

As students read, invite them to share what they notice. Use some of the suggestions below to encourage observations and talk about the book.

Pages 2–5
Key Concept Words *continent, lake*

Support Comprehension Read the names of the lakes on pages 4–5. Point out that the map on pages 2–3 also shows the lakes but does not give the names.

Pages 6–9
Key Concept Words *river, mountain*

Support Comprehension Point out that this map shows only some of the largest rivers in North America. There are many other rivers, which are not shown. (The same is true for lakes, mountains, and cities.)

Pages 10–13
Key Concept Words *country, border*

Check Understanding What do you notice about the countries shown on the map? What symbol do you notice? *(Countries are labeled, are different colors, and are separated by dot-dash lines as symbols for the borders.)*

Pages 14–15

Apply the Comprehension Strategy

Encourage students to **Determine Importance** to help them understand pages 14–15.

When I read these pages, I noticed _____.

The picture shows _____.

The important idea must be _____.

Discuss the Book

Invite students to use the Word Bank to tell about the book. What have they learned about what different kinds of maps show us? What information about lakes, rivers, and mountains did the two theme books provide? Remind students to add words to their Vocabulary Logs.

Use *Learning Masters* page 61.

Reread for Fluency

Have students reread the entire book independently to build fluency. See *Customize the Reading*.

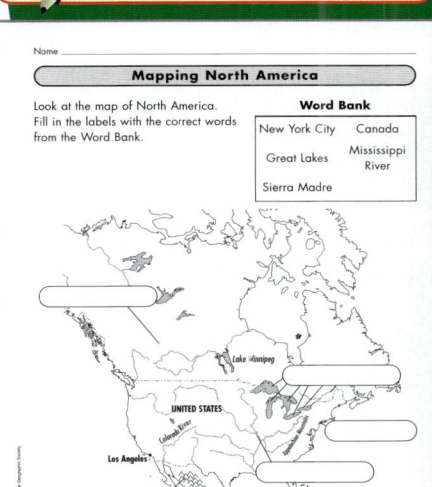

Learning Masters/page 61

Customize the Reading

Students reread and talk about Mapping North America using one of the following options:

- Look through the pages and find the map that brings all of the important information together.
- Reread the book while following along with the audiolesson.
- Read independently or aloud with a partner.

Guided Writing

Distribute copies of the *Take-Home Book Masters*. Read the title and page through the book. Explain that they will write books about different kinds of maps. Work with students to:

- Understand the text on the even-numbered pages.
- Fill in the blank labels in the book.
- Share writing ideas for each set of pages.

Record students' writing ideas for the pages of their books on chart paper.

Have learning partners talk together to plan what to write. Have each student complete a graphic organizer. Display the Word Bank and remind students to check their Vocabulary Logs as they begin to write.

Use *Learning Masters* page 62.

Learning Masters/page 62

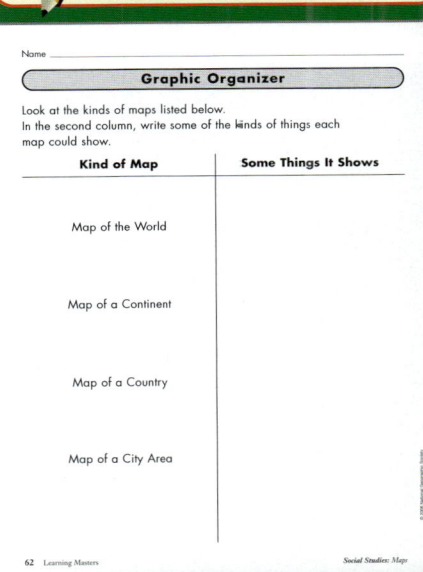

OBJECTIVES

- Use Key Concepts and Key Concept Words in writing
- Demonstrate oral language proficiency
- Demonstrate comprehension of theme selections
- Read related titles to reinforce Key Concepts and vocabulary

Materials

Take-Home Book Masters: *Maps*

Learning Masters pages 6–7, 63–64

Assessment Masters pages 179, 180, 198, 214, 215, 222, 228

Take-Home Book Masters

Maps

by _____

Rereading and Assessments

Allow time for students to independently reread the theme selections. Display the Word Bank for students' reference as they read.

As students reread, meet with individuals. Use the assessment tools listed on page 115 to evaluate students' progress and to update their records.

Guided Writing

Students continue writing the Take-Home Books they began in Lesson 4. Review the group list of writing ideas. Display the Word Bank.

Page through the theme books to review the text features, including graphic symbols and maps. Talk about text features that students could add to their Take-Home Books. For example, they might create a map key. Encourage students to use some of the ideas they have recorded on their graphic organizers.

Point out that good writers:

- Use examples. Students might explain why people use each kind of map. For example, people might use a map to find landforms or to locate different states.

- Revise their work. Have students check that each paragraph has a main idea.

- Read over their work. Have students capitalized proper nouns?

Have students complete the Index and About the Author last.

As students write, circulate to coach and support individuals. If students need help, try having partners talk together to decide how to solve a writing problem.

Have partners exchange books and discuss what they like in each other's book. For example, a partner may like the way the writer has made a main idea clearer. Each writer decides what changes to make and adds any final touches.

Customize Instruction for ELLs

Newcomers/Beginning Have students provide drawings to expand on or support their writing.

Developing Ask questions with simple answers to help students to recall additional information on what each type of map includes.

Expanding/Bridging Have students provide reasons why people might use each of the types of maps in the book.

Assessment Tools

Self-Assessment

Allow students to reflect and assess their own learning by completing *Learning Masters* pages 6–7.

- What I Learned, page 6
- How I Learned, page 7

Reading

The following assessment tools can help you evaluate and record students' progress in reading and understanding the theme books.

- Retelling Guide and Scoring Rubric, page 179
- Fluency Scoring Guide, page 180
- Oral Reading Record, page 198

Writing

Use the completed Take-Home Books and the following tools to assess students' development as writers.

- Writing Rubric, page 214
- Writing Traits Checklist, page 215

Content Assessment

Give small groups different types of maps. Have them look for appropriate items listed in the Word Bank, such as *lake* and *road*. Students should also use the map key and read the graphic symbols. Each group presents its information to another group.

Vocabulary and Oral Language

Use the following resources, in addition to the Think and Discuss scene on the *Theme Builder,* to assess oral language development.

- Content Vocabulary Checklist, page 222
- Oral Language Developmental Checklist, page 228

Optional Reading

Reading related titles allows students to explore concepts and vocabulary at different levels. It also allows them to use reading strategies in different types of texts. Encourage students to compare the theme books to the books in the next column.

Optional Titles

These related *Windows on Literacy* titles reinforce Key Concepts of the *Maps* theme.

Nonfiction Titles

Zoo Map Level 10

On a Treasure Hunt Level 16

The Key to Maps Level 17

Places to Visit Level 17

More Places to Visit Level 18

Fiction Titles

The Treasure Map: A Play Level 15

The Bike Trail Level 16

Home Connection

The Family Focus letters on *Learning Masters* pages 63–64 summarize key concepts about maps.

In the Share and Learn activity, family members use a map to find a destination.

Learning Masters/pages 6–7

What I Learned

List the three most important things you learned in this theme. Tell why you listed each one.

1.

2.

3.

6   Learning Masters

Learning Masters   7

Related Fiction Titles

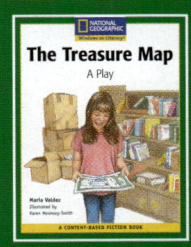

The Treasure Map
A Play

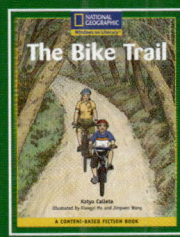

The Bike Trail

Learning Masters/pages 63–64

Family Focus

Dear Family,
Your child has been reading the books *Maps, All Kinds of Maps,* and *Mapping North America* in our unit of study on maps. Please use this page to talk about different kinds of maps with your child.

Your child has written a Take-Home Book. Invite your child to read the book to you. Also, share your child's Vocabulary Log for the theme. Use these questions to discuss the Take-Home Book together:
- What kind of map is this?
- What does this map show?
- Why do people use this kind of map?

Key Concepts
Your child has been learning these important ideas about maps:
- Maps represent landforms, bodies of water, and places.
- People can use maps and their symbols to identify and locate continents, oceans, lakes, rivers, mountains, countries, cities, roads, and buildings.
- Maps that show the same place in different ways can be used for different purposes.

Words to Know	
• border	• landforms
• continent	• mountain
• country	• ocean
• highway	• river
• lake	• road

Share and Learn
Go to an area where you can find a local map. This may be an area of the city, a nature trail, or a museum or a shopping mall map. On the map, help your child identify north. If there are symbols on the map, ask your child what they may mean. Then together pick out a destination, and let your child explain how to find it.

Social Studies: Maps

Learning Masters   63

64   Learning Masters

Social Studies: Maps

Overview

STANDARDS

ACADEMIC LANGUAGE/ELD

- Use academic vocabulary related to the study of patterns, shapes, and symmetry
- Use appropriate language forms to ask questions and to make connections
- Develop fluency in reading, writing, listening to, and speaking English

MATH

- Recognize patterns, shapes, and symmetry in many living and nonliving things
- Discuss and create patterns, shapes, and symmetry

READING/LANGUAGE ARTS

- Learn and apply the comprehension strategy: Making Connections
- Use the text features: Labels and Numbered Steps
- Write about patterns, shapes, and symmetry
- Learn and use vocabulary related to patterns, shapes, and symmetry

Before Theme Assessment

To compare progress before and after teaching this theme, use one or more of the following informal assessment tools before beginning the theme.

- Oral Reading Record, page 200
- Fluency Scoring Guide, page 180
- Content Vocabulary Checklist, page 223
- Oral Language Developmental Checklist, page 228

Theme Materials

Concept Book

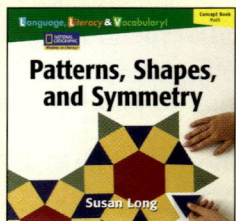

Nonfiction Books

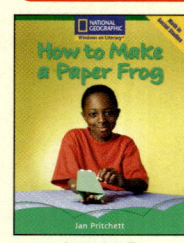
Level 15

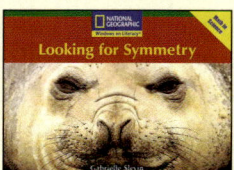
Level 16

Theme Builder

Learning Masters

Audiolesson on CD

Take-Home Book Masters

Optional Reading

Windows on Literacy
Content-Based Fiction

The Family Quilt Level 15
The Fly-Right Kite Level 16

Windows on Literacy
Nonfiction

Patterns Around the World Level 8
Thanks to the Triangle Level 11
The Eiffel Tower Level 15

Instructional Highlights

Key Concepts

- There are patterns, shapes, and symmetry in many living and nonliving things.
- People can look for patterns, shapes, and symmetry.
- People can create patterns, shapes, and symmetry.

Comprehension Strategy

Making Connections

Key Concept Words

circle

half

line of symmetry

pattern

rectangle

shape

square

symmetry

triangle

Text Features

Labels

Numbered Steps

Theme Planner

Lesson 1*

Teacher's Guide
pp. 118–119

Read
Patterns, Shapes, and Symmetry

- Introduce Concepts and Vocabulary
- Model and Share the Reading

* Before you begin Lesson 1, you may want to use the Before Theme Assessment tools listed on page 116.

Lesson 2

Teacher's Guide
pp. 120–121

Reread
Patterns, Shapes, and Symmetry

- Develop Concepts and Vocabulary
- Introduce the Comprehension Strategy: Making Connections
- Small Group Reading
- Modeled Writing

Lesson 3

Teacher's Guide
pp. 122–123

Read
How to Make a Paper Frog

- Develop Concepts and Vocabulary
- Small Group Reading
- Practice the Comprehension Strategy: Making Connections
- Shared Writing

Lesson 4

Teacher's Guide
pp. 124–125

Read
Looking for Symmetry

- Review Concepts and Vocabulary
- Small Group Reading
- Apply the Comprehension Strategy: Making Connections
- Guided Writing

Lesson 5

Teacher's Guide
pp. 126–127

Assess and Extend

- Rereading and Assessments
- Guided Writing
- Assessment Tools
- Optional Reading
- Home Connection

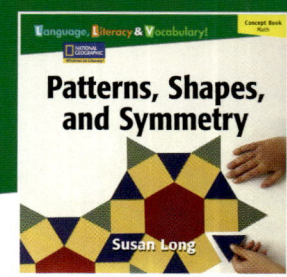

Language, Literacy & Vocabulary!

Patterns, Shapes, and Symmetry

Susan Long

OBJECTIVES

- Understand that objects may have shapes and show patterns or symmetry
- Learn and use vocabulary related to patterns, shapes, and symmetry
- Use photographs to predict vocabulary
- Use text features, such as labels and ordered steps, to understand shapes and patterns

Materials

Realia: paper shapes: red squares, yellow rectangles, blue triangles; other random assortments of paper shapes

Theme Builder

Patterns, Shapes, and Symmetry

Learning Masters page 65

Audiolesson 8

Theme Builder (Chant)

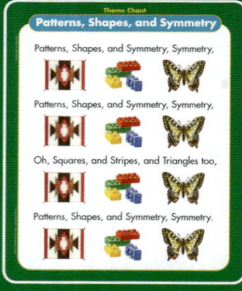

Theme Builder (Scene)

Introduce Concepts and Vocabulary

Introduce Theme Question

Ask students: How would you talk about the shapes you see in this room? How would you talk about patterns you see on the clothes your friends are wearing? Explain that students will learn about patterns, shapes, and symmetry. They will also learn the language used when describing and asking questions about shapes and patterns.

Turn and Talk Provide learning partners with randomly cut paper shapes. Have them sort the shapes according to the number of sides each shape has and talk about their groupings.

Develop Oral Language

Give a paper square to each student. Have students count the number of sides in a square. A square has four sides that are the same length.

Give a paper rectangle to each student. Have students compare the square and rectangle. Ask students to describe the difference between a square and a rectangle. What is the same about a square and a rectangle? What is different?

Turn and Talk Have students work with partners to identify rectangle shapes in the room, such as doors and windows.

Introduce Theme Chant

Display the Theme Chant on the *Theme Builder*. Have students say the chant in unison. Have learning partners use *Learning Masters* page 65 to practice saying the Theme Chant.

Introduce Key Vocabulary

Use the Think and Discuss scene to teach Key Concept Words and model language forms.

What shapes do you see?

The paper pattern includes square and triangle shapes. The butterfly wings have circle shapes.

Continue to model sentences using the words listed below to help identify shapes and objects in the scene. As you introduce words, jot them down on chart paper. Display this Word Bank throughout the theme.

Turn and Talk Have students work with partners to practice using the words and the language forms for asking questions. For example:

What pattern does this _____ have?

The butterfly has a pattern with _____.

circle	pattern	square
half	rectangle	symmetry
line of symmetry	shape	triangle

Build Background

Display the Think and Discuss scene on the *Theme Builder* again. Ask students to describe the patterns.

Turn and Talk Have partners talk about where the patterns are the same and where they are different. For example: The butterfly pattern is the same on both wings.

Model and Share the Reading

Preview the Book

Distribute copies of *Patterns, Shapes, and Symmetry*. Read aloud the title and the author's name. As you page through the book, point out:

- Most pages show patterns.
- There are labels to help define some shapes and patterns.
- There are steps to show how to make a pattern.

Predict Vocabulary

Encourage students to use pictures to predict vocabulary: Which words do you expect to see in this book?

Display pages 6–7 and cover the words: Which words do you expect to see on these pages?

Students may mention the types of patterns seen on these pages, such as alternating color patterns. Have learning partners use *pattern* and *line* when describing the patterns. Continue the activity with other pages as time allows.

Model the Reading

Invite students to follow along as you read aloud pages 4–7 in *Patterns, Shapes, and Symmetry*. Read fluently, modeling smooth, accurate reading with appropriate expression. After reading each pair of pages, pause to think aloud. Encourage students to ask questions and make observations.

Pages 4–5

Think Aloud This is like the Think and Discuss scene on the ***Theme Builder***. The pictures show different kinds of patterns and shapes. We can find patterns and shapes in many different places.

Pages 6–7

Think Aloud The words next to each picture help me think about the kinds of patterns I see.

Share the Reading

Now have partners complete the reading. Encourage them to pause after reading one or two pages and have conversations about what they have read. Ask them to share what they notice about the patterns and shapes on these pages.

Reread for Fluency

To have students practice fluent reading, read the sentences and questions on pages 4–7 aloud. Have students read each sentence and question with you a second time. Then have students reread the entire book independently to build fluency. See *Customize the Reading*.

Learning Masters/page 65

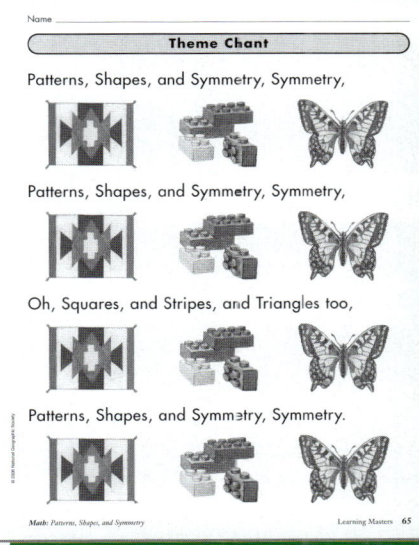

Customize the Reading

Students reread and talk about Patterns, Shapes, and Symmetry on their own to build fluency.

- Students who are not yet able to read the book can identify shapes in the room.
- Students who need extra support can reread the book while listening to the audiolesson.
- Students who can read the book might read independently or aloud with partners.

Customize Instruction for ELLs

Newcomers/Beginning During reading, have students find and stand by appropriate shapes or patterns in the room.

Developing Point to shapes in the room and ask questions such as, "What shape is the window?" "What shape is the fish tank?" Encourage students to respond using the language form: The _____ is a _____ shape.

Expanding/Bridging Ask students to choose an object in the room and say two sentences describing the shape of the object or pattern shown.

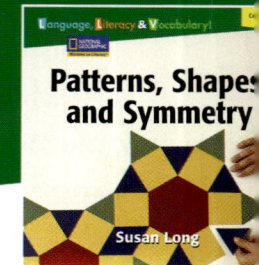

OBJECTIVES

- Understand that objects can have shapes and patterns, and that the patterns can show symmetry
- Use vocabulary to describe an object's form
- Learn the comprehension strategy: Making Connections
- Read to gain fluency in oral and silent reading
- Write descriptions of objects

Materials

Realia: paper shapes: red squares, yellow rectangles, blue triangles, green circles; pattern card; shapes card; symmetry card

Theme Builder

Patterns, Shapes, and Symmetry

Learning Masters pages 8, 66, 67

 Audiolesson 8

Theme Builder (Graphic Organizer)

Develop Concepts and Vocabulary

Develop Oral Language

Display a red square, yellow rectangle, and blue triangle. Ask students to describe each shape as it is presented. Next, create a shapes pattern on the board, such as a square–circle–square–circle. What pattern did I make with the shapes?

Turn and Talk Have learning partners use paper shapes to create patterns. Have one partner create a pattern for the other partner to describe. Encourage partners to create and describe several different patterns.

Revisit the Theme Chant Display the Theme Chant on the *Theme Builder*. Give three students pattern, shapes, and symmetry cards. Say the chant about Patterns, Shapes, and Symmetry again. Have students hold up the correct cards as the group says the chant.

Build Background

Display the graphic organizer on the *Theme Builder*. Have students look at the middle photo. Ask them to find a rectangle. Continue with the other three shapes. Point out that these are shapes on a nonliving thing—a house.

Turn and Talk Encourage partners to identify other shapes and patterns in the photo.

Begin Vocabulary Log As students read, encourage them to use sticky notes to tag words that they would like to save. After reading, students can record the words and their notes about them.

Use *Learning Masters* page 8.

Introduce the Comprehension Strategy

Introduce Making Connections

Students make connections to what they are reading by connecting a new concept to something they have read, experienced, or know.

Think Aloud When I read a book, I look at the words and the pictures. Sometimes these remind me of a book I have read. Sometimes they remind me of things in real life that I have seen and touched. I connect what I already know to what I am reading. When I do this, I am **making a connection.** This helps me better understand the book.

Model Making Connections

Turn to page 7 and model the comprehension strategy and language forms for making connections.

I can connect to the pattern I see on the fish.

It reminds me of my favorite beach towel. I liked counting the number of blue stripes in the pattern.

This connection helps me understand that the same kind of pattern can be found in different places.

For additional practice in making connections, have partners work on *Learning Masters* page 66.

Small Group Reading

As students read, invite them to share what they notice. Use some of the suggestions below to encourage observations and talk about the book.

Pages 4–9

Support Comprehension Help students think of other places they have seen patterns, such as on a favorite shirt or pair of socks. Tell them that they are making connections.

Pages 10–15

Check Understanding Explain what the headings on pages 6–7, 10–11, and 14–15 tell you about patterns, shapes, and symmetry. *(They say that patterns, shapes, and symmetry are everywhere.)*

Pages 16–17

Support Comprehension Have a volunteer explain what the line of symmetry shows. *(two sides that match)*

Pages 18–19

Check Understanding Have students use the Word Bank to help them identify patterns, shapes, and symmetry in the images. What patterns can you find? What shapes can you find? Which pictures show symmetry?

Discuss the Book

Invite students to share what they learned. Ask them to describe shapes and patterns in the real world. Encourage them to use the words in the Word Bank to discuss what they have read. Remind students to add words to their Vocabulary Logs.

Students can complete *Learning Masters* page 67.

Reread for Fluency

Have students follow along as you read pages 10–11 in a flat tone. Ask how you can improve your reading. *(Read with more expression.)* Demonstrate reading the same text with expression. Ask students which way was more interesting. Have a volunteer read the page with expression. Have partners reread pages 12–13. Ask them to focus on improving the expression in their reading. For other suggestions, see *Customize the Reading*.

Learning Masters/pages 8, 66

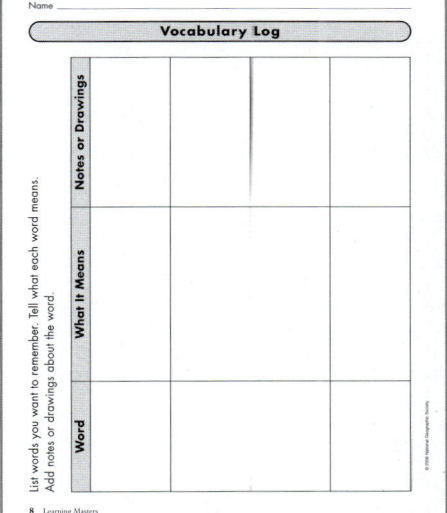

Customize the Reading

Students reread and talk about Patterns, Shapes, and Symmetry using one of the following options:

- Look through the pages, identifying objects with patterns.
- Reread the book while following along with the audiolesson.
- Read independently or read aloud with a partner.

Modeled Writing

Use the graphic organizer on the *Theme Builder* to review some Key Concepts of the theme. Prepare to model writing, including how to use precise nouns and adjectives.

Think Aloud When I look around, I see shapes all around me. The wheels on the cars are circles. Some buildings look like tall rectangles. I remember a sign that was in the shape of a triangle. My purpose is to describe shapes I see around me. My audience is the students in this group. I'm going to write about my own experiences, so I'll use the pronoun *I*. First, I'll write my main idea.

Shapes are all around me. Some shapes are big. Some shapes are small. Some shapes have shapes inside them.

Continue by identifying the shapes of other objects found outside, such as the sidewalk (squares) or the billboard (rectangle).

Think Aloud I'll use precise nouns and adjectives to describe the shapes.

The buildings look like tall rectangles. Cars zoom past the buildings. Their tires look like spinning circles. I walk on the hard squares of the sidewalk. The squares of the sidewalk make a long rectangle. A red circle shines, and I stop. It's the traffic light.

Learning Masters/page 67

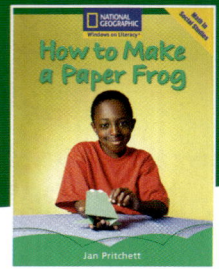

OBJECTIVES

- Read to gain fluency in oral and silent reading
- Practice the comprehension strategy: Making Connections
- Develop an understanding that people can create shapes and patterns
- Use numbered steps to create a shape
- Understand sequence

Materials

Realia: green paper squares, scissors, glue, pencil, small paper circles, pictures of frogs

Theme Builder

How to Make a Paper Frog

Learning Masters page 68

Audiolesson 8

Develop Concepts and Vocabulary

Develop Oral Language

Model the Key Concept Words *square, shape, triangle, circle,* and *half.* Display a green paper square. Have students identify the shape. Fold the square in half to make a triangle. Have students identify the shape. Point out that the fold is a line of symmetry. Fold each triangle point again to make three small triangles. I can use a square shape to make a triangle. I can use the big triangle to make three small triangle shapes.

Turn and Talk Give students green paper squares. Have students work together to fold the square to make a triangle. Have them

identify the shapes. What shape am I giving you? What shape do you make when you fold it in half?

Revisit the Theme Chant Display the chant on the *Theme Builder.* Say the chant in unison. Then, using their green squares and triangles, have students hold up the correct shape as they say the chant again.

Build Background

Distribute copies of *How to Make a Paper Frog.* Show pictures of frogs. Talk about where frogs live and how they look and move. Ask students to share experiences they have had with frogs.

Small Group Reading

Get Ready to Read

Preview the Book Read aloud the title, the author's name, and the Think and Discuss question on the back cover: What shapes do you use to make a paper frog?

Page through the book and do the following:

- Point out the labels on pages 2–3.
- Point out the steps on pages 4–12. Point out sequencing words such as *first, next,* and *last.*
- Ask students to predict what they will learn.

Predict Vocabulary Encourage students to use photos to predict vocabulary: Which words do you expect to see in this book?

Display a page and cover the words: Which words do you expect to see on this page?

List the words students mention. Add Key Concept Words in the book that students do not mention.

Text Feature: Numbered Steps

Introduce Explain that steps are used to show how to make things. When you make something, it is important to follow the steps in order.

Model Have students look at page 6. Hold up the starting square from Step One. I have a square, but Step Two shows a triangle. I missed what I needed to do. I go back to Step One.

Practice Have students look at page 7. Have them explain how Step Three shows how to fold the right side of the triangle.

Read the Book

As students read, invite them to share what they notice. Use some of the suggestions below to encourage observations and talk about the book.

Pages 2–3

Practice the Comprehension Strategy

Encourage students to **Make Connections.** When have you used these materials before? What did you make?

Pages 4–7

Key Concept Words *square, half, shape, triangle*

Support Comprehension Prepare students to make the paper frogs as they read the book. Distribute needed supplies. Ask students to think about how they used a square to make a triangle (in Develop Oral Language). Have partners connect how Step One shows how they can make a triangle from a square.

Pages 8–11

Check Understanding Ask students to explain Step Six. Demonstrate the step. Complete Step Six together. Have students explain Step Seven. Have partners complete Step Seven.

Page 12

Key Concept Word *circle*

Check Understanding Have students identify the shape used for the frog's eyes and complete Step Eight. Have them work with partners to retell the steps to make the frog.

Discuss the Book

Invite students to use the Word Bank to discuss the book and to share what they learned. Ask students to explain why it was important to follow the numbered steps. Have students name all the shapes they used. *(square, triangles, circles)* Have students add words to their Vocabulary Logs.

Use *Learning Masters* page 68.

Reread for Fluency

Have students reread the entire book independently to build fluency. See *Customize the Reading.*

Learning Masters/page 68

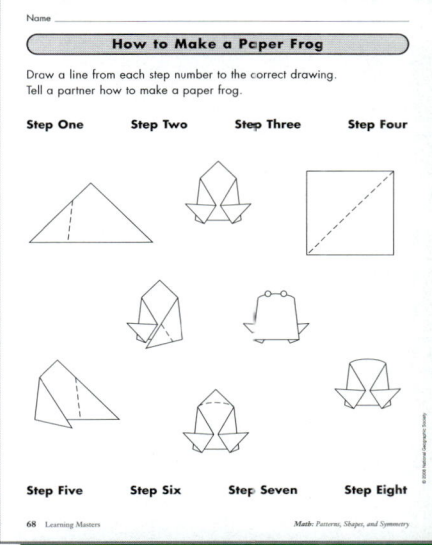

Customize the Reading

Students reread and talk about How to Make a Paper Frog *using one of the following options:*

- *Look through the pages, pointing out the numbered steps.*
- *Reread the book while following along with the audiolesson.*
- *Read independently or aloud with a partner.*

Shared Writing

Review the writing you modeled in Lesson 2. Point out that writers sometimes label pictures. Draw shapes to go with your writing and label them with students' help.

Guide students to frame questions about shapes and answers that describe shapes and patterns. Ask them to suggest sentences that tell how the shapes are identified.

Customize Instruction for ELLs

Newcomers/Beginning Have students add details to the writing such as the color or the size of shapes.

Developing Help students think about the shapes that are found on buildings by having them finish sentences such as: "I see *(windows)* on the building. They have a *(square)* shape."

Expanding/Bridging Have students think about where circles are found outside. Encourage students to add another sentence to the writing.

Read *Looking for Symmetry*

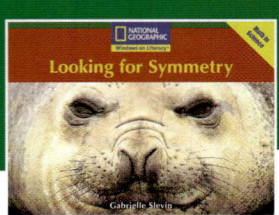

OBJECTIVES

- Read to gain fluency in oral and silent reading
- Apply the comprehension strategy: Making Connections
- Understand the fundamentals of symmetry
- Use labels to comprehend text
- Evaluate information

Materials

Realia: symmetrical star with a symmetrical pattern drawn on it, paper rectangles

Theme Builder

Looking for Symmetry

Learning Masters pages 69, 70

Take-Home Book Masters: *Patterns, Shapes, and Symmetry*

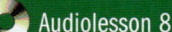 Audiolesson 8

 Take-Home Book Masters

Patterns, Shapes, and Symmetry

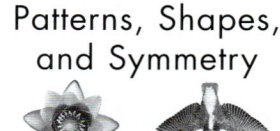

by _____

Review Concepts and Vocabulary

Develop Oral Language

Model the Key Concept Words *symmetry* and *line of symmetry*. For example, hold up the star. Fold it to make identical halves.

When I unfold the star, I can see that each side is exactly the same. The star has symmetry. The fold in the paper is the line of symmetry.

Turn and Talk Give each student a paper rectangle. Have students fold the rectangle in half and open it. Have conversation partners identify the line of symmetry in the rectangle. Then have students make matching patterns on the two sides of the rectangle.

Revisit the Theme Chant Display the chant on the *Theme Builder*. Assign three students to read line three, as the group reads the rest of the chant. Say the chant. On a second reading, have each student hold up his or her symmetrical rectangle when the word "symmetry" is sung.

Build Background

Distribute copies of *Looking for Symmetry*. Ask students to look at the cover and title page of the book. Then ask them to use the word *symmetry* to describe the animal's face and the butterfly.

Small Group Reading

Get Ready to Read

Preview the Book Read aloud the title, the author's name, and the Think and Discuss question on the back cover: Is this a line of symmetry?

Page through the book and do the following:

- Point out the labels next to the pictures.
- Invite students to identify the possible line of symmetry in each picture.
- Ask students to predict what they will learn.

Predict Vocabulary Encourage students to use photos to predict vocabulary: Which words do you expect to see in this book?

Display a page and cover the words: Which words do you expect to see on this page?

List the words students mention. Add Key Concept Words in the book that students do not mention.

Text Feature: Labels

Introduce Point out and read the label on page 5 aloud. This is a label. It helps you identify what the picture shows.

Model I know this is a flower on page 5, but I'm not sure about the name of the flower. I read the label. It says this flower is called a *sunflower.*

Practice Have partners look at pages 7, 9, and 11 and read each label.

Read the Book

As students read, invite them to share what they notice. Use some of the suggestions below to encourage observations and talk about the book.

Pages 2–5

Key Concept Words *symmetry, line of symmetry*

Support Comprehension Ask students to identify the line of symmetry. Have them count the legs on the spider and the petals on the flower to make sure there are the same number on both sides of the line of symmetry.

Pages 6–7

Check Understanding The crab looks very much the same on both sides, but it does not have symmetry. Explain why this crab does not have symmetry. (*The two sides of the crab are not the same because one side has a claw.*)

Pages 10–11

Check Understanding Look on both sides of the line. Why is this line not a line of symmetry? (*There are four sea star arms on one side of the line and only two on the other side. The two sides do not match.*)

Page 12

Apply the Comprehension Strategy

Encourage students to **Make Connections** to help them better understand page 12.

I can connect to _____.

It reminds me of _____.

This connection helps me understand _____.

Guide students to realize that their connections helps them to understand what *symmetry* and *line of symmetry* mean.

Discuss the Book

Invite students to use the Word Bank to tell about the book. What have they learned about symmetry? Can they give examples of symmetry? Remind students to add words to their Vocabulary Logs.

Use *Learning Masters* page 69.

Reread for Fluency

Have students reread the entire book independently to build fluency. See *Customize the Reading*.

Learning Masters/page 69

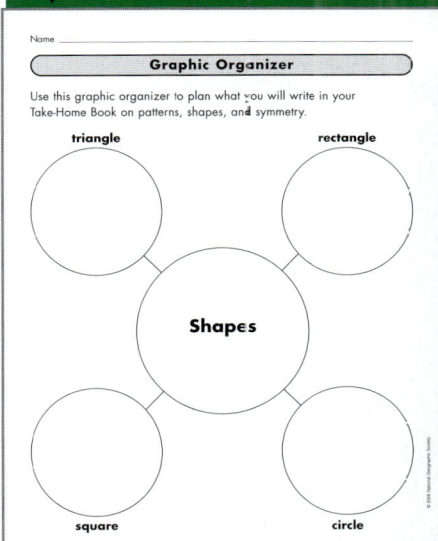

Customize the Reading

Students reread and talk about Looking for Symmetry *using one of the following options:*

- *Look through the pages, finding the lines of symmetry.*
- *Reread the book while following along with the audiolesson.*
- *Read independently or aloud with a partner.*

Guided Writing

Distribute copies of the *Take-Home Book Masters*. Explain that students will write books about symmetry, shapes, and patterns around them. Work with students to:

- Describe the shapes, patterns, and symmetry shown in the photos in their Take-Home Books.
- Share writing ideas for each set of pages.
- Complete the labels.

Record students' writing ideas for the pages of their books on chart paper.

Have partners talk together about the shapes around them as they plan what to write.

Have each partner complete a graphic organizer. In each attached circle, have students list words to describe the shape and tell where they might see this shape. Students may include these words and ideas in their writing.

Display the Word Bank and remind students to check their Vocabulary Logs as they begin to write.

Use *Learning Masters* page 70.

Learning Masters/page 70

OBJECTIVES

- Use Key Concepts and Key Concept Words in writing
- Demonstrate oral language proficiency
- Demonstrate comprehension of theme selections
- Read related titles to reinforce Key Concepts and vocabulary

Materials

Take-Home Book Masters: *Patterns, Shapes, and Symmetry*

Learning Masters pages 6–7, 71–72

Assessment Masters pages 179, 180, 200, 214, 215, 223, 228

Take-Home Book Masters

Patterns, Shapes,
and Symmetry

by _____

Rereading and Assessments

Allow time for students to independently reread the theme selections. Display the Word Bank for students' reference as they read.

As students reread, meet with individuals. Use the assessment tools listed on page 127 to evaluate students' progress and to update their records.

Guided Writing

Students continue writing the Take-Home Books they began in Lesson 4. Review the group list of writing ideas. Display the Word Bank.

Page through the theme books to review the text features, including labels and numbered steps. Talk about text features that students could add to their Take-Home Books. For example, they might write steps for figuring out symmetry.

Point out that good writers:

- Use precise words to help the reader picture what is described. Remind students to include adjectives.
- Sometimes connect to their own experiences. Students may tell where they have seen a similar pattern or shape.

- Revise their work. Students can check that subjects and verbs agree and that their sentences make sense.

Have students complete the Picture Glossary and About the Author last.

As students write, circulate to coach and support individuals. If students need help, guide them to think about the kinds of patterns and shapes they see every day.

Have partners exchange books and discuss what they like in each other's book. For example, partners may point out an interesting word that is fun to read. Partners can also offer suggestions, such as adding an adjective to better describe a shape or pattern. Each writer decides what changes to make and adds any final touches.

Customize Instruction for ELLs

Newcomers/Beginning Have students work with a bridging partner to help them frame sentences.

Developing Have students suggest a different way to write a sentence. Encourage students to add color words and size words to their sentences.

Expanding/Bridging Have students check the text for correct capitalization. Encourage students to use interjections such as "Stripes!"

Assessment Tools

Self-Assessment

Allow students to reflect and assess their own learning by completing *Learning Masters* pages 6–7.

- What I Learned, page 6
- How I Learned, page 7

Reading

The following assessment tools can help you evaluate and record students' progress in reading and understanding the theme books.

- Retelling Guide and Scoring Rubric, page 179
- Fluency Scoring Guide, page 180
- Oral Reading Record, page 200

Writing

Use the completed Take-Home Books and the following tools to assess students' development as writers.

- Writing Rubric, page 214
- Writing Traits Checklist, page 215

Content Assessment

Display the Key Concept Words. Have students choose one Key Concept Word and group students according to the word they chose. Then have each group make a poster that illustrates the Key Concept Word and shows how it can apply to things we see around us. Encourage students to label their poster. Have students present their posters.

Vocabulary and Oral Language

Use the following resources, in addition to the Think and Discuss scene on the *Theme Builder*, to assess oral language development.

- Content Vocabulary Checklist, page 223
- Oral Language Developmental Checklist, page 228

Optional Reading

Reading related titles allows students to explore concepts and vocabulary at different levels. It also allows them to use reading strategies in different types of texts. Encourage students to compare the theme books to the books in the next column.

Optional Titles

These related *Windows on Literacy* titles reinforce Key Concepts of the *Patterns, Shapes, and Symmetry* theme.

Nonfiction Titles

Patterns Around the World Level 8

Thanks to the Triangle Level 11

The Eiffel Tower Level 15

Fiction Titles

The Family Quilt Level 15

The Fly-Right Kite Level 16

Home Connection

The Family Focus letters on *Learning Masters* pages 71–72 summarize key concepts about identifying patterns, shapes, and symmetry in living and nonliving things.

In the Share and Learn activity, family members take a walk and identify shapes in the neighborhood.

Learning Masters/pages 6–7

Related Fiction Titles

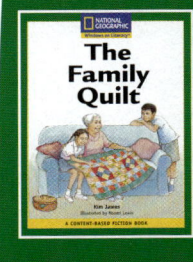
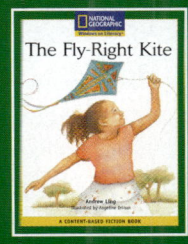

Learning Masters/pages 71–72

Overview

States of Matter

STANDARDS

ACADEMIC LANGUAGE/ELD

- Use academic vocabulary related to the study of states of matter
- Use appropriate language forms to discuss and predict states of matter, and to make inferences
- Develop fluency in reading, writing, listening to, and speaking English

SCIENCE

- Identify the three states of matter—solid, liquid, gas—and describe the properties of each
- Explain how temperature can cause matter to change from one state to another state

READING/LANGUAGE ARTS

- Learn and apply the comprehension strategy: Making Inferences
- Use the text features: Graphic Organizers/Charts, and Contents/Headings
- Write about states of matter in everyday life
- Learn and use vocabulary related to states of matter

Before Theme Assessment

To compare progress before and after teaching this theme, use one or more of the following informal assessment tools before beginning the theme.

- Oral Reading Record, page 203
- Fluency Scoring Guide, page 180
- Content Vocabulary Checklist, page 224
- Oral Language Developmental Checklist, page 228

Theme Materials

Concept Book

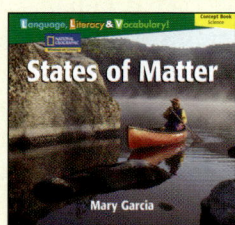

States of Matter
Mary Garcia

Nonfiction Books

Water Can Change
Brian Birchall

Level 17

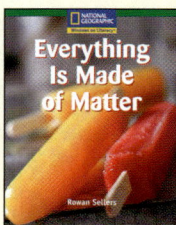

Everything Is Made of Matter
Rowan Sellers

Level 18

Theme Builder

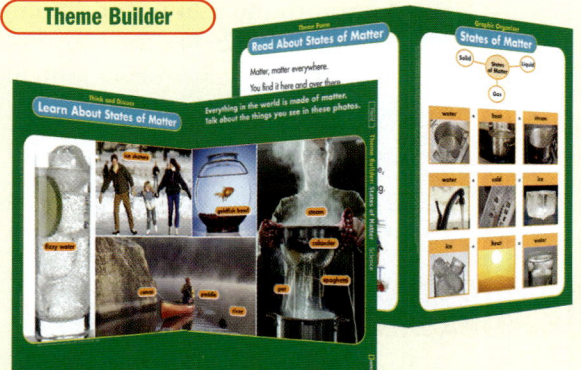

Learning Masters

Audiolesson on CD

Take-Home Book Masters

States of Matter
by

Optional Reading

Windows on Literacy Content-Based Fiction

Uncle Terry's Glasses Level 17

Summer Day Slushes Level 18

Windows on Literacy Nonfiction

Heat Changes Things Level 7

Water Level 12

Where Do the Puddles Go? Level 18

Instructional Highlights

Key Concepts

- Matter can take the form of a solid, a liquid, or a gas.
- Each state of matter has its own unique properties.
- Changes in temperature can cause matter to change from one state to another state.

Comprehension Strategy

Making Inferences

Key Concept Words

change	matter
gas	melt
heat	solid
ice	steam
liquid	temperature

Text Features

Charts/Graphic Organizers

Contents/Headings

Theme Planner

Lesson 1*
Teacher's Guide
pp. 130–131

Read
States of Matter

- Introduce Concepts and Vocabulary
- Model and Share the Reading

* Before you begin Lesson 1, you may want to use the Before Theme Assessment tools listed on page 128

Lesson 2
Teacher's Guide
pp. 132–133

Reread
States of Matter

- Develop Concepts and Vocabulary
- Introduce the Comprehension Strategy: Making Inferences
- Small Group Reading
- Modeled Writing

Lesson 3
Teacher's Guide
pp. 134–135

Read
Water Can Change

- Develop Concepts and Vocabulary
- Small Group Reading
- Practice the Comprehension Strategy: Making Inferences
- Shared Writing

Lesson 4
Teacher's Guide
pp. 136–137

Read
Everything Is Made of Matter

- Review Concepts and Vocabulary
- Small Group Reading
- Apply the Comprehension Strategy: Making Inferences
- Guided Writing

Lesson 5
Teacher's Guide
pp. 138–139

Assess and Extend

- Rereading and Assessments
- Guided Writing
- Assessment Tools
- Optional Reading
- Home Connection

Lesson 1

Read *States of Matter*

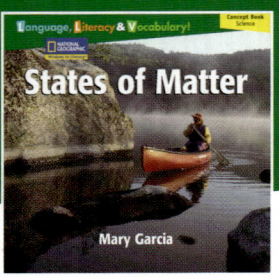

States of Matter

Mary Garcia

OBJECTIVES

- Understand that matter has three states, each with unique properties, and that temperature can cause matter to change states
- Learn and use vocabulary related to states of matter
- Use photos to predict vocabulary
- Use text features, such as headings, to understand text

Materials

Realia: three small resealable plastic bags, crayon, water

Theme Builder

States of Matter

Learning Masters page 73

Audiolesson 9

Theme Builder (Poem)

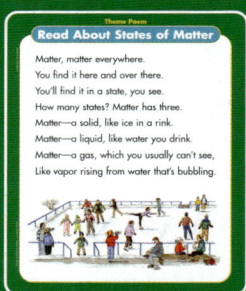

Read About States of Matter

Matter, matter everywhere.
You find it here and over there.
You'll find it in a state, you see.
How many states? Matter has three.
Matter—a solid, like ice in a rink.
Matter—a liquid, like water you drink.
Matter—a gas, which you usually can't see,
Like vapor rising from water that's bubbling.

Theme Builder (Scene)

Learn About States of Matter

Everything in the world is made of matter. Talk about the things you see in these photos.

Introduce Concepts and Vocabulary

Introduce Theme Question

Ask students: Think about something such as a book you can hold in your hand. How is the book different from something you pour? How is it different from the air you breathe? Explain that students will learn about different kinds of matter and the language to use to talk about matter.

Turn and Talk Provide learning groups with small plastic bags—one with a solid object such as a crayon, one with water, and one with only air. Have students touch the bags and describe differences. *(The crayon keeps its shape. It is hard. The water changes shape. I can't see the air.)*

Develop Oral Language

Show the bag with the solid. Model sentences such as the following: The crayon is hard. It keeps its shape. The crayon is a solid.

Continue in the same way with the other two bags.

Turn and Talk Have learning partners name and describe one item that is a solid, one that is a liquid, and one that is a gas.

Introduce Theme Poem

Display the Theme Poem on the *Theme Builder*. Have students echo-read the poem, reading line by line after you. Then read the poem in unison. Ask partners to use *Learning Masters* page 73 to practice reading the poem.

Introduce Key Vocabulary

Use the Think and Discuss scene to teach Key Concept Words and model language forms.

There are three states of matter—solid, liquid, and gas.

The people skate on ice. Ice is a solid.

It will change to a liquid when the sun _____ it.

Continue to model sentences, using the words listed below to help identify objects in the scene. As you introduce words, jot them on chart paper. Display this Word Bank throughout the theme.

Turn and Talk Have students work with partners to practice using the words and language forms: The _____ is a _____. It will change to a _____ when you _____ it.

NAMING WORDS	ACTION WORDS
gas	change
ice	heat
liquid	melt
matter	
solid	
steam	
temperature	

Build Background

Display the Think and Discuss scene on the *Theme Builder* again. Ask students to describe the state of matter in each photo.

Turn and Talk Have partners use the language forms to discuss states of matter and how they can change.

Model and Share the Reading

Preview the Book

Distribute copies of *States of Matter*. Read aloud the title and the author's name. As you page through the book, point out:

- The Contents page tells what students will read about.
- Each entry from the Contents appears as a heading in the book. The heading tells what the pages are about.
- The sidebar on page 7 adds information about the states of matter.

Predict Vocabulary

Encourage students to use pictures to predict vocabulary: Which words do you expect to see in this book?

Display pages 6–7 and cover the words: Which words do you expect to see on these pages?

Students may mention objects on the pages, such as rocks. Add these words to the Word Bank. Have students talk with partners and use *solid*, *liquid*, and *gas* to describe the objects. Continue the activity with other pages, as time allows.

Model the Reading

Invite students to follow along as you read aloud pages 4–12 in *States of Matter*. Read fluently, modeling smooth, accurate reading with appropriate expression. After reading each group of pages, pause to think aloud. Also, encourage students to ask questions and make observations.

Pages 4–7

Think Aloud This is like the Think and Discuss scene on the **Theme Builder.** I know the labels name the people and things.

Pages 8–13

Think Aloud When I look through the headings, I see that the next three pairs of pages each describes one of the states of matter. This tells me that each pair of pages gives information about the kind of matter named in the heading.

Share the Reading

Now have partners complete the reading. Encourage them to pause after reading one or two pages and have conversations about what they have read. Ask them to share questions they may have.

Reread for Fluency

To have students practice fluent reading, read aloud pages 6–7 of *States of Matter*, sentence by sentence. Have students echo-read each sentence in unison, imitating your model. Then have students reread the entire book independently to build fluency. See *Customize the Reading*.

Name _____

Theme Poem

Matter, matter everywhere.
You find it here and over there.
You'll find it in a state, you see.
How many states? Matter has three.
Matter—a solid, like ice in a rink.
Matter—a liquid, like water you drink.
Matter—a gas, which you usually can't see,
Like vapor rising from water that's bubbling.

Science: States of Matter   Learning Masters **73**

Customize the Reading

Students reread and talk about States of Matter on their own to build fluency.

- *Students who are not yet able to read the book can name objects they know and tell the state of matter of each.*
- *Students who need extra support can reread the book while listening to the audiolesson.*
- *Students who can read the book might read independently or aloud with partners.*

Customize Instruction for ELLs

Newcomers/Beginning During reading, ask, "Which is a solid/liquid/gas?" Have students point to objects or say their names.

Developing During reading, ask, "What is the state of matter of this object?" Encourage students to respond with the language form: The _____ is a _____.

Expanding/Bridging Ask students to speak in complete sentences as they identify objects and tell the state of matter of each. Extend the activity to classroom objects.

Lesson 2

Reread *States of Matter*

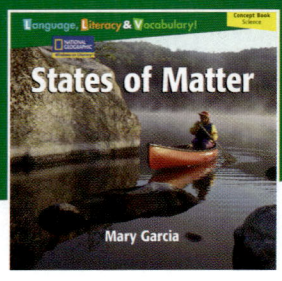

Language, Literacy & Vocabulary!
States of Matter
Mary Garcia

OBJECTIVES

- Understand that matter has three states and that temperature can cause matter to change states
- Use vocabulary to discuss the states of matter and how they can change
- Learn the comprehension strategy: Making Inferences
- Read to gain fluency in oral and silent reading
- Write about states of matter

Materials

Realia: three clear glasses, tap water, club soda

Theme Builder

States of Matter

Learning Masters pages 8, 74, 75

Audiolesson 9

Theme Builder (Graphic Organizer)

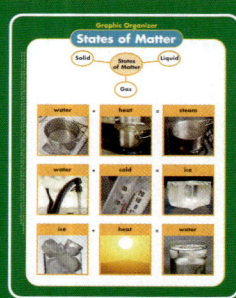

Develop Concepts and Vocabulary

Develop Oral Language

Display several objects, such as an empty glass, a glass filled with tap water, and a glass filled with club soda. Ask students to describe the states of matter. Next, ask: What will happen when you heat water in a pot?

Turn and Talk Have learning partners describe objects in the classroom by their shape, size, and state of matter. The listening partner can guess what the objects are.

Revisit the Theme Poem Display the theme poem on the *Theme Builder*. Assign students to read lines 5, 6, and 7. Have the group read the other lines in unison. Read the poem together.

Build Background

Display the graphic organizer on the *Theme Builder* and identify the three states of matter shown on the web. Then review changes in matter as shown on the graphic organizer. For example: When you heat water, the water will change to steam. When you freeze water, the water will change to ice.

Turn and Talk Encourage partners to describe the processes shown on the graphic organizer and say the state of matter in each picture.

Begin Vocabulary Log As students read, encourage them to use sticky notes to tag words they would like to save. After reading, students can record the words and their notes about them.

Use *Learning Masters* page 8.

Introduce the Comprehension Strategy

Introduce Making Inferences

Students make inferences when they combine information from the text with things they already know to infer meaning.

Think Aloud When I read a book, sometimes the author doesn't tell me everything I need to know. I have to think about what I'm reading and what I see in the pictures and combine that information with what I already know. That's called **making inferences.**

Model Making Inferences

Turn to pages 14–15 and model the comprehension strategy and language forms for making inferences.

The words tell me that the water has become a solid—ice.

The picture shows me the ice on a small river or canal. I can see the boats frozen in the ice.

I know that water in a river is usually a liquid. I know that when the temperature is very cold, water will change to a solid.

I infer that the cold temperature changed the water in the river into a solid **because** I know that water freezes when it's very cold.

For additional practice in making inferences, have partners work on *Learning Masters* page 74.

Small Group Reading

As students read, invite them to share what they notice. Use some of the suggestions below to encourage observations and talk about the book.

Pages 6–15

Check Understanding Tell about the differences between a solid, a liquid, and a gas. *(The size and shape of a solid stay the same. The shape of a liquid depends on where it is. You can see solids and liquids, but you can't always see gases. You can see signs, like air bubbles in water, that show that gases are there.)*

Pages 16–17

Check Understanding In your own words, tell about the states of matter in the water cycle. *(When the sun heats water in the puddle, the water changes into vapor, a gas. In clouds, the water changes back into a liquid. The liquid then falls as rain.)*

Pages 18–19

Check Understanding Have students use the words from the Word Bank and make inferences about changes in the states of matter shown in the pictures.

Pages 20–21

Check Understanding Have students discuss the pictures. How are solids, liquids, and gases the same? *(They all take up space.)* Which does not change shape easily? *(a solid)* Which do we not see easily? *(a gas)*

Discuss the Book

Invite students to share what they learned. Ask them to describe the three states of matter and give examples of each. Also, ask students to describe how states of matter can change and to provide examples of the changes. Encourage students to use the words in the Word Bank to discuss what they have read. Remind students to add words to their Vocabulary Logs.

Students can complete ***Learning Masters*** page 75.

Reread for Fluency

Read aloud the paragraph on page 8, without pausing at the periods or commas. Ask students why it was hard to understand you. *(You didn't pause.)* Explain that a period is a place to stop at the end of a sentence; a comma shows a place to pause within a sentence. Guide students to improve in phrasing by being sure to pause for each comma and period as they read the page in unison with you. For other suggestions, see *Customize the Reading.*

Learning Masters/pages 8, 74

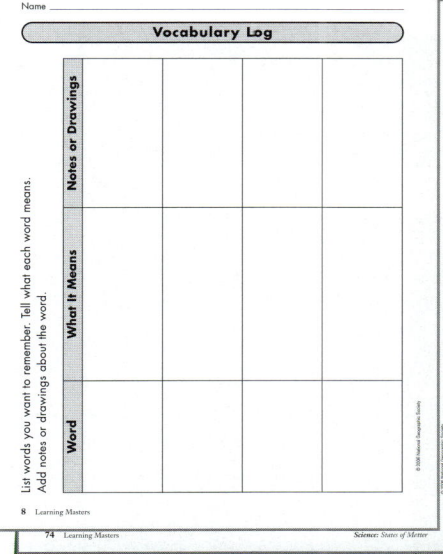

Learning Masters/page 75

Customize the Reading

Students reread and talk about States of Matter *using one of the following options:*

- *Look through the pages, pointing to objects and telling their state of matter.*
- *Reread the book while following along with the audiolesson.*
- *Read independently or read aloud with a partner.*

Modeled Writing

Use the graphic organizer on the ***Theme Builder*** to review some Key Concepts of the theme. Prepare to model writing, including how to use details to support main ideas.

Think Aloud I'm going to write about an amusement park and things I might find there in different states of matter. I'll draw a web like the one on the ***Theme Builder*** and list ideas for each state of matter—solid, liquid, or gas. *(Ideas for solids should include rides, such as a roller coaster. Liquids and gas could include soda.)*

Think Aloud I'm going to create an interesting beginning by describing the roller coaster. I'll begin by telling where we are.

At an amusement park, a red roller coaster goes slowly up the hill. The roller coaster is a solid. It has a shape. When it moves from place to place, it still keeps its shape.

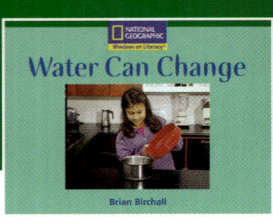

OBJECTIVES

- Read to gain fluency in oral and silent reading
- Practice the comprehension strategy: Making Inferences
- Understand that changes in temperature can cause matter to change from one state to another
- Use Charts/Graphic Organizers to comprehend text
- Use new information to make predictions

Materials

Realia: items that will melt in the sun, such as ice cubes, butter, chocolate; ice tray with water

Theme Builder

Water Can Change

Learning Masters page 76

Audiolesson 9

Develop Concepts and Vocabulary

Develop Oral Language

Model the Key Concept Words *melt*, *ice*, and *solid*. Display an ice cube. Model the following language: What will happen when the ice is put in the sun? It will melt. If possible, put the object in the sun to demonstrate melting. Next, display an ice tray filled with water. Model the following language: What will happen when the water is put into the freezer? It will change into ice. It will change into a solid.

Turn and Talk Have learning partners examine the other items you have brought in—butter and chocolate. Have them use your model to ask questions and make predictions.

Revisit the Theme Poem Display the poem on the *Theme Builder*. Invite students to point to appropriate pictures beneath the poem as they read with you.

Build Background

Distribute copies of *Water Can Change*. Have students describe the objects on the cover. Ask them to predict what will happen. *(The water will be heated. The girl, with help from an adult, may cook something in the water. There will be steam.)*

Small Group Reading

Get Ready to Read

Preview the Book Read aloud the title, the author's name, and the Think and Discuss question on the back cover: What makes the water boil?

Page through the book and do the following:

- Point out how the chapter titles in the Contents match the headings in the book.
- Ask students to describe the state of matter of the water on the pages.
- Ask students to predict what they will learn.

Predict Vocabulary Encourage students to use photos to predict vocabulary: Which words do you expect to see in this book?

Display a page and cover the words: Which words do you expect to see on this page?

List the words students mention. Add Key Concept Words in the book that students do not mention.

Text Feature: Chart

Introduce Display the chart on page 12. This chart summarizes information in the book about how water changes.

Model I see that the top row of this chart shows how ice changes as a result of being heated. It changes into a liquid.

Practice Direct students' attention to the second row at the bottom of the page. Ask what it shows. *(It shows how water changes to steam as a result of being heated.)*

Read the Book

As students read, invite them to share what they notice. Use some of the suggestions below to encourage observations and talk about the book.

Pages 3–5
Key Concept Words *ice, solid, heat, change*

Practice the Comprehension Strategy

Encourage students to **Make Inferences** about the change in the state of matter to help them better understand pages 4–5.

What change in state is happening? In the first picture, what state is the water in? In the third picture, what state is the water in? What causes the change?

Guide students in recognizing how they added what they already knew to what they saw and read on these pages.

Pages 6–9
Key Concept Words *liquid, steam*

Support Comprehension Ask students to make predictions: The girl is going to heat the water. What will happen to the water? (*It will change to steam.*)

Pages 10–11
Key Concept Word *gas*

Check Understanding Describe the change that happened when the water was heated. (*It changed from a liquid to a gas.*) How is a gas different from a solid or a liquid? (*A gas is hard to see.*)

Page 12

Check Understanding Tell about the changes that the chart shows. What causes the changes?

Discuss the Book

Invite students to use the Word Bank to tell about the book. What have they learned about two ways that water can change? Can they explain what causes the change? Remind students to add words to their Vocabulary Logs.

Use *Learning Masters* page 76.

Reread for Fluency

Have students reread the entire book independently to build fluency. See *Customize the Reading.*

Learning Masters/page 76

Shared Writing

Review the paragraphs you modeled in Lesson 2. Invite students to help you write a paragraph about other activities at an amusement park, such as throwing darts at balloons tacked to a dart board or riding down a water slide. Be sure to help students tie in properties of matter they have learned about.

Customize Instruction for ELLs

Newcomers/Beginning Show a photo or sketch of an amusement park. Guide students as they point out objects and tell the state of matter of each.

Developing Encourage students to finish sentences such as, "The liquids at the park include *(the water at the water slide)."*

Expanding/Bridging Have students call on prior knowledge to add details as they describe items from the amusement park.

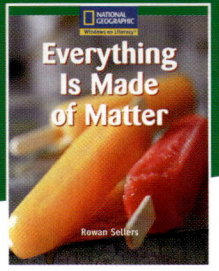

OBJECTIVES

- Read to gain fluency in oral and silent reading
- Apply the comprehension strategy: Making Inferences
- Develop an understanding that the three states of matter—solid, liquid, and gas—have unique properties
- Use the Contents/Headings to comprehend text
- Use making connections to understand the text better

Materials

Theme Builder

Everything Is Made of Matter

Learning Masters pages 77, 78

Take-Home Book Masters: *States of Matter*

 Audiolesson 9

 Take-Home Book Masters

States of Matter

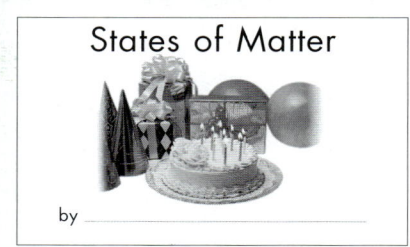

by _____

Review Concepts and Vocabulary

Develop Oral Language

If possible, take students to a different place in the school, such as the cafeteria. Have students identify various items as a solid, liquid, or gas. Have them describe any changes in states of matter they see.

Turn and Talk Ask learning partners to take turns describing what they remember from the visit about states of matter. Invite them to add information about states of matter in restaurants they have visited.

Revisit the Theme Poem Display the song on the *Theme Builder*. Ask students to practice reading the poem. Students should read a line silently to themselves, then look up and say the line to a partner.

Build Background

Distribute copies of *Everything Is Made of Matter*. Ask students to identify what kind of matter is on the cover. What is happening to it?

Small Group Reading

Get Ready to Read

Preview the Book Read aloud the title, the author's name, and the Think and Discuss question on the back cover: What makes the balloons rise?

Page through the book and do the following:

- Point out the question at the top of page 3. Explain that the next sentence answers the question. Point out a similar format on page 14.
- Read through the Contents.
- Ask students to predict what they will learn.

Predict Vocabulary Encourage students to use photos to predict vocabulary: Which words do you expect to see in this book?

Display a page and cover the words: Which words do you expect to see on this page?

List the words students mention. Add Key Concept Words in the book that students do not mention.

Text Feature: Contents/Headings

Introduce Read the listings in the Contents. The listings show me what pages have information on different topics.

Model When I turn to page 14, I see that the heading at the top of the page is the same as the one listed in the Contents.

Practice Ask students to pick two listings from the Contents and find them within in the book.

Read the Book

As students read, invite them to share what they notice. Use some of the suggestions below to encourage observations and talk about the book.

Pages 3–7

Key Concept Words *matter, solid, liquid, gas, change, heat, melt*

Support Comprehension Encourage students to make connections between personal experiences and the text. For example, ask them to name other solids they know of that melt. *(ice cream, chocolate)*

Apply the Comprehension Strategy

Encourage students to use these language forms as they **Make Inferences** about states of matter:

I infer _____ because _____ .

Pages 8–16

Check Understanding Have students compare the two bottles on page 9. Why are they different?

Check Understanding What makes the balloons on page 13 rise in the air?

Discuss the Book

Invite students to use the Word Bank to discuss the book and to share what they have learned. Ask them to share anything surprising they learned about states of matter. Have them name the things in the book that they have experienced in real life. Tell students to add words to their Vocabulary Logs.

Use *Learning Masters* page 77.

Reread for Fluency

Have students reread the entire book independently to build fluency. See *Customize the Reading.*

Learning Masters/page 77

Name _____

Everything Is Made of Matter

Here is a Contents page for a book about matter. Read the Contents. Then read each question. Tell the page number you would check to answer the question.

Contents

Solids	3
Liquids	6
Gas	8
Cooking: From Liquid to Solid	10
Glossary	12

1. Is juice a liquid? Look on page _____ .
2. Is ice a solid? Look on page _____
3. Where is the list of words from the book? Look on page _____ .
4. Is steam a gas? Look on page _____ .
5. Are pancakes a solid or a liquid? Look on page _____ .
6. How can heat change matter? Look on page _____ .
7. What are some solids? Look on page _____ .
8. What does "liquid" mean? Look on page _____ .

Science: States of Matter   Learning Masters **77**

Guided Writing

Distribute copies of the *Take-Home Book Masters.* Read the title and page through the book. Explain that students will write books about states of matter—and changes in states of matter—of objects at a birthday party. Work with students to:

- Complete the Contents.
- Describe and name the objects.
- Share writing ideas for each pair of pages.

Record students' writing ideas for the pages of their books on chart paper.

Have partners talk together to plan what to write. Explain that each student will complete a graphic organizer. They may wish to identify solids, liquids, and gases they see in each picture of their Take-Home Books. Display the Word Bank, and remind students to check their Vocabulary Logs as they begin to write.

Use *Learning Masters* page 78.

Customize the Reading

Students reread and talk about Everything Is Made of Matter using one of the following options:

- Look through the pages, naming the items and the state of matter of each.
- Reread the book while following along with the audiolesson.
- Read independently or aloud with a partner.

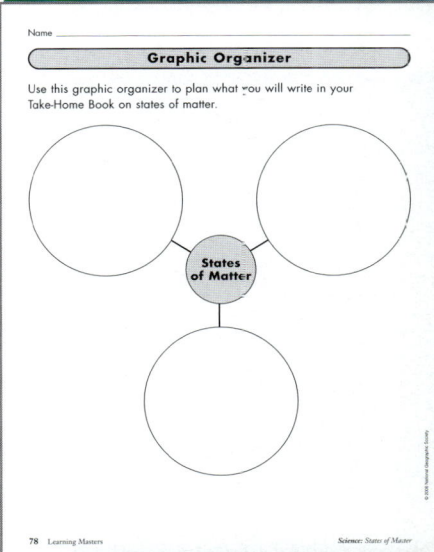

Learning Masters/page 78

Name _____

Graphic Organizer

Use this graphic organizer to plan what you will write in your Take-Home Book on states of matter.

States of Matter

78 Learning Masters   *Science: States of Matter*

OBJECTIVES

- Use Key Concepts and Key Concept Words in writing
- Demonstrate oral language proficiency
- Demonstrate comprehension of theme selections
- Read related titles to reinforce Key Concepts and vocabulary

Materials

Take-Home Book Masters:
States of Matter

Learning Masters pages 6–7, 79–80

Assessment Masters 179, 180, 203, 214, 215, 224, 228

Take-Home Book Masters

States of Matter

by _____

Rereading and Assessments

Allow time for students to independently reread the theme selections. Display the Word Bank for students' reference as they read.

As students reread, meet with individuals. Use the assessment tools listed on page 139 to evaluate students' progress and to update their records.

Guided Writing

Students continue writing the Take-Home Books they began in Lesson 4. Review the group list of writing ideas. Display the Word Bank.

Page through the theme books to review the text features, including the Contents page and headings. Talk about text features students could add to their Take-Home Books. For example, they might include a chart to show the change in the state of matter they describe for pages 10–11 in their Take-Home Books.

Point out that good writers:

- Often start with a sentence that tells where something is happening.
- Add describing details.

- Read over their work. Have students check to be certain they capitalized the first word in each sentence and included a period at the end of each sentence.

Have students complete the Picture Glossary and About the Author last.

As students write, circulate to coach and support individuals. If students need help, try suggesting one or two words that will remind the student of a Key Concept.

Have partners exchange books and discuss what they like in one another's books. For example, a reader may like a detail that the writer added from personal experience. Tell students to decide which changes to make and add any final touches.

Customize Instruction for ELLs

Newcomers/Beginning Have students dictate what they want to write to a bridging partner.

Developing Tell students to write simple sentences in their Take-Home Books describing objects and their states of matter.

Expanding/Bridging Encourage students to vary the types of sentences they use. Have students look through the theme selections for patterns.

Assessment Tools

Self-Assessment

Allow students to reflect and assess their own learning by completing *Learning Masters* pages 6–7.

- What I Learned, page 6
- How I Learned, page 7

Reading

The following assessment tools can help you evaluate and record students' progress in reading and understanding the theme books.

- Retelling Guide and Scoring Rubric, page 179
- Fluency Scoring Guide, page 180
- Oral Reading Record, page 203

Writing

Use the completed Take-Home Books and the following tools to assess students' development as writers.

- Writing Rubric, page 214
- Writing Traits Checklist, page 215

Content Assessment

Have groups choose or draw a picture of a place, such as a kitchen, a fair, a cafeteria, or an ice rink. Have students label objects in the scene to represent the three states of matter. Encourage groups to find at least one object that can change its state of matter. Have groups present their labeled pictures to other groups.

Vocabulary and Oral Language

Use the following resources, in addition to the Think and Discuss scene on the *Theme Builder,* to assess oral language development.

- Content Vocabulary Checklist, page 224
- Oral Language Developmental Checklist, page 228

Optional Reading

Reading related titles allows students to explore concepts and vocabulary at different levels. It also allows them to use reading strategies in different types of texts. Encourage students to compare the theme books to the books in the next column.

Optional Titles

These related *Windows on Literacy* titles reinforce Key Concepts of the *States of Matter* theme.

Nonfiction Titles

Heat Changes Things Level 7

Water Level 12

Where Do the Puddles Go? Level 13

Fiction Titles

Uncle Terry's Glasses Level 17

Summer Day Slushes Level 18

Home Connection

The Family Focus letters on *Learning Masters* pages 79–80 summarize key concepts about states of matter.

In the Share and Learn activity, family members look for things in the kitchen that illustrate states of matter and the way these states can change.

Name _____

What I Learned

List the three most important things you learned in this theme. Tell why you listed each one.

1. _____
2. _____
3. _____

6 Learning Masters

Learning Masters

Uncle Terry's Glasses

Summer Day Slushes

Name _____

Family Focus

Dear Family,
Your child has been reading the books *States of Matter, Water Can Change,* and *Everything Is Made of Matter* in our unit of study on states of matter. Please use this page to talk together about what your child has learned in this theme.

Your child has written a Take-Home Book. Invite your child to share the book with you. Also, share your child's Vocabulary Log for the theme. Here are some sample questions to help you discuss the Take-Home Book together:

- What are the three states of matter?
- What are examples of solids you find in everyday life?
- What are examples of liquids?
- What are examples of gases?
- What are examples of matter changing from one state to another because of a change in temperature?

Key Concepts

Your child has been learning these important ideas:
- Matter can take the form of a solid, a liquid, or a gas.
- Each state of matter has its own unique properties.
- Changes in temperature can cause matter to change from one state to another state.

Words to Know

- change
- gas
- heat
- ice
- liquid
- matter
- melt
- solid
- steam
- temperature

Share and Learn

Look for examples of the three states of matter—solid, liquid, and gas—in your kitchen. Demonstrate changes in states of matter with these activities: To show a liquid changing to a solid, make ice cubes with your child. To show liquid changing to a gas, spill a few drops of water and check later to see if they have evaporated, or turned into water vapor. To show a solid changing to a liquid, let an ice cube melt on a plate.

Science: States of Matter Learning Masters **79**

80 Learning Masters *Science: States of Matter*

Overview

Animal Habitats

Theme Materials

Concept Book

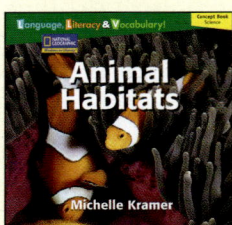

Nonfiction Books

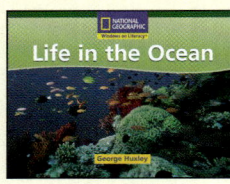

Level 18

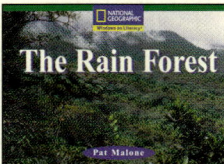

Level 18

Theme Builder

Learning Masters

Audiolesson on CD

Take-Home Book Masters

Optional Reading

Windows on Literacy
Content-Based Fiction

Rain Forest Discovery Level 17

Turtle Beach Mystery Level 18

Windows on Literacy
Nonfiction

Mud, Mud, Mud Level 7

Polar Bears Level 8

What Lives in a Tide Pool? Level 14

Going Up the Mountain Level 18

Instructional Highlights

Key Concepts

- Animals live in many different kinds of habitats.
- Animals live in habitats that provide for their basic needs, which include food, water, air, and shelter.
- Animal adaptations help animals survive in their habitats.

Comprehension Strategy

Summarizing

Key Concept Words

Arctic	ocean
desert	prairie
habitat	rain forest
level	zone

Text Features

Charts/Graphic Organizers

Graphic Locators

Theme Planner

Lesson 1*

Teacher's Guide
pp. 142–143

Read
Animal Habitats

- Introduce Concepts and Vocabulary

- Model and Share the Reading

*Before you begin Lesson 1, you may want to use the Before Theme Assessment tools listed on page 140.

Lesson 2

Teacher's Guide
pp. 144–145

Reread
Animal Habitats

- Develop Concepts and Vocabulary

- Introduce the Comprehension Strategy: Summarizing

- Small Group Reading

- Modeled Writing

Lesson 3

Teacher's Guide
pp. 146–147

Read
Life in the Ocean

- Develop Concepts and Vocabulary

- Small Group Reading

- Practice the Comprehension Strategy: Summarizing

- Shared Writing

Lesson 4

Teacher's Guide
pp. 148–149

Read
The Rain Forest

- Review Concepts and Vocabulary

- Small Group Reading

- Apply the Comprehension Strategy: Summarizing

- Guided Writing

Lesson 5

Teacher's Guide
pp. 150–151

Assess and Extend

- Rereading and Assessments

- Guided Writing

- Assessment Tools

- Optional Reading

- Home Connection

Read *Animal Habitats*

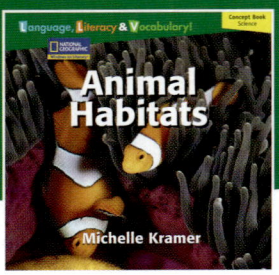

Language, Literacy & Vocabulary!
Concept Book Science

Animal Habitats

Michelle Kramer

Theme Builder (Readers Theater)

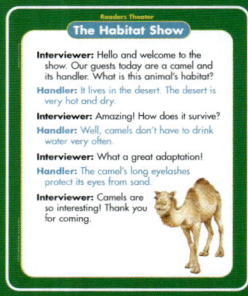

Theme Builder (Scene)

Introduce Concepts and Vocabulary

Introduce Theme Question

Ask students: What do you know about the places, or habitats, where animals live? What do these habitats provide to help animals survive? Explain that they will learn about animal habitats. They will also learn the language to use when describing animal habitats.

Have students draw a picture of an animal in its habitat. Ask them to write a sentence under the picture telling what the animal has or does that helps it survive in its habitat.

Turn and Talk Provide learning partners with photos of different habitats. Have them write at least one question about each habitat.

Develop Oral Language

Display a photo of a rain forest. Ask students to describe the scene. Model a sentence using *rain forest* and *levels:* A rain forest has many levels. A level is a specific part of the rain forest where different animals live.

Then display a photo of a desert. Ask students to describe the scene. Model sentences using *desert* and *habitat:* The desert is a habitat for many animals.

Tell students that they just described two different kinds of habitats—rain forest and desert. Explain that the ocean, Arctic, and prairie are other habitats for animals.

Turn and Talk Have partners take turns describing the photos of the other habitats.

Introduce Readers Theater

Display the Readers Theater selection on the ***Theme Builder***.

Assign the roles of the interviewer and the handler to groups of students to read in unison. Encourage students to add appropriate expression and gestures to their reading. Have learning partners use ***Learning Masters*** page 81 to practice reading the Readers Theater selection.

Introduce Key Vocabulary

Use the Think and Discuss scene to teach Key Concept Words and model language forms.

The Arctic is one kind of habitat.

The Arctic has snow and ice.

Continue to model sentences using the words listed below. As you introduce words, jot them down on chart paper. Display this Word Bank throughout the theme.

Turn and Talk Have students work with partners to practice using the language forms for describing. For example: The _____ is very _____.

Arctic	level	rain forest
desert	ocean	zone
habitat	prairie	

Build Background

Display the Think and Discuss scene on the ***Theme Builder*** again. Ask students to describe the habitats.

Turn and Talk Then have partners talk about one habitat and practice using the language forms for describing. For example: A (rain forest) has (many tall trees).

Model and Share the Reading

Preview the Book

Distribute copies of *Animal Habitats*. Read aloud the title and the author's name. As you page through the book, point out:

- There is a Contents page showing the sections in the book.
- Important words are highlighted in bold or in color bars.
- Diagrams called graphic locators are used to show levels or zones.

Predict Vocabulary

Encourage students to use photos to predict vocabulary: Which words do you expect to see in this book?

Display pages 8–9 and cover the words: Which words do you expect to see on these pages?

Students may mention the animals on the pages and the things they need. Add these words to the Word Bank. Have students talk with partners and use *Arctic, desert,* and *rain forest* to name the habitats. Continue the activity with other pages as time allows.

Model the Reading

Invite students to follow along as you read aloud pages 4–7 in *Animal Habitats*. Read fluently, modeling smooth, accurate reading with appropriate expression. After reading each pair of pages, pause to think aloud. Also, encourage students to ask questions and make observations.

Pages 4–5

Think Aloud This is like the Think and Discuss scene on the **Theme Builder.** The labels help identify different kinds of habitats.

Pages 6–7

Think Aloud The highlighted words in the captions identify the habitats.

Share the Reading

Now have partners complete the reading. Encourage them to pause after reading one or two pages and have conversations about what they have read. Ask them to share what they already know about the animals and their habitats.

Reread for Fluency

To have students practice fluent reading, model reading pages 12–13. Have students echo-read in unison each sentence as you finish, imitating your model. Then have students reread the entire book independently to build fluency. See *Customize the Reading.*

Customize the Reading

Students reread and talk about Animal Habitats *on their own to build fluency.*

- *Students who are not yet able to read the book can point to unique features in each habitat.*
- *Students who need extra support can reread the book while listening to the audiolesson*
- *Students who can read the book might read independently or aloud with partners.*

Customize Instruction for ELLs

Newcomers/Beginning During reading, have students point to the animal in each photo of a habitat. Have them show what they know about the animal by pantomiming its movements or making its sounds.

Developing Ask students simple questions to review and reinforce content, such as, "Is the Trench Zone at the top or at the bottom of the ocean?"

Expanding/Bridging Ask students to say two sentences about a particular habitat and the animals that live in it, such as, "The Arctic is cold and snowy. Polar bears have fur to keep them warm."

Lesson 2

Reread *Animal Habitats*

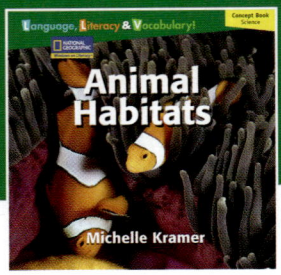

OBJECTIVES

- Understand that animals live in many different kinds of habitats and that animal adaptations help them survive in their habitats
- Use vocabulary to talk about various animal habitats
- Learn the comprehension strategy: Summarizing
- Read to gain fluency in oral and silent reading
- Write descriptions of animal habitats

Materials

Realia: photo of flying fish

Theme Builder

Animal Habitats

Learning Masters pages 8, 82, 83

Audiolesson 10

Theme Builder (Graphic Organizer)

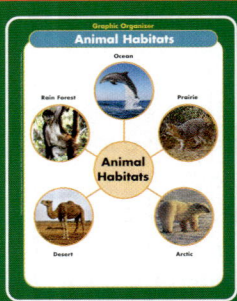

Develop Concepts and Vocabulary

Develop Oral Language

Display the photo of the flying fish. Ask students to describe the fish. What adaptation does this fish have that helps it survive? What words describe this adaptation?

Turn and Talk Encourage conversation partners to talk about the wing-like fins of the flying fish and how they help the fish fly out of the water to escape danger. Have them use these language forms:

The *(flying fish)* has large *(fins)*. These *(fins)* are like *(wings)*.

Revisit Readers Theater Display the Readers Theater selection on the *Theme Builder*. This time, have the handler bring a polar bear on the show. Change the information to fit polar bears. Assign the roles of the interviewer and the handler to groups of students and read in unison.

Build Background

Display the graphic organizer on the *Theme Builder* with the photos covered with sticky notes. Point to the label of one habitat and read it aloud. Ask students what would be included in such a habitat. What animals would live there? How would they survive? Follow the same procedure for the other habitats.

Turn and Talk Encourage partners to describe habitats and tell how each gives animals the things they need.

Begin Vocabulary Log As students read, encourage them to use sticky notes to tag words that they would like to save. After reading, students can record the words and their notes about them.

Use *Learning Masters* page 8.

Introduce the Comprehension Strategy

Introduce Summarizing

When students summarize, they condense information in a text to the most important ideas. By looking carefully at the facts, graphics, and photos in a nonfiction text, students can synthesize information into a meaningful summary.

Think Aloud When I read a book on a topic, I want to be able to pull all the information together so I can talk about the topic quickly and easily. That's called **summarizing.**

Model Summarizing

Turn to pages 16–17 and model the comprehension strategy and language forms for summarizing.

The important information on these pages is that the animals shown are able to survive in the desert because they know how to find shelter, food, and water.

This text is about the fact that desert animals do things or have adaptations that help them survive.

For additional practice in summarizing, have partners work on *Learning Masters* page 82.

Small Group Reading

As students read, invite them to share what they notice. Use some of the suggestions below to encourage observations and talk about the book.

Pages 4–9

Support Comprehension Guide students to summarize by having them name the things that all animals need to survive. *(Animals need food, water, oxygen, and shelter to survive.)*

Pages 10–13

Check Understanding How would you summarize the information shown on the graphic locators on pages 10 and 12? *(There are four levels in the rain forest habitat. There are four zones in the ocean habitat. Different animals live in each level or zone.)*

Pages 14–19

Support Comprehension Have students study the photos and sentences containing the following words to explain the words' meanings: *wide-open, floes, blubber,* and *gather.*

Pages 20–21

Check Understanding Have students use the Word Bank to help them talk about each habitat. What is each habitat like? What plants and animals does it have? How are the habitats alike? How are they different?

Discuss the Book

Invite students to share what they learned. Ask them to name a fact about the habitats or animals that they found interesting or surprising. Encourage them to use the words in the Word Bank to discuss what they have read. Remind students to add words to their Vocabulary Logs.

Students can complete *Learning Masters* page 83.

Reread for Fluency

Read the captions on pages 10–11 aloud very slowly and ask students how you might improve your fluency. *(Read faster.)* Point out that it is important to use a speed that makes sense. Now have partners prepare to read these pages. First, discuss the meaning of any difficult words. Have partners review and practice reading these words. Then have partners practice reading the pages aloud. For other suggestions, see *Customize the Reading.*

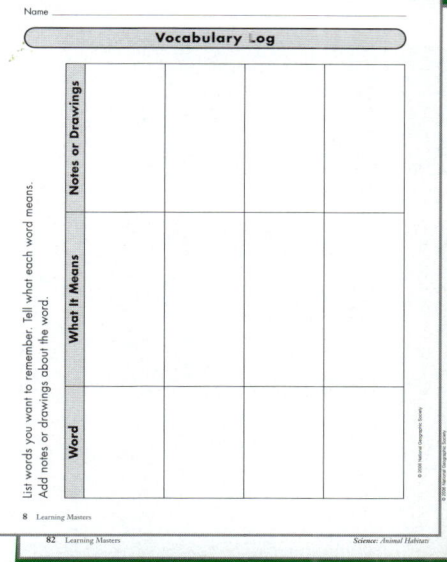

Learning Masters/pages 8, 82

Customize the Reading

Students reread and talk about Animal Habitats *using one of the following options:*

- Look through the pages, pointing out and naming the colors of the animals and their habitats.
- Reread the book while following along with the audiolesson.
- Read independently or read aloud with a partner.

Learning Masters/page 83

Modeled Writing

Use the graphic organizer on the *Theme Builder* to review some Key Concepts of the theme. Prepare to model writing, including providing details through examples.

Think Aloud I know that animals in a habitat find what they need to live. I will choose one habitat—the rain forest—and give examples that show animals meeting their needs.

An orange and black jaguar drinks water from a pool. Busy ants carry leaves near the jaguar's feet. The ants will eat the leaves. Above, two bright red macaws climb a tree. They are building a nest. All these animals find what they need in the rain forest.

Continue, using animals from another habitat. Give examples of the animals meeting their basic needs in a habitat.

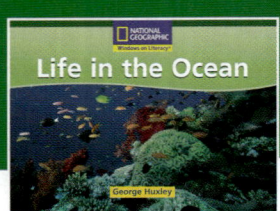

OBJECTIVES

- Read to gain fluency in oral and silent reading
- Practice the comprehension strategy: Summarizing
- Understand that animal adaptations help animals survive in their habitats
- Use a chart to comprehend text
- Use context clues to find word meanings

Materials

Realia: world map or globe

Theme Builder

Life in the Ocean

Learning Masters page 84

Audiolesson 10

Develop Concepts and Vocabulary

Develop Oral Language

Model the Key Concept Words *ocean* and *zone*. For example, point out oceans on a world map or globe.

Much of the Earth is covered by oceans. Oceans have different zones. A zone is a layer or section. Different animals live in these zones.

Turn and Talk Have conversation partners take turns creating sentence stems that can be completed with *ocean* and *zone*. For example:

The east coast of the United States is on the Atlantic *(Ocean)*.

Many fish that live in the deep *(zones)* of the *(ocean)* have adaptations that help them see.

Revisit Readers Theater Display the Readers Theater selection on the *Theme Builder*. Assign the roles of the interviewer and the handler to groups of students to read in unison. Encourage students to add gestures or motions.

Build Background

Distribute copies of *Life in the Ocean*. Invite students to talk about sea creatures that they have seen. Encourage them to use the language forms for describing:

A squid is _____.

Its tentacles have _____.

Small Group Reading

Get Ready to Read

Preview the Book Read aloud the title, the author's name, and the Think and Discuss question on the back cover: Which zone do hatchet fish live in?

Page through the book and do the following:

- Point out the highlighted words in the text and their placement in the graphic locators.
- Point out the Index and have students use it to find information.
- Ask students to predict what they will learn.

Predict Vocabulary Encourage students to use photos to predict vocabulary: Which words do you expect to see in this book?

Display a page and cover the words: Which words do you expect to see on this page?

List the words students mention. Add Key Concept Words in the book that students do not mention.

Text Feature: Charts

Introduce Display the chart on pages 22–23. A chart shows groups of information. This chart shows information in rows.

Model If I want to know which animals live in the Twilight Zone, I find the row labeled "Twilight Zone" and follow it to see which animals are shown there.

Practice Have students use the chart to answer these questions: What is the name of the bottom zone? Name the animals that live there.

Read the Book

As students read, invite them to share what they notice. Use some of the suggestions below to encourage observations and talk about the book.

Pages 2–3

Key Concept Words *ocean, zone*

Support Comprehension Explain the meaning of words that students may not understand, such as *surface*. Show students how they can find this meaning using context clues. (Contrast with "very deep water.")

Pages 4–9

Check Understanding Describe the adaptations of flying fish and sea turtles that help them survive in the Sunlit Zone. *(Flying fish have fins like wings. Sea turtles have strong flippers to swim quickly. These adaptations can help them catch food or get away from their enemies.)*

Pages 10–17

Support Comprehension Draw students' attention to the highlighted words in the text and their placement in the graphic locators on pages 10 and 14.

Pages 18–23

Practice the Comprehension Strategy

Encourage students to **Summarize** to help them understand pages 18–21.

What do we know from reading these pages? What do you think is the most important information? How can we give this information in two sentences?

Guide students to understand that summaries give only the most important information, not all the information.

Discuss the Book

Invite students to use the Word Bank to tell about the book. What have they learned about the ocean zones in both *Life in the Ocean* and *Animal Habitats?* What new information did *Life in the Ocean* provide? Remind students to add words to their Vocabulary Logs.

Use *Learning Masters* page 84.

Reread for Fluency

Have students reread the entire book independently to build fluency. See *Customize the Reading*.

Name _____

Life in the Ocean

List adjectives to describe the water and an animal found in each zone of the ocean. Then use some of the words in a sentence about the zone.

Sunlit Zone
Adjectives: _____
Sentence: _____
_____

Twilight Zone
Adjectives: _____
Sentence: _____

Midnight Zone
Adjectives: _____
Sentence: _____

Trench Zone
Adjectives: _____
Sentence: _____
_____

84   Learning Masters   *Science: Animal Habitats*

Customize the Reading

Students reread and talk about Life in the Ocean *using one of the following options:*

- *Look through the pages, pointing out the adaptations of the animals.*
- *Reread the book while following along with the audiolesson.*
- *Read independently or aloud with a partner.*

Shared Writing

Review the writing you modeled in Lesson 2. Point out that writers sometimes add a chart to their writing to make their ideas clearer. Work with students to create a chart with a column for each habitat.

Now invite students to help you to continue to write about animals and their habitats. Help students frame a sentence stating a new main idea.

Customize Instruction for ELLs

Newcomers/Beginning Have students make drawings of ocean animals and write the name of the zone in which they live.

Developing Encourage students to describe the water in the various zones by asking questions such as, "Is the light bright?" "Is the water cold?"

Expanding/Bridging Have students describe in detail what animals do and the adaptations they have to survive in the various zones.

Lesson 4

Read *The Rain Forest*

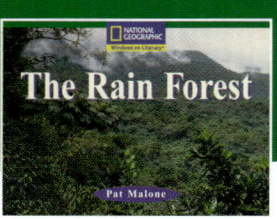

The Rain Forest
Pat Malone

148

OBJECTIVES

- Read to gain fluency in oral and silent reading
- Apply the comprehension strategy: Summarizing
- Develop an understanding that animals live in habitats that provide for their basic needs, which include food, water, air, and shelter
- Use Graphic Locators to comprehend text
- Make inferences

Materials

Photos: animals in different levels of a rain forest, such as the forest floor and the emergent level

Theme Builder

The Rain Forest

Learning Masters pages 85, 86

Take-Home Book Masters: *Animal Habitats*

Audiolesson 10

Take-Home Book Masters

Animal Habitats

by _____

Review Concepts and Vocabulary

Develop Oral Language

Model the Key Concept Words *level* and *rain forest*. Display and discuss the photos of different levels of a rain forest: Rain forests have four levels. Different kinds of animals live on each level.

Turn and Talk Have partners take turns describing the photos of different levels of a rain forest. For example:

There are ants and other insects on the bottom level of the rain forest.

Encourage students to use language forms for describing.

Revisit Readers Theater Display the Readers Theater selection on the *Theme Builder*. Repeat the Readers Theater with information on a new animal. Assign the roles of the interviewer and the handler to groups of students to read in unison.

Build Background

Distribute copies of *The Rain Forest*. Invite students to share what they know about rain forests and the animals that live there. Are the animals they know insects, reptiles, mammals, or birds? What does the rain forest provide these animals?

Small Group Reading

Get Ready to Read

Preview the Book Read aloud the title, the author's name, and the Think and Discuss questions on the back cover: Would you like to live in a rain forest? Which level would you choose?

Page through the book and do the following:

- Describe the animals in the photos.
- Point out the colors of the labels and how they correspond to the colors on the graphic locators.
- Ask students to predict what they will learn.

Predict Vocabulary Encourage students to use photos to predict vocabulary: Which words do you expect to see in this book?

Display a page and cover the words: Which words do you expect to see on this page?

List the words that students mention. Add Key Concept Words in the book that students do not mention.

Text Feature: Graphic Locators

Introduce Have students look at the graphic locator on the left side of page 4. A graphic locator is a kind of key that shows location or order.

Model Point to the bottom level of the graphic locator. This graphic locator shows the four levels of a rain forest. We are looking at the bottom one, the forest floor.

Practice Have students tell what the graphic locators on pages 8, 12, and 14 indicate.

Read the Book

As students read, invite them to share what they notice. Use some of the suggestions below to encourage observations and talk about the book.

Pages 2–3

Key Concept Words *level, rain forest*

Check Understanding What do you notice about the picture on the chart on page 3? How does this help you understand the levels of the rain forest? *(It shows trees and plants at each level of the rain forest. I can see the trees or plants at each level.)*

Pages 4–7

Check Understanding Why are there so many leaves on the ground? *(They may fall from the trees or from animals above eating them.)*

Pages 8–15

Apply the Comprehension Strategy

Use language forms to help students **Summarize** the information on pages 8–15.

The important information on these pages is _____.

This text is about _____.

Page 16

Support Comprehension Guide students to use the Index to find information about different animals and levels of the rain forest.

Discuss the Book

Invite students to use the Word Bank to discuss the book and to share what they learned. Were they surprised by what they learned about the rain forest habitat? How is the rain forest habitat similar to the ocean habitat described in *Life in the Ocean*? *(Both habitats are divided into layers, or sections, in which specific animals live. The rain forest has levels, and the ocean has zones.)* Have students add words to their Vocabulary Logs.

Use *Learning Masters* page 85.

Reread for Fluency

Have students reread the entire book independently to build fluency. See *Customize the Reading*.

Customize the Reading

Students reread and talk about The Rain Forest *using one of the following options:*

- *Look through the pages, pointing out the animals that they would like to learn more about.*
- *Reread the book while following along with the audiolesson.*
- *Read independently or aloud with a partner.*

Guided Writing

Distribute copies of the *Take-Home Book Masters*. Read the title and page through the book. Explain to students that they will write books about animal habitats. Work with students to:

- Complete the Contents page.
- Name and describe animals in each habitat.
- Share writing ideas for each pair of pages.

Record students' writing ideas for the pages of their books on chart paper. Have them suggest details or graphic locators to add to the photos as appropriate.

Now have partners talk together to plan what to write. Have each student complete a graphic organizer to plan writing. Students may name each habitat and list such information as animals that live in the habitat and words to describe the habitat.

Display the Word Bank and remind students to check their Vocabulary Logs as they begin to write.

Use *Learning Masters* page 86.

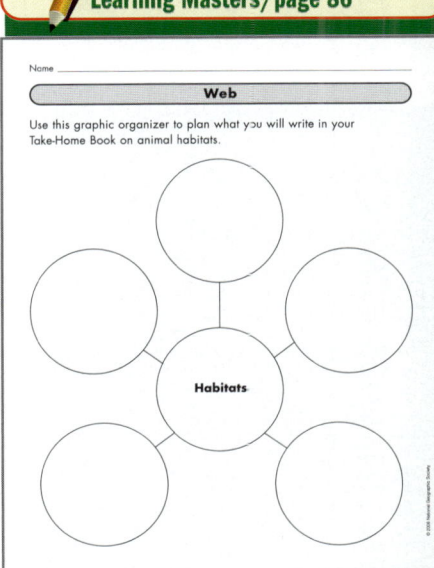

OBJECTIVES

- Use Key Concepts and Key Concept Words in writing
- Demonstrate oral language proficiency
- Demonstrate comprehension of theme selections
- Read related titles to reinforce Key Concepts and vocabulary

Materials

Take-Home Book Masters: *Animal Habitats*

Learning Masters pages 6–7, 87–88

Assessment Masters pages 179, 180, 205, 214, 215, 225, 228

Take-Home Book Masters

Animal Habitats

by _____

Rereading and Assessments

Allow time for students to independently reread the theme selections. Display the Word Bank for students' reference as they read.

As students reread, meet with individuals. Use the assessment tools listed on page 151 to evaluate students' progress and to update their records.

Guided Writing

Students continue writing the Take-Home Books they began in Lesson 4. Review the group list of writing ideas. Display the Word Bank.

Page through the theme books to review the text features, including charts and graphic locators. Talk about text features that students could add to their Take-Home Books. For example, they might add graphic locators to illustrate the rain forest and ocean habitats.

Point out that good writers:

- Plan what they are going to write. Have students use their completed graphic organizers to guide their writing.
- Add details or examples to make their ideas clearer. Students can add examples of adaptations.

- Revise their work. Have students check that they gave a clear main idea with each paragraph.

Have students complete the Picture Glossary and About the Author last.

As students write, circulate to coach and support individuals. If students need help, have them use their graphic organizers to recall or prioritize information they can add.

Have partners exchange books and discuss what they like in each other's book. For example, a partner may point out a good opening sentence that hooks the reader. Each writer decides what changes to make and adds any final touches.

Customize Instruction for ELLs

Newcomers/Beginning Provide sentence frames that reinforce the language forms for describing, such as, "Deserts are hot and dry."

Developing Ask questions with simple answers to help students think of what they will write, such as, "In the ocean, are the animals in the Sunlit Zone the same as in the Trench Zone?"

Expanding/Bridging Encourage students to use a variety of sentences and sentence lengths.

Assessment Tools

Self-Assessment

Allow students to reflect and assess their own learning by completing *Learning Masters* pages 6–7.

- What I Learned, page 6
- How I Learned, page 7

Reading

The following assessment tools can help you evaluate and record students' progress in reading and understanding the theme books.

- Retelling Guide and Scoring Rubric, page 179
- Fluency Scoring Guide, page 180
- Oral Reading Record, page 205

Writing

Use the completed Take-Home Books and the following tools to assess students' development as writers.

- Writing Rubric, page 214
- Writing Traits Checklist, page 215

Content Assessment

Have students work in groups to create a picture album of animals grouped by habitat. Students should share ideas about adaptations animals have and how an adaptation helps an animal live in the habitat. Have students include captions for their drawings.

Vocabulary and Oral Language

Use the following resources, in addition to the Think and Discuss scene on the *Theme Builder,* to assess oral language development.

- Content Vocabulary Checklist, page 225
- Oral Language Developmental Checklist, page 228

Learning Masters/pages 6–7

Name _____

What I Learned

List the three most important things you learned in this theme. Tell why you listed each one.

1. _____
2. _____
3. _____

6 Learning Masters

Learning Masters 7

Optional Reading

Reading related titles allows students to explore concepts and vocabulary at different levels. It also allows them to use reading strategies in different types of texts. Encourage students to compare the theme books to the books in the next column.

Optional Titles

These related *Windows on Literacy* titles reinforce Key Concepts of the *Animal Habitats* theme.

Nonfiction Titles

Mud, Mud, Mud Level 7

Polar Bears Level 8

What Lives in a Tide Pool? Level 14

Going Up the Mountain Level 18

Fiction Titles

Rain Forest Discovery Level 17

Turtle Beach Mystery Level 18

Related Fiction Titles

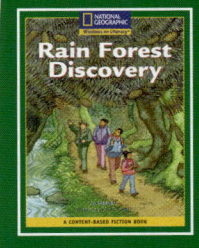
Rain Forest Discovery

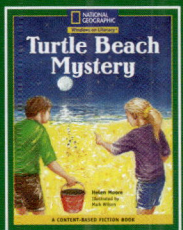
Turtle Beach Mystery

Home Connection

The Family Focus letters on *Learning Masters* pages 87–88 summarize key concepts about animal habitats and adaptations.

In the Share and Learn activity, family members take a walk to observe animals and talk about how the animals survive in their habitat.

Learning Masters/pages 87–88

Name _____

Family Focus

Dear Family,
Your child has been reading the books *Animal Habitats, Life in the Ocean,* and *The Rain Forest* in our unit of study on animal habitats. Please use this page to talk about animal habitats with your child.

Your child has written a Take-Home Book. Invite your child to share the book with you. Also, share your child's Vocabulary Log for the theme. Here are some sample questions to help you discuss the Take-Home Book together:
- What is a habitat?
- What do animals need in their habitats?
- Which habitat or animal you have read about is most interesting to you? Why?
- What are some animal adaptations?

Key Concepts
Your child has been learning these important ideas:
- Animals live in many different kinds of habitats.
- Animals live in habitats that provide for their basic needs, which include food, water, air, and shelter.
- Animal adaptations help animals survive in their habitats.

Words to Know
- Arctic
- desert
- habitat
- level
- ocean
- prairie
- rain forest
- zone

Share and Learn
Take a walk with your child to observe animals in your neighborhood or in a park or forest preserve. As you see animals, have your child describe the animal and what it is doing. Ask your child questions about how the animal survives, such as, "What does this animal eat? Where does it find food, shelter, and water?" Ask your child to use the *Words to Know* and any new vocabulary he or she learned about habitats and animals.

Science: Animal Habitats

Learning Masters **87**

88 Learning Masters

Science: Animal Habitats

Overview

Producing Goods

STANDARDS

ACADEMIC LANGUAGE/ELD
- Use academic vocabulary related to the study of producing goods
- Use appropriate language forms to sequence and to ask questions
- Develop fluency in reading, writing, listening to, and speaking English

SOCIAL STUDIES
- Describe how people take raw materials found in nature and turn them into finished products
- Understand that workers follow a sequence of steps to turn raw materials into finished goods
- Discuss the special words that describe the process of turning raw materials into finished goods

READING/LANGUAGE ARTS
- Learn and apply the comprehension strategy: Asking Questions
- Use the text features: Inset Photos and Captions
- Write about producing goods
- Learn and use vocabulary related to producing goods

Before Theme Assessment

To compare progress before and after teaching this theme, use one or more of the following informal assessment tools before beginning the theme.
- Oral Reading Record, page 209
- Fluency Scoring Guide, page 180
- Content Vocabulary Checklist, page 226
- Oral Language Developmental Checklist, page 228

Theme Materials

Concept Book

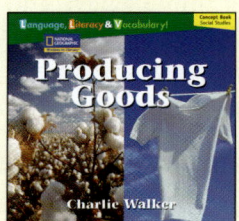

Nonfiction Books

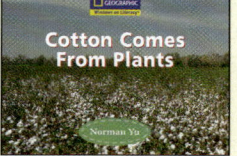

Level 17   Level 17

Theme Builder

Learning Masters

Audiolesson on CD

Take-Home Book Masters

Optional Reading

**Windows on Literacy
Content-Based Fiction**

Curious Charlotte Level 17

Our Lucky Day Level 18

**Windows on Literacy
Nonfiction**

Food Comes From Farms Level 8

Popcorn and Candy Level 12

Chocolate Level 16

Ice Cream for You Level 18

Instructional Highlights

Key Concepts

- People take raw materials found in nature and turn them into finished products.

- Workers follow a sequence of steps to turn raw materials into finished goods.

- There are special words to describe the process of turning a raw material into a finished product that can be sold in stores.

Comprehension Strategy

Asking Questions

Key Concept Words

factory	machine
goods	product
harvest	raw material

Text Features

Inset Photos

Captions

Theme Planner

Lesson 1 *

Teacher's Guide
pp. 154–155

Read
Producing Goods

- Introduce Concepts and Vocabulary

- Model and Share the Reading

* Before you begin Lesson 1, you may want to use the Before Theme Assessment tools listed on page 152.

Lesson 2

Teacher's Guide
pp. 156–157

Reread
Producing Goods

- Develop Concepts and Vocabulary

- Introduce the Comprehension Strategy: Asking Questions

- Small Group Reading

- Modeled Writing

Lesson 3

Teacher's Guide
pp. 158–159

Read
Wool Keeps Me Warm

- Develop Concepts and Vocabulary

- Small Group Reading

- Practice the Comprehension Strategy: Asking Questions

- Shared Writing

Lesson 4

Teacher's Guide
pp. 160–161

Read
Cotton Comes From Plants

- Review Concepts and Vocabulary

- Small Group Reading

- Apply the Comprehension Strategy: Asking Questions

- Guided Writing

Lesson 5

Teacher's Guide
pp. 162–163

Assess and Extend

- Rereading and Assessments

- Guided Writing

- Assessment Tools

- Optional Reading

- Home Connection

Lesson 1

Read *Producing Goods*

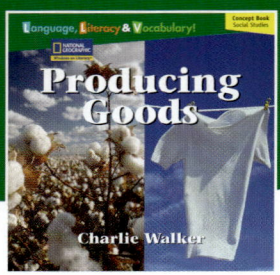

Producing Goods
Charlie Walker

OBJECTIVES

- Understand that people take raw materials and turn them into finished goods that can be sold in stores
- Learn and use vocabulary related to producing goods
- Use photos to predict vocabulary
- Use text features, such as captions, to learn new words

Materials

Realia: small pieces of wood

Theme Builder

Producing Goods

Learning Masters page 89

Audiolesson 11

Theme Builder (Poem)

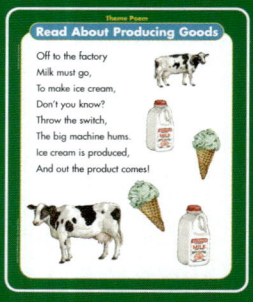

Theme Builder (Scene)

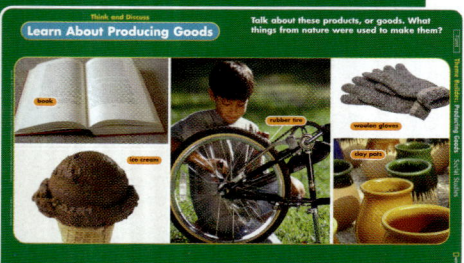

Introduce Concepts and Vocabulary

Introduce Theme Question

Ask students: How would you explain where ice cream comes from? How is it made? Explain that they will learn about producing, or making, goods. They will also learn the language to use when talking about turning things from nature into finished products.

Turn and Talk Have learning partners make a list of items used in the classroom. Then ask partners to speculate what materials were used to make the items.

Develop Oral Language

Display a piece of wood. Ask students to tell where wood is found. (*Wood comes from trees.*)

Then ask students to name some things that are made from wood. (*Houses are made from wood. Wood is also used to make furniture and paper.*)

Explain that goods are products that can be sold. Many goods are made from something in nature.

Turn and Talk Have partners pick a classroom item and ask each other questions about what it could be made from.

Introduce Theme Poem

Display the Theme Poem on the *Theme Builder*. Have students say the poem in unison. Then divide the class into two groups and have each group say four lines. Have learning partners use *Learning Masters* page 89 to practice reading the poem.

Introduce Key Vocabulary

Use the Think and Discuss scene and the theme graphic organizer to teach Key Concept Words and model language forms.

Ice cream is a product, or good. First, you get milk from a cow. Milk is a raw material. Then you put the milk in a machine at a factory.

Continue to model sentences using the words listed below to help talk about items in the scene. As you introduce words, jot them down on chart paper. Display this Word Bank throughout the theme.

Turn and Talk Have partners practice using the words and the language forms for sequencing. For example: First, _____. Then _____.

| factory | harvest | product |
| goods | machine | raw material |

Build Background

Display the Think and Discuss scene on the *Theme Builder* again. Ask students to tell how each picture relates to producing goods.

Turn and Talk Have partners talk about one item and practice using the language forms for sequencing. For example, for "book": First, (trees were cut down). Next, (the wood was made into paper at the factory). Finally, (the book was made).

Model and Share the Reading

Preview the Book

Distribute copies of *Producing Goods*. Read aloud the title and the author's name. As you page through the book, point out:

- Many of the pictures have captions.
- The highlighted words are vocabulary words.
- Some pages use arrows to show the order in which actions happen.

Predict Vocabulary

Encourage students to use pictures to predict vocabulary: Which words do you expect to see in this book?

Display pages 6–7 and cover the words: Which words do you expect to see on these pages?

Students may mention the animals, plants, and worker shown in the pictures. Add these words to the Word Bank. Have students talk with partners and use *goods* and *raw materials* to describe the pictures. Continue the activity with other pages as time allows.

Model the Reading

Invite students to follow along as you read aloud pages 4–7 in *Producing Goods*. Read fluently, modeling smooth, accurate reading with appropriate expression. After reading each pair of pages, pause

to think aloud. Also, encourage students to ask questions and make observations.

Pages 4–5
Think Aloud This is like the Think and Discuss scene on the *Theme Builder*. The labels name the goods, or products. Some labels tell me the raw material the product is made from.

Pages 6–7
Think Aloud This page will tell me where goods come from. The captions will give me more information about the raw materials used to made goods.

Share the Reading

Now have partners complete the reading. Ask students to pause after reading one or two pages and discuss what they have read. Ask them to share connections that they were able to make with the text.

Reread for Fluency

To have students practice fluent reading, read aloud page 10 of *Producing Goods* with expression. Have students echo-read the sentences, imitating your model. Then have students reread the entire book independently to build fluency. See *Customize the Reading*.

Learning Masters/page 89

Theme Poem

Off to the factory
Milk must go,
To make ice cream,
Don't you know?
Throw the switch,
The big machine hums.
Ice cream is produced,
And out the product comes!

Social Studies: Producing Goods   Learning Masters **89**

Customize the Reading

Students reread and talk about Producing Goods on their own to build fluency.

- Students who are not yet able to read the book can look at the photos and name items in the pictures.
- Students who need extra support can reread the book while listening to the audiolesson.
- Students who can read the book might read independently or aloud with partners.

Customize Instruction for ELLs

Newcomers/Beginning During reading, have students point to the pictures that show the sequence of producing goods. Use prompts such as, "Point to the step that happens first."

Developing Point to a sequence of pictures. Ask: "What happens first? What happens next?" Encourage students to respond using these language forms: First, _____. Next, _____. Then _____. Finally, _____.

Expanding/Bridging Have students tell in sequence the steps for making woolly socks or a cotton shirt.

Lesson 2

Reread *Producing Goods*

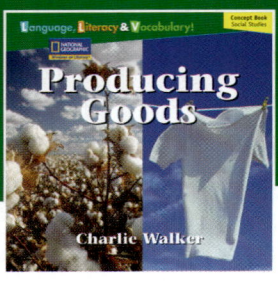

Language, Literacy & Vocabulary!
Concept Book
Social Studies
NATIONAL GEOGRAPHIC
Producing Goods
Charlie Walker

OBJECTIVES

- Understand that workers follow a sequence of steps to turn raw materials into finished goods
- Use vocabulary to describe the process of turning raw materials into goods that people want and need
- Learn the comprehension strategy: Asking Questions
- Read to gain fluency in oral and silent reading
- Write about producing a good, using a sequence of steps

Materials

Realia: bark, pine cones, rocks
Theme Builder
Producing Goods
Learning Masters pages 8, 90, 91
Audiolesson 11

Theme Builder (Graphic Organizer)

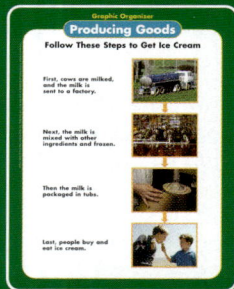

Develop Concepts and Vocabulary

Develop Oral Language

Display some raw materials found in nature, such as bark, pine cones, and rocks. Ask students to tell where each raw material could be found. Next, ask: What good, or product, could you make from each of these raw materials?

Turn and Talk Encourage learning partners to talk about making a product using a raw material. Have them use the language forms:

First, *(you gather pine cones from the ground)*. Next, *(you glue them to a foam circle)*. Then *(you hang the wreath)*.

Revisit the Theme Poem Display the Theme Poem on the ***Theme Builder***. Say the poem again. Then have students suggest other words for the raw material and product such as *wood* and *paper*.

Build Background

Display the graphic organizer on the ***Theme Builder***. Have students identify the sequence word in each step. Discuss the steps in making a product.

Turn and Talk Encourage partners to use sequence words to tell about the steps in making a cotton shirt.

Begin Vocabulary Log As students read, encourage them to use sticky notes to tag words that they would like to save. After reading, students can record the words and their notes about them.

Use ***Learning Masters*** page 8.

Introduce the Comprehension Strategy

Introduce Asking Questions

When students ask questions, they generate questions as they read, look for answers that may or may not be in the text, and self-monitor their comprehension.

Think Aloud When I read a book, I often wonder about things I am reading and seeing in the pictures. That's called **asking questions.** I ask myself questions about what the words mean, what is happening in the book, how well I understand the information, and other things I want to learn.

Model Asking Questions

Turn to pages 10–11 and model the comprehension strategy and the language forms for asking questions.

Think Aloud Before I read, I wondered what a cotton picker machine is.

While I read, I wondered if the arrows show me the order of steps in making a cotton shirt.

After I read, I wondered whether cotton balls from the plant look like the cotton balls I can buy at the store.

For additional practice in Asking Questions, have partners work on ***Learning Masters*** page 90.

Small Group Reading

As students read, invite them to share what they notice. Use some of the suggestions below to encourage observations and talk about the book.

Pages 4–7

Support Comprehension Guide students to ask questions as they read. Students may ask themselves:

Do I understand what I'm reading? What is happening on these pages? What else do I want to know?

Pages 8–11

Check Understanding Tell the importance of sheep in the making of woolly socks. (*Sheep supply the wool, or raw material, for the socks.*)

Pages 12–15

Support Comprehension Have students summarize the steps in making paper. (*First, trees are cut and taken to the paper mill. Then the cut trees are processed and turned into paper. Last, it is sold in stores.*)

Pages 16–19

Support Comprehension Point out and talk about the captions and the information given in them. Ask what a *kiln* is. (*a hot oven used to make pottery*)

Pages 20–21

Check Understanding Have students use the Word Bank to help describe how raw materials are turned into goods.

Discuss the Book

Invite students to share what they learned. Ask students to tell something that surprised them. Encourage students to use the words in the Word Bank to discuss what they have read. Remind students to add words to their Vocabulary Logs.

Students can complete **Learning Masters** page 91.

Reread for Fluency

Have students follow along as you read page 16 slowly. Then ask students to tell how you might improve your reading. (*Read faster.*) Remind students that they should read fast enough to sound interesting, but not so fast as to be confusing. Have partners reread pages 18–19. Ask them to focus on improving the pace of their reading. For other suggestions, see *Customize the Reading*.

Learning Masters/pages 8, 90

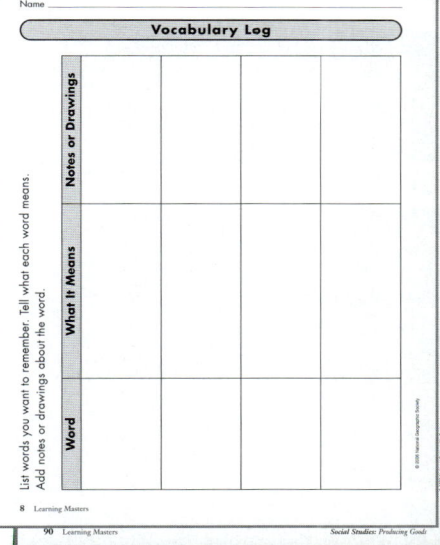

Customize the Reading

Students reread and talk about Producing Goods using one of the following options:

- *Look through the pages, finding and naming the products, or goods, and raw materials.*
- *Reread the book while following along with the audiolesson.*
- *Read independently or read aloud with a partner.*

Learning Masters/page 91

Modeled Writing

Use the graphic organizer on the *Theme Builder* to review some Key Concepts of the theme. Prepare to model writing, including planning and using words that show order.

Think Aloud My purpose is to write about how to make clay pots. My audience is the students in this group. To plan, I'll complete a sequence chart like the one on the *Theme Builder.* First, clay is dug from the ground. Then the clay is shaped on a potter's wheel. Next, the clay is baked in a kiln. Finally, a vase or bowl is painted. Now I'll introduce my topic.

Some people make beautiful bowls and vases. They put the bowls and vases in special places in their homes. They may make extra bowls and vases to sell.

Think Aloud Now I'll tell the steps of making these products.

Everything starts with a sticky, gray mud. It's clay. The clay is dug from the ground. This gray clay will go through many changes.

Lesson 3   Read *Wool Keeps Me Warm*

OBJECTIVES

- Read to gain fluency in oral and silent reading
- Practice the comprehension strategy: Asking Questions
- Understand that workers follow a sequence of steps to turn a raw material into a finished product
- Use inset photos to comprehend text
- Use context clues to find the meaning of words

Materials

Realia: clothing made from wool, preferably with tags showing the content of the fabric

Theme Builder

Wool Keeps Me Warm

Learning Masters page 92

 Audiolesson 11

Develop Concepts and Vocabulary

Develop Oral Language

Model the Key Concept Words *factory* and *machine*. For example, talk about a specific kind of factory and a machine that would be in it. Then model:

A toy factory has a machine that makes dolls.

Turn and Talk Have learning partners talk about factories and the machines that may be used in them. For example:

A bread factory has a machine that makes the bread.

Revisit the Theme Poem Display the poem on the *Theme Builder*. This time, use wool as the raw material and have students suggest a product made from wool. Substitute *milk* with *wool* and *ice cream* with the product students suggest. Have students say the poem together, using the new words.

Build Background

Distribute copies of *Wool Keeps Me Warm*. Let students examine the wool clothing you have brought in. Point out any tags that tell that the fabric is made from wool. Explain that some clothing labels show a symbol for the raw material used in the fabric, such as cotton or wool. Also, point out that wool clothing is not fluffy and white like the sheep's wool.

Small Group Reading

Get Ready to Read

Preview the Book Read aloud the title, the author's name, and the Think and Discuss question on the back cover: What is a sheep's coat used for?

Page through the book and do the following:

- Point out captions that go with the photos.
- Invite students to share what they know about wool.
- Ask students to predict what they will learn.

Predict Vocabulary Encourage students to use photos to predict vocabulary: Which words do you expect to see in this book?

Display a page and cover the words: Which words do you expect to see on this page?

List the words students mention. Add Key Concept Words in the book that students do not mention.

> **Text Feature: Inset Photos**
>
> **Introduce** Point out the small inset photo on page 5. This photo is called an inset photo because it is put inside another photo on the page.
>
> **Model** This inset photo helps me see how thick, white, and fluffy a sheep's coat is.
>
> **Practice** Have students describe the inset photo on page 13. Ask them how the inset photo helps them understand the larger photo.

Read the Book

As students read, invite them to share what they notice. Use some of the suggestions below to encourage observations and talk about the book.

Pages 2–5
Support Comprehension Explain that products made from wool, such as clothes, scarves, and hats, can keep people warm. Tell students that Russia is a country that has very cold winters.

Check Understanding On page 5, have students tell what the inset photo helps them understand about outer wool and interior wool on the sheep.

Pages 6–9
Key Concept Word *factory*

Support Comprehension Help students use the photos and context clues to figure out what the words *shearing* and *bales* mean. (Shearing *is cutting the wool off sheep.* Bales *are very large and heavy bundles.*)

Pages 10–11

Practice the Comprehension Strategy

Encourage students to **Ask Questions** to help them better understand pages 10–11.

As you read, ask yourself, "What is the roller doing? Which words are important? What else do I want to know?"

Help students understand that asking questions as they read will help them understand the text.

Pages 12–16
Check Understanding Explain why you would want yarn in many colors. (So that we can have colorful clothes)

Discuss the Book

Invite students to use the Word Bank to tell about the book. What have they learned about making wool products? Remind students to add words to their Vocabulary Logs.

Use *Learning Masters* page 92.

Reread for Fluency

Have students reread the entire book independently to build fluency. See *Customize the Reading.*

Learning Masters/page 92

92 Learning Masters

Customize the Reading

Students reread and talk about Wool Keeps Me Warm *using one of the following options:*

- *Have students answer questions about sequence, such as, "What happens after the yarn is made?"*
- *Reread the book while following along with the audiolesson.*
- *Read independently or aloud with a partner.*

Shared Writing

Review the paragraphs you modeled in Lesson 2. Invite students to help you continue writing the steps involved in making bowls and vases from clay. Follow the graphic organizer you completed in Lesson 2.

Ask volunteers to suggest phrasings for what needs to be done at each step. For example, students may say that people next shape the clay with their hands. Guide students to use sequence words as they help you frame sentences.

Customize Instruction for ELLs

Newcomers/Beginning Have students draw pictures of clay pots to go with the writing.

Developing Provide students with sentence frames such as: "The first step is _____. The second step is _____."

Expanding/Bridging Have students add details to each step by suggesting adjectives and adverbs to make the writing more vivid.

Read *Cotton Comes From Plants*

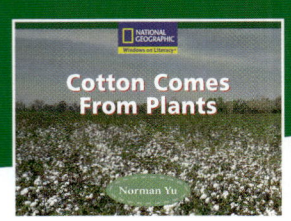

OBJECTIVES

- Read to gain fluency in oral and silent reading
- Apply the comprehension strategy: Asking Questions
- Develop an understanding that people take raw materials found in nature and turn them into finished products
- Use captions to comprehend text
- Make inferences using photos

Materials

Realia: ear of corn, bag of popcorn, clothing and fabric made of cotton, preferably with tags showing the content of the fabric

Theme Builder

Cotton Comes From Plants

Learning Masters pages 93, 94

Take-Home Book Masters:
Producing Goods

Audiolesson 11

Review Concepts and Vocabulary

Develop Oral Language

Model the Key Concept Words *harvest*, *factory*, and *machine*. Display an ear of corn and a bag of popcorn. Ask: What raw material turns into something we can buy at the movies? Describe what happens first in the process. First, farmers use a machine to harvest ears of corn. Continue describing the steps.

Turn and Talk Have learning partners take turns creating and answering riddles about raw materials turning into finished products. For example: What raw material can be turned into mittens? *(wool)* What raw material can be turned into something sweet? *(milk)*

Revisit the Theme Poem Display the poem on the *Theme Builder*. This time, have students suggest a raw material that is a plant to substitute for *milk* and a product made from it to substitute for *ice cream*. Have students say the poem together, using the new words.

Build Background

Distribute copies of *Cotton Comes From Plants*. Let students examine the cotton clothing and fabric you brought in. Point out the tags showing the cotton content. Have students compare cotton to wool. Ask students to share experiences they have had wearing cotton or wool clothing.

Small Group Reading

Get Ready to Read

Preview the Book Read aloud the title, the author's name, and the Think and Discuss question on the back cover: What machines do farmers use to pick cotton?

Page through the book and do the following:

- Point out the inset photo.
- Invite students to share what they know about cotton.
- Ask students to predict what they will learn.

Predict Vocabulary Encourage students to use photos to predict vocabulary: Which words do you expect to see in this book?

Display a page and cover the words: Which words do you expect to see on this page?

List the words that students mention. Add Key Concept Words in the book that students do not mention.

Text Feature: Captions

Introduce Display page 4. Point out the caption. This is a caption. It gives information about the photo and also adds information to what I read in the text.

Model This caption tells me that a cotton plant grows more than one seed pod. I wonder how many pods can grow on one cotton plant.

Practice Have students read other captions in the book. Have them talk about the information that the captions provide.

Read the Book

As students read, invite them to share what they notice. Use some of the suggestions below to encourage observations and talk about the book.

Pages 2–7
Key Concept Word *harvest*

Support Comprehension Point out the inset photo and talk about how it gives a close-up view of the inside of a seed pod.

Check Understanding Why would a farmer use a machine to harvest cotton? *(It's fast and efficient.)*

Pages 8–9
Key Concept Words *factory, machine*

Apply the Comprehension Strategy

Help students **Ask Questions** to better understand what they read on pages 8–9.

Before I read, I wondered _____.

While I read, I wondered _____.

After I read, I wondered _____.

Encourage students to explain how the questions they are asking will help them understand more about cotton.

Pages 10–13
Support Comprehension Have students suggest what should be included in a summary of these pages. *(The cotton is combed and straightened in the factory. Then it is woven into fabric.)*

Page 14–16
Check Understanding Describe what the women in the picture on pages 14–15 are doing. Tell the importance of their work.

Discuss the Book

Invite students to use the Word Bank to discuss the book and to share what they learned. Ask them what new information they learned about cotton. Ask students to compare the processes of turning the raw materials of wool, and of cotton, into finished products. Have students add words to their Vocabulary Logs.

Use *Learning Masters* page 93.

Reread for Fluency

Have students reread the entire book independently to build fluency. See *Customize the Reading*.

Learning Masters/page 93

Name _____

Cotton Comes From Plants

Fill in each blank with a word from the Word Bank. Use the book *Cotton Comes From Plants* if you need help.

Word Bank
clothes fabric factory harvest
machine mill yarn

First, the farmer must _____ the cotton.

Second, the cotton is sent to a _____.

Next, the cotton is cleaned in a _____.

Then the cotton goes to a spinning _____.

Next, a machine twists the cotton into _____.

Then looms weave the yarn into _____.

Last, people sew the fabric into _____.

Draw a picture showing one of the steps in turning cotton into clothes. Write a sentence about your picture.

Social Studies: Producing Goods   Learning Masters **93**

Customize the Reading

Students reread and talk about Cotton Comes From Plants *using one of the following options:*

- *Look through the pages, finding the machines and telling what they do.*
- *Reread the book while following along with the audiolesson.*
- *Read independently or aloud with a partner.*

Guided Writing

Distribute copies of the **Take-Home Book Masters**. Read the title and page through the book. Explain that students will write books telling how trees are used to make paper. Work with students to:

- Describe steps in the sequence.
- Complete the Contents page and captions.
- Share writing ideas for each pair of pages.

Record students' writing ideas for the pages of their books on chart paper. Have them suggest captions for the photos.

Have partners work together to plan what to write. Have each student complete a sequence chart before writing. Remind students to match their sequence chart to the order of photos in their Take-Home Books.

Use *Learning Masters* page 94.

Learning Masters/page 94

Name _____

Sequence Chart

Write about the steps used to turn trees into paper. Use the sequence words to begin your sentences. If you need help, look at pages 12–13 in *Producing Goods*.

First,

↓

Next,

↓

Then

↓

Last,

94   Learning Masters   *Social Studies: Producing Goods*

OBJECTIVES

- Use Key Concepts and Key Concept Words in writing
- Demonstrate oral language proficiency
- Demonstrate comprehension of theme selections
- Read related titles to reinforce Key Concepts and vocabulary

Materials

Take-Home Book Masters:
Producing Goods

Learning Masters pages 6–7, 95–96

Assessment Masters pages 179, 180, 209, 214, 215, 226, 228

Take-Home Book Masters

Producing Goods

by _____

Rereading and Assessments

Allow time for students to independently reread the theme selections. Display the Word Bank for students' reference as they read.

As students reread, meet with individuals. Use the assessment tools listed on page 163 to evaluate students' progress and to update their records.

Guided Writing

Students continue writing the Take-Home Books they began in Lesson 4. Review the group list of writing ideas. Display the Word Bank.

Page through the theme books to review the text features, including captions and inset photos. Talk about text features that students could add to their Take-Home Books. For example, they might add inset "photos" that show additional information.

Point out that good writers:

- Organize their ideas before writing. Have students use their graphic organizers and sequence words to clarify the order of steps.
- Add details to their sentences to help the reader picture what is happening in each step.

- Read over their work. Have students check that the steps are in the correct order and that their writing makes sense.

Have students complete the Picture Glossary and About the Author last.

As students write, circulate to coach and support individuals. Ask students what ideas are most important to add to the writing.

Have partners exchange books and discuss what they like in each other's book. For example, a partner may point out a good way of varying sentences rather than always using the word *next*. Each writer decides what changes to make and adds any final touches.

Customize Instruction for ELLs

Newcomers/Beginning Have students provide simple spellings or initial consonants of words for the captions. Help students complete the spellings.

Developing Have students suggest adjectives to add more details about the raw material, machines, and finished products. Encourage them to use the words from their Vocabulary Logs.

Expanding/Bridging Have students check that they have used words that tell order, such as *first*, *next*, *then*, and *last*.

Assessment Tools

Self-Assessment

Allow students to reflect and assess their own learning by completing *Learning Masters* pages 6–7.

- What I Learned, page 6
- How I Learned, page 7

Reading

The following assessment tools can help you evaluate and record students' progress in reading and understanding the theme books.

- Retelling Guide and Scoring Rubric, page 179
- Fluency Scoring Guide, page 180
- Oral Reading Record, page 209

Writing

Use the completed Take-Home Books and the following tools to assess students' development as writers.

- Writing Rubric, page 214
- Writing Traits Checklist, page 215

Content Assessment

Have partners pick a raw material they read about and make a pictorial sequence chart about turning the raw material into a finished product. Suggest that they use arrows between pictures to show the sequence of steps.

Vocabulary and Oral Language

Use the following resources, in addition to the Think and Discuss scene on the *Theme Builder,* to assess oral language development.

- Content Vocabulary Checklist, page 226
- Oral Language Developmental Checklist, page 228

Optional Reading

Reading related titles allows students to explore concepts and vocabulary at different levels. It also allows them to use reading strategies in different types of texts. Encourage students to compare the theme books to the books in the next column.

Optional Titles

These related *Windows on Literacy* titles reinforce Key Concepts of the *Producing Goods* theme.

Nonfiction Titles

Food Comes From Farms Level 8

Popcorn and Candy Level 12

Chocolate Level 16

Ice Cream for You Level 18

Fiction Titles

Curious Charlotte Level 17

Our Lucky Day Level 18

Home Connection

The Family Focus letters on *Learning Masters* pages 95–96 summarize key concepts about how goods are produced.

In the Share and Learn activity, family members talk about the raw materials that are used to make finished products students use in their home.

Learning Masters/pages 6–7

Related Fiction Titles

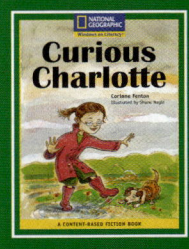

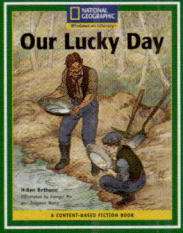

Learning Masters/pages 95–96

Overview

United States Geography

STANDARDS

ACADEMIC LANGUAGE/ELD
- Use academic vocabulary related to the study of United States geography
- Use appropriate language forms to compare and to ask questions
- Develop fluency in reading, writing, listening to, and speaking English

SOCIAL STUDIES
- Recognize famous places in the United States of America
- Identify natural landmarks and landmarks made by people
- Use maps to identify the locations of landmarks

READING/LANGUAGE ARTS
- Learn and apply the comprehension strategy: Asking Questions
- Use the text features: Index and Maps
- Write about United States geography features
- Learn and use vocabulary related to United States geography

Before Theme Assessment

To compare progress before and after teaching this theme, use one or more of the following informal assessment tools before beginning the theme.

- Oral Reading Record, page 211
- Fluency Scoring Guide, page 180
- Content Vocabulary Checklist, page 227
- Oral Language Developmental Checklist, page 228

Theme Materials

Concept Book

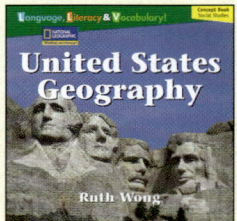

Nonfiction Books

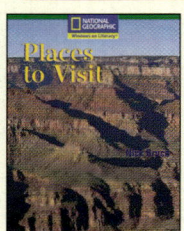

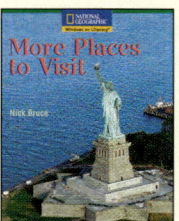

Level 17   Level 18

Theme Builder

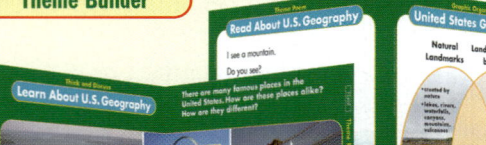

Learning Masters

Audiolesson on CD

Take-Home Book Masters

Optional Reading

**Windows on Literacy
Content-Based Fiction**

The Sleeping Bear Dune: An Ojibway Legend Level 18

Anna at Ellis Island Level 18

**Windows on Literacy
Nonfiction**

Mapping North America Level 16

I Live in the Rockies Level 18

Hawaii Level 18

See the USA Level 19

Instructional Highlights

Key Concepts

- There are many famous places in the United States of America.
- Some of these places are natural landmarks, and some are landmarks made by people.
- People can use maps to identify the locations of landmarks.

Comprehension Strategy

Asking Questions

Key Concept Words

canyon	monument
cave	national park
geography	volcano
landmark	waterfall

Text Features

Index

Maps

Theme Planner

Lesson 1*

Teacher's Guide
pp. 166–167

Read
United States Geography

- Introduce Concepts and Vocabulary
- Model and Share the Reading

* Before you begin Lesson 1, you may want to use the Before Theme Assessment tools listed on page 164.

Lesson 2

Teacher's Guide
pp. 168–169

Reread
United States Geography

- Develop Concepts and Vocabulary
- Introduce the Comprehension Strategy: Asking Questions
- Small Group Reading
- Modeled Writing

Lesson 3

Teacher's Guide
pp. 170–171

Read
Places to Visit

- Develop Concepts and Vocabulary
- Small Group Reading
- Practice the Comprehension Strategy: Asking Questions
- Shared Writing

Lesson 4

Teacher's Guide
pp. 172–173

Read
More Places to Visit

- Review Concepts and Vocabulary
- Small Group Reading
- Apply the Comprehension Strategy: Asking Questions
- Guided Writing

Lesson 5

Teacher's Guide
pp. 174–175

Assess and Extend

- Rereading and Assessments
- Guided Writing
- Assessment Tools
- Optional Reading
- Home Connection

Read *United States Geography*

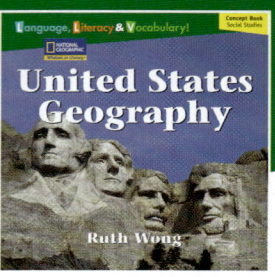

Language, Literacy & Vocabulary! Concept Book Social Studies

United States Geography

Ruth Wong

OBJECTIVES

- Understand that there are many famous landmarks in the United States
- Learn and use vocabulary related to United States geography
- Use photos to predict vocabulary
- Use text features, such as maps, to understand the text

Materials

Photos: several famous landmarks in the United States, Mount St. Helens, the Mississippi River

Theme Builder

United States Geography

Learning Masters page 97

Audiolesson 12

Theme Builder (Poem)

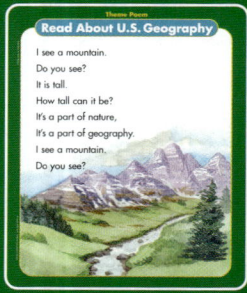

Theme Poem
Read About U.S. Geography

I see a mountain.
Do you see?
It is tall.
How tall can it be?
It's a part of nature,
It's a part of geography.
I see a mountain.
Do you see?

Theme Builder (Scene)

Think and Discuss
Learn About U.S. Geography

There are many famous places in the United States. How are these places alike? How are they different?

Lake Superior, which borders Michigan, Wisconsin, and Minnesota

Gateway Arch, St. Louis, Missouri

Grand Canyon National Park, Arizona

Brooklyn Bridge, New York, New York

Introduce Concepts and Vocabulary

Introduce Theme Question

Ask students: What famous places have you visited in the United States? How would you describe those places? Explain that students will learn about United States geography. They will also learn the language to use when describing the geography of the United States and comparing and contrasting.

Turn and Talk Provide learning partners with several pictures of famous landmarks in the United States. Encourage students to talk about which landmarks were made by nature and which were made by humans.

Develop Oral Language

Display a picture of Mount St. Helens. Ask students to describe the geography of the mountain. Model a sentence using *mountain* and *volcano*. Mount St. Helens is a mountain that was formed by a volcano.

Then display a picture of the Mississippi River. Ask students to describe the river. Model a sentence using *landmark*. The Mississippi River is a landmark that many early explorers used when traveling.

Tell students that they just talked about two of the natural landmarks found in the United States. Explain that some of the landmarks in the United States are natural, and some are made by humans.

Turn and Talk Have partners each describe famous landmarks that they have visited or have seen in books or on television.

Introduce Theme Poem

Display the Theme Poem on the *Theme Builder*. Have students say the poem together. Have learning partners use *Learning Masters* page 97 to practice reading the poem.

Introduce Key Vocabulary

Use the Think and Discuss scene to teach Key Concept Words and model language forms. The Grand Canyon is wide and deep.

Continue to model sentences using the words listed below as you identify objects in the scene. As you introduce words, jot them down on chart paper. Display this Word Bank throughout the theme.

Turn and Talk Have students work with partners to practice using the words and the language forms for comparing. For example: Both the _____ and the _____ are landmarks made by people.

canyon	landmark	volcano
cave	monument	waterfall
geography	national park	

Build Background

Display the Think and Discuss scene on the *Theme Builder* again. Ask students to tell how the landmarks are different.

Turn and Talk Have partners choose landmarks to contrast and practice using the language forms for contrasting. The Grand Canyon shows rock patterns, while Lake Superior shows wide blue water.

Model and Share the Reading

Preview the Book

Distribute copies of *United States Geography*. Read aloud the title and the author's name. As you page through the book, point out:

- Most pages show at least two examples of different types of landmarks in the United States.
- Most of the photographs have captions or labels.
- The boldfaced words are vocabulary words.

Predict Vocabulary

Encourage students to use pictures to predict vocabulary: Which words do you expect to see in this book?

Display pages 6–7 and cover the words: Which words do you expect to see on these pages?

Students may mention objects shown on the pages, such as a map, mountains, lakes, a desert, and a city. Add any new words to the Word Bank. Ask students to talk with a partner about the different types of landmarks shown on these pages. Continue the activity with other pages as time allows.

Model the Reading

Invite students to follow along as you read aloud pages 6–9 in *United States Geography*. Read fluently, modeling smooth, accurate reading with appropriate expression. After reading each pair of pages, pause to think aloud. Also, encourage students to ask questions and make observations.

Pages 6–7
Think Aloud These pages show three different landmarks in the United States. Lines between the photos and the map show where these places are located. I have many questions about each landmark such as, "How did Death Valley get its name?" I would like to read more and see if my questions are answered.

Pages 8–9
Think Aloud When I read each caption, I notice that it gives specific information about the landmark in the photo.

Share the Reading

Now have partners complete the reading. Encourage them to pause after reading two pages and talk about what they read. Ask them to share questions they have about the pages.

Reread for Fluency

To have students practice fluent reading, read aloud pages 10–11 with expression. Then have the whole group reread the pages in unison. Also, have students reread the entire book independently to build fluency. See *Customize the Reading*.

Name _____

Theme Poem

I see a mountain.

Do you see?

It is tall.

How tall can it be?

It's a part of nature,

It's a part of geography.

I see a mountain.

Do you see?

Social Studies: United States Geography Learning Masters **97**

Customize the Reading

Students reread and talk about United States Geography *on their own to build fluency.*

- *Students who are not yet able to read the book can describe what they see in each photograph.*
- *Students who need extra support can reread the book while listening to the audiolesson.*
- *Students who can read the book might read independently or aloud with partners.*

Customize Instruction for ELLs

Newcomers/Beginning During reading, have students point to the photos in the text that are being described. Use prompts such as, "Point to the mountain."

Developing Point to photos in the text and ask questions such as, "What is the name of this waterfall?" Encourage students to respond in complete sentences.

Expanding/Bridging Ask students to choose one photo in the book and say two or more sentences describing what they see.

Lesson 2

Reread *United States Geography*

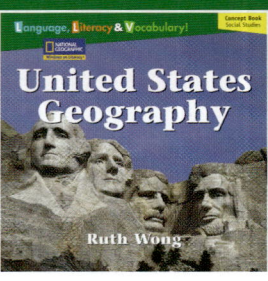

Language, Literacy & Vocabulary!
Concept Book Social Studies

United States Geography

Ruth Wong

OBJECTIVES

- Understand that there are many famous landmarks in the United States made by nature and made by humans, and we can use maps to locate these landmarks
- Use vocabulary to talk about landmarks
- Learn the comprehension strategy: Asking Questions
- Read to gain fluency in oral and silent reading
- Write about a natural landmark

Materials

Realia: information about some national parks

Photo: a canyon

Theme Builder

United States Geography

Learning Masters pages 8, 98, 99

Audiolesson 12

Theme Builder (Graphic Organizer)

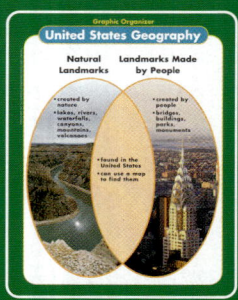

Develop Concepts and Vocabulary

Develop Oral Language

Display fliers or information and pictures from the Internet on key national parks. Talk about some of the geographic features found in these parks. What natural features are present in these national parks?

Turn and Talk Encourage learning partners to describe and compare features in national parks you have discussed.

Revisit the Theme Poem Display the theme poem on the *Theme Builder*. Say the poem again, replacing *mountain* with *canyon* and *tall* with *deep*. Then show students a photo of a canyon as students say the poem in unison.

Build Background

Display the graphic organizer on the *Theme Builder*. Have students read the labels aloud. Read through the lists. Ask students if they can add to any of the lists.

Turn and Talk Ask partners to talk about other natural landmarks they know.

Begin Vocabulary Log As students read, encourage them to use sticky notes to tag words that they would like to save. After reading, students can record the words and their notes about them.

Use *Learning Masters* page 8.

Introduce the Comprehension Strategy

Introduce Asking Questions

When students ask questions, they think of questions as they read, look for answers that may or may not be in the text, and monitor their comprehension.

Think Aloud When I read a book, I often wonder about things I am reading and seeing in the pictures. That is called **asking questions.** I look for answers in the text and make sure I understand what I am reading before I continue.

Model Asking Questions

Turn to pages 8–9 and model the comprehension strategy and language forms for asking questions.

Before I read, I wondered what were some natural landmarks in my state.

While I read, I wondered why some natural landmarks have become famous.

After I read, I wondered what are some other natural landmarks.

For additional practice in asking questions, have partners work on *Learning Masters* page 98.

Small Group Reading

As students read, invite them to share what they notice. Use some of the suggestions below to encourage observations and talk about the book.

Pages 6–9

Support Comprehension Guide students to ask questions about what they read.

Do I understand what I'm reading? What is happening in the text? What else do I want to know?

Pages 10–13

Check Understanding Explain how using a map can help us find a natural landmark. *(The map shows where in the country the landmark is located.)*

Pages 14–19

Support Comprehension Encourage students to summarize what they read about landmarks built by people. *(Some landmarks are famous bridges, buildings, and parks. Others were built to help us remember important people and events. Landmarks can be found using a map.)*

Pages 20–21

Check Understanding Have students use the words in the Word Bank to talk about and compare the landmarks shown in the photos.

Discuss the Book

Invite students to share what they learned. Ask them to describe some of the landmarks they read about. Encourage them to use the words in the Word Bank to discuss what they have read. Remind students to add words to their Vocabulary Logs.

Students can complete *Learning Masters* page 99.

Reread for Fluency

Read the paragraph on page 8 in a flat tone and ask what's wrong with how you read. *(You should read with expression.)* Model by reading the paragraph again with expression. Now have students reread pages 14–19 to build fluency. You might pair a proficient student with a less-proficient partner. Have the more proficient student read a paragraph, modeling fluent reading. Then have the partner echo-read the same paragraph, imitating the first reading. For other suggestions, see *Customize the Reading*.

Learning Masters/pages 8, 98

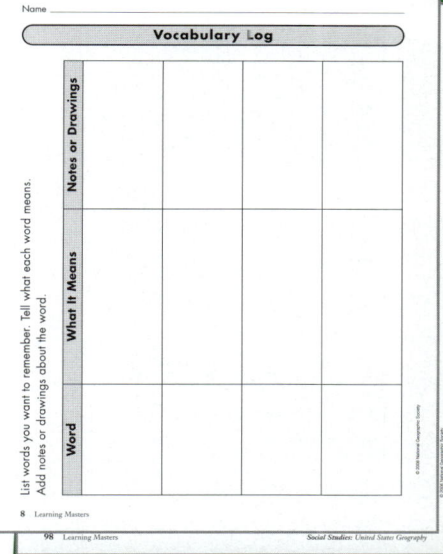

Name _____
Vocabulary Log

List words you want to remember. Tell what each word means. Add notes or drawings about the word.

Word	What It Means	Notes or Drawings

8   Learning Masters

98   Learning Masters   *Social Studies: United States Geography*

Customize the Reading

Students reread and talk about United States Geography *using one of the following options:*

- *Look through the pages, pointing to landmarks and stating their names.*
- *Reread the book while following along with the audiolesson.*
- *Read independently or read aloud with a partner.*

Modeled Writing

Use the graphic organizer on the *Theme Builder* to review some Key Concepts of the theme. Prepare to model writing, including using active verbs.

Think Aloud I'll describe a famous natural landmark I've seen—Niagara Falls. That is my purpose for writing. My audience is the students in this group. I'll use the picture on page 8 in *United States Geography* and what I remember to describe the waterfall.

At Niagara Falls, a sightseeing boat bounces in the bumpy water. On the boat, people watch. Ahead is the waterfall. White water crashes near them. A soft mist hangs above the place where the water hits. The noise from the falls is like thunder.

Think Aloud Now I'll tell what a waterfall is.

At a falls, water pours over land or rocks. It crashes to water below. A waterfall is a beautiful and powerful natural landmark.

Learning Masters/page 99

Name _____
United States Geography

Find the Contents page from *United States Geography*. The Contents page tells the sections in the book and the page each section starts on.

Answer the questions below using the Contents page.

1. On which page does the chapter "The United States" begin? _____

2. If you turn to page 12, what chapter begins on that page? _____

3. On which page does the chapter "Landmarks Built by People" begin? _____

4. How many pages long is the chapter "Natural Landmarks"? _____

5. What heading is found on page 8? _____

6. Where would you look to find definitions for important words? _____

Social Studies: United States Geography   Learning Masters   99

Read *Places to Visit*

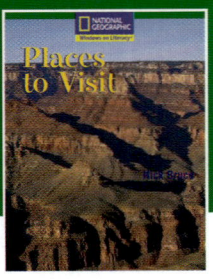

Develop Concepts and Vocabulary

Develop Oral Language

Model the Key Concept Words *cave*, *canyon*, *national park*, and *waterfall*. For example, read this sentence aloud and model how to fill in the blank.

The _____ has steep sides and is very deep.

The *canyon* has steep sides and is very deep.

Turn and Talk Have conversation partners take turns creating sentence stems that can be completed with one of these words: *cave*, *national park*, or *waterfall*.

Revisit the Theme Poem
Display the poem on the *Theme Builder*. This time, replace *mountain* with *cave* and *tall* with *dark*. Invite students to close their eyes so they are "in the dark" as they say the poem.

Build Background

Distribute copies of *Places to Visit*. Invite students to share some of the interesting places they have visited. Ask students to tell where those places are located and describe what they saw. Encourage them to use this language form for comparing.

_____ is the _____-est _____ in the United States.

Small Group Reading

Get Ready to Read

Preview the Book Read aloud the title, the author's name, and the Think and Discuss question on the back cover: What are the two waterfalls that make up Niagara Falls?

Page through the book and do the following:

- Point out that a new location is described on each pair of pages.
- Point out that for each location, there is a map that shows where the landmark can be found.
- Ask students to predict what they will learn.

Predict Vocabulary Encourage students to use photos to predict vocabulary: Which words do you expect to see in this book?

Display a page and cover the words: Which words do you expect to see on this page?

List the words students mention. Add Key Concept Words in the book that students do not mention.

Text Feature: Index

Introduce Point out the Index on page 16. This is the Index. It shows you where each topic can be found in the book.

Model According to the Index, Montana can be found on page 4.

Practice Have students use the Index to find three different topics.

OBJECTIVES

- Read to gain fluency in oral and silent reading
- Practice the comprehension strategy: Asking Questions
- Understand that people can use maps to identify locations of landmarks
- Use the Index to find information
- Summarize to better understand text

Materials

Theme Builder

Places to Visit

Learning Masters page 100

Audiolesson 12

Read the Book

As students read, invite them to share what they notice. Use some of the suggestions below to encourage observations and talk about the book.

Pages 2–5

Key Concept Words *canyon, national park*

Support Comprehension Encourage students to summarize the information they read on pages 2–5.

Pages 6–9

Key Concept Words *waterfall, volcano*

Check Understanding What formed Mount St. Helens, and where is Mount St. Helens located? *(Mount St. Helens is a volcano, and it is located in Washington.)*

Pages 10–13

Key Concept Word *cave*

Support Comprehension Have students look at the cave on page 11. Explain that *stalactites* are formations that look like icicles hanging from the roof of a cave. Have students look up *Kentucky* in the Index.

Pages 14–15

Practice the Comprehension Strategy

Encourage students to **Ask Questions** to help them better understand pages 14–15.

What famous places did you see in this book? What do you remember about each place? What questions can you ask yourself to help you remember what you read?

Guide students to think of questions they can ask about the reading that will help them better understand and remember what they read.

Discuss the Book

Invite students to use the Word Bank to tell about the book. What have they learned about natural landmarks from both *Places to Visit* and *United States Geography*? What new information does this book provide? Remind students to add words to their Vocabulary Logs.

Use **Learning Masters** page 100.

Reread for Fluency

Have students reread the entire book independently to build fluency. See *Customize the Reading*.

Learning Masters/page 100

Name _____

Places to Visit

In this book, you read about six places to visit. Write the name of the place that goes with each number shown on the map. Then write one word to describe each place.

Word Bank
Yellowstone National Park
Grand Canyon
Mammoth Cave
Mount St. Helens
Niagara Falls
the Everglades

1. _____
2. _____
3. _____
4. _____
5. _____
6. _____

100 Learning Masters *Social Studies: United States Geography*

Shared Writing

Review the writing you modeled in Lesson 2. Invite students to help you write about other natural landmarks, such as mountains. Encourage students to think about the information they read about Mount St. Helens.

Have volunteers give information about the crater that formed on top of the mountain. Help students frame a sentence stating the main idea of the new paragraph. Ask them to suggest phrases or sentences that describe a mountain.

Customize the Reading

Students reread and talk about Places to Visit *using one of the following options:*

- Look through the pages, pointing to each location on the map.
- Reread the book while following along with the audiolesson.
- Read independently or aloud with a partner.

Customize Instruction for ELLs

Newcomers/Beginning Have students suggest words to describe Mount St. Helens and then list those words as a group.

Developing Encourage students to finish sentences such as, "Mount St. Helens has a *(crater)* because it is a *(volcano)*."

Expanding/Bridging Have students explain in complete sentences what they know about how Mount St. Helens formed.

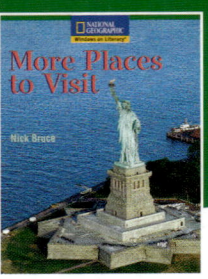

Read *More Places to Visit*

OBJECTIVES

- Read to gain fluency in oral and silent reading
- Apply the comprehension strategy: Asking Questions
- Develop an understanding that there are many famous places in the United States
- Use maps to comprehend text
- Recognize landmarks made by people

Materials

Photo: a monument

Theme Builder

More Places to Visit

Learning Masters pages 101, 102

Take-Home Book Masters:
United States Geography

Audiolesson 12

Take-Home Book Masters

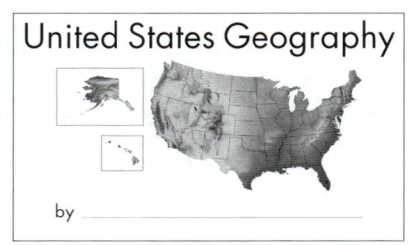

United States Geography

by _____

Review Concepts and Vocabulary

Develop Oral Language

Model the Key Concept Word *monument*. Display a photo of a monument. This is a monument. A monument is something built by humans to honor a person or an event.

Turn and Talk Have learning partners talk about monuments they have seen—in person, in books, or on television. For example: I visited the Washington Monument. It is a very tall, white building. It was built to honor George Washington, the first president of the United States.

Revisit the Theme Poem Display the poem on the *Theme Builder*. Replace *mountain* with *monument*, *tall* with *big*, and *part of nature* with *made by people*. Have students point to the photo of the monument as they say the poem with you.

Build Background

Distribute copies of *More Places to Visit*. Have students look at the cover of the book. Ask a volunteer to name the landmark shown on the cover. (*the Statue of Liberty*) Invite students to share what they already know about this famous statue.

Small Group Reading

Get Ready to Read

Preview the Book Read aloud the title, the author's name, and the Think and Discuss question on the back cover: Which presidents' faces are carved into Mount Rushmore?

Page through the book and do the following:

- Point out the maps that show the location of each landmark.
- Talk about the places that are included in the Index on page 16.
- Ask students to predict what they will learn.

Predict Vocabulary Encourage students to use photos to predict vocabulary: Which words do you expect to see in this book?

Display a page and cover the words: Which words do you expect to see on this page?

List the words students mention. Add Key Concept Words in the book that students do not mention.

Text Feature: Maps

Introduce Have students look at the map on page 15. This map shows different famous places that are discussed in this book. Maps help us find places we want to visit or learn about.

Model Point to the star for the Gateway Arch. I have never visited the Gateway Arch. If I want to go there in the future, I can tell from the map that it is located in the Midwestern section of the United States. I know from page 6 that the Gateway Arch is in St. Louis.

Practice Have students point to landmarks on the map and tell the general locations of each landmark. (*in the east, west, and so on*)

Read the Book

As students read, invite them to share what they notice. Use some of the suggestions below to encourage observations and talk about the book.

Pages 2–3

Apply the Comprehension Strategy

Encourage students to **Ask Questions** to help them better understand pages 2–3 and the rest of the book.

Before I read, I wondered _____.

While I read, I wondered _____.

After I read, I wondered _____.

Pages 4–7

Key Concept Word *monument*

Support Comprehension Ask students to summarize what they have read about the Washington Monument and the Gateway Arch.

Pages 8–13

Check Understanding Have students explain why the Space Needle in Seattle was built. (*It was built for the 1962 World's Fair.*)

Pages 14–15

Support Comprehension Have students read the names of the famous places. Have volunteers tell a little about each famous place.

Discuss the Book

Invite students to use the Word Bank to discuss the book and to share what they learned. Encourage students to discuss what they learned about landmarks made by humans from *More Places to Visit* and *United States Geography*. (*Humans build monuments to honor people or events. Humans have also built famous bridges and other structures for everyone to use.*) Have students add words to their Vocabulary Logs.

Use *Learning Masters* page 101.

Reread for Fluency

Have students reread the entire book independently to build fluency. See *Customize the Reading*.

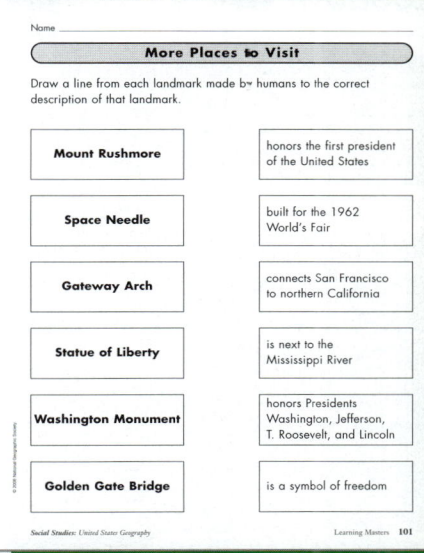

Learning Masters/page 101

More Places to Visit

Draw a line from each landmark made by humans to the correct description of that landmark.

Mount Rushmore	honors the first president of the United States
Space Needle	built for the 1962 World's Fair
Gateway Arch	connects San Francisco to northern California
Statue of Liberty	is next to the Mississippi River
Washington Monument	honors Presidents Washington, Jefferson, T. Roosevelt, and Lincoln
Golden Gate Bridge	is a symbol of freedom

Social Studies: United States Geography   Learning Masters **101**

Customize the Reading

Students reread and talk about More Places to Visit using one of the following options:

• Look through the pages and point to a unique feature of each place.

• Reread the book while following along with the audiolesson.

• Read independently or aloud with a partner.

Guided Writing

Distribute copies of the *Take-Home Book Masters.* Read the title and page through the book. Explain that students will write books about a few of the landmarks found in the United States. Work with students to:

• Describe the landmarks shown.

• Find the landmarks on a map.

• Share writing ideas for each pair of pages.

Record students' writing ideas for the pages of their books on chart paper.

Have partners talk together to plan what to write. Ask each student to complete a graphic organizer. On their graphic organizers, students can list and give describing words for each landmark shown in their Take-Home Books. Display the Word Bank and remind students to check their Vocabulary Logs as they begin to write.

Use *Learning Masters* page 102.

Learning Masters/page 102

Graphic Organizer

Use this graphic organizer to plan what you will write in your Take-Home Book about United States geography.

Natural Landmarks   Landmarks Made by People

102 Learning Masters   *Social Studies: United States Geography*

OBJECTIVES

- Use Key Concepts and Key Concept Words in writing
- Demonstrate oral language proficiency
- Demonstrate comprehension of theme selections
- Read related titles to reinforce Key Concepts and vocabulary

Materials

Take-Home Book Masters:
United States Geography

Learning Masters pages 6–7, 103–104

Assessment Masters pages 179, 180, 211, 214, 215, 227, 228

Take-Home Book Masters

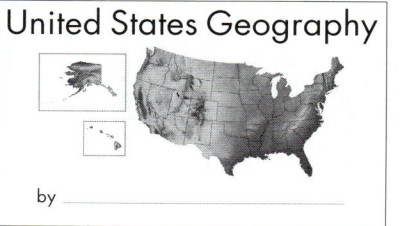

United States Geography

by _____

Rereading and Assessments

Allow time for students to independently reread the theme selections. Display the Word Bank for students' reference as they read.

As students reread, meet with individuals. Use the assessment tools listed on page 175 to evaluate students' progress and to update their records.

Guided Writing

Students continue writing the Take-Home Books they began in Lesson 4. Review the group list of writing ideas. Display the Word Bank.

Page through the theme books to review the text features, including maps and indexes. Talk about text features that students could add to their Take-Home Books. For example, they might add another landmark made by people and include it in the Index.

Point out that good writers:

- Plan their writing. Have students use their completed graphic organizer to guide their writing.
- Use appropriate comparison words. Students may compare landmarks telling how they are the same and different.

- Read over their work. Have students check to make sure that each sentence has the correct end punctuation.

Have students complete the Index and About the Author last.

As students write, circulate to coach and support individuals. If students need help, try suggesting a Key Concept Word to include.

Have partners exchange books and discuss what they like in each other's book. For example, a partner may point out an interesting fact. Partners can also offer ways to improve the book, such as by suggesting interesting words. Each writer decides what changes to make and adds any final touches.

Customize Instruction for ELLs

Newcomers/Beginning Prompt contributions to writing by asking yes/no questions about each heading, such as, "Is this a picture of Niagara Falls?"

Developing Ask questions with simple answers to prompt contributions to writing, such as, "What words describe Niagara Falls?"

Expanding/Bridging Have students suggest complete sentences or ways to phrase an idea. For example, they might say, "Niagara Falls is the largest waterfall in North America."

Assessment Tools

Self-Assessment

Allow students to reflect and assess their own learning by completing *Learning Masters* pages 6–7.

- What I Learned, page 6
- How I Learned, page 7

Reading

The following assessment tools can help you evaluate and record students' progress in reading and understanding the theme books.

- Retelling Guide and Scoring Rubric, page 179
- Fluency Scoring Guide, page 180
- Oral Reading Record, page 211

Writing

Use the completed Take-Home Books and the following tools to assess students' development as writers.

- Writing Rubric, page 214
- Writing Traits Checklist, page 215

Content Assessment

Have students draw pictures of natural landmarks or landmarks made by humans. Ask students to write a caption for each picture describing the landmark. Invite students to display their pictures and captions on a class map of the United States. Have groups talk together about the landmarks and their locations.

Vocabulary and Oral Language

Use the following resources, in addition to the Think and Discuss scene on the *Theme Builder,* to assess oral language development.

- Content Vocabulary Checklist, page 227
- Oral Language Developmental Checklist, page 228

Optional Reading

Reading related titles allows students to explore concepts and vocabulary at different levels. It also allows them to use reading strategies in different types of texts. Encourage students to compare the theme books to the books in the next column.

Optional Titles

These related *Windows on Literacy* titles reinforce Key Concepts of the *United States Geography* theme.

Nonfiction Titles

Mapping North America Level 16

I Live in the Rockies Level 18

Hawaii Level 18

See the USA Level 19

Fiction Titles

The Sleeping Bear Dune: An Ojibway Legend Level 18

Anna at Ellis Island Level 18

Home Connection

The Family Focus letters on *Learning Masters* pages 103–104 summarize key concepts about United States geography.

In the Share and Learn activity, family members can use craft materials to create a model of a famous landmark.

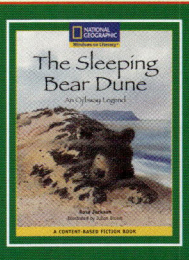
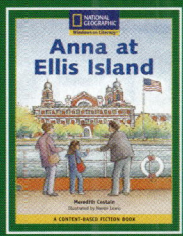

Learning Masters/pages 6–7

Related Fiction Titles

Learning Masters/pages 103–104

Assessment Overview

Although one purpose of assessment is to measure performance so that results can be shared with parents and school administrators, its primary purpose is to gather information to inform instruction. Assessment offers valuable insights into students' learning and allows teachers to plan instruction that supports and challenges students based on their individual needs. Assessment deals with both the knowledge students attain, as well as the process of learning.

- An assessment program needs to be ongoing so that changes over time in students' learning can be noted and appropriate adjustments to an instructional program can be made in a timely fashion.

- An assessment program also needs to be multidimensional, as no one assessment tool can measure the many dimensions of the complex process of reading.

- An assessment program needs to include both formal and informal tools so that evaluation of performance is reliable and useful.

Managing Assessment

Before the Theme

- Fluency Scoring Guide (page 180)
- * Oral Reading Record (page 185)
- * Content Vocabulary Checklist (page 216)
- Oral Language Developmental Checklist (page 228)

After the Theme

- * Content Vocabulary Checklist (page 216)
- Oral Language Developmental Checklist (page 228)
- Writing Rubric (page 214)
- Writing Traits Checklist (page 215)
- Retelling Guide and Scoring Rubric (page 179)
- Fluency Scoring Guide (page 180)
- * Oral Reading Record (page 185)
- What I Learned (*Learning Masters*, page 6)
- How I Learned (*Learning Masters*, page 7)

* Assessments specific to theme

Before the Theme

Oral Reading Record Using an Oral Reading Record, also known as a running record, allows you to assess a student's accuracy in word recognition. As the student reads, use the coding system to record each word that is read accurately, as well as errors, self-corrections, and the strategies and cueing systems used to figure out challenging words. The notations made during the oral reading can help you diagnose the kinds of challenges the student is experiencing and plan instruction to match that student's needs. Plan a schedule so that you meet with each student at regular intervals during the course of the year.

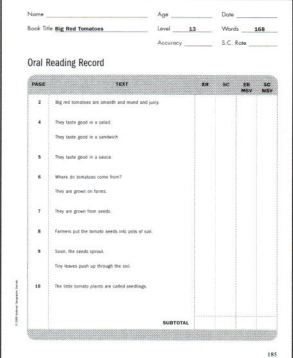

page 185

page 180

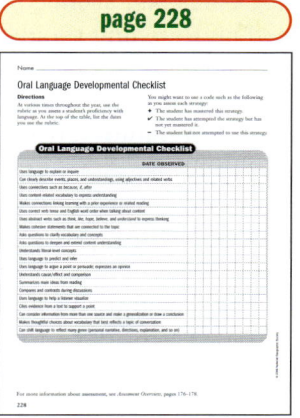

Fluency Scoring Guide
The Fluency Scoring Guide provides a snapshot of students' development as fluent readers. Consider using the Fluency Scoring Guide with one of the theme books before instruction of the theme. As you listen to an individual, use the rubric to assign a score. After the theme, listen to the student read the selection again to check progress with fluency.

Content Vocabulary Checklist (page 216) Use the Content Vocabulary Checklist before and after reading. Have students read the Key Concept Words and assess their own knowledge of the words. Circulate among the students to quickly assess gaps in content knowledge in individuals and the whole group. Encourage students to use their knowledge of vocabulary words to complete the activity on the master.

page 228

Oral Language Developmental Checklist The Oral Language Developmental Checklist provides ongoing assessment of students' growth in using language. Because the checklist relies on observation of speaking behaviors, you might want to use this checklist as small groups of students discuss the Think and Discuss scene on the *Theme Builder*.

After the Theme

page 216

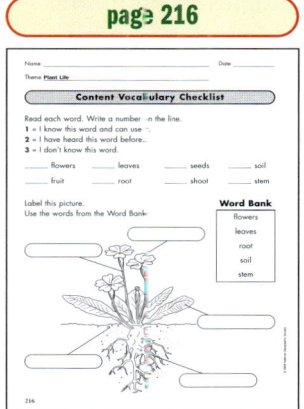

Content Vocabulary Checklist
Revisit the Content Vocabulary Checklist after completing the theme. By having students repeat the activity on the top of the page, you will be able to tell at a glance whether students have gained in their understanding of Key Concept Words. The activity on the bottom of the page will provide more insight as students complete cloze and other activities that help show their understanding of vocabulary and concepts.

Oral Language Developmental Checklist (page 228)
If you worked with several groups before reading to assess oral language development, consider working with other groups after reading theme materials. To provide opportunities for using oral language, you might have students talk with you about their Take-Home Books. You might also complete this checklist of oral language development during the Content Assessment activity.

Writing Rubric and Writing Traits Checklist
Both assessments are appropriate for use with students' Take-Home Books, as well as with other writing assignments. The Writing Rubric evaluates a student's writing performance on a particular assignment. The Writing Traits Checklist shows a student's progress over time, making it a way to monitor long-term growth and a useful tool to share with parents.

page 214

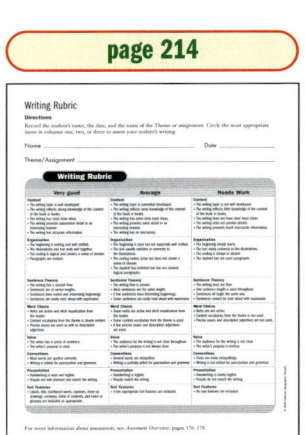

page 215

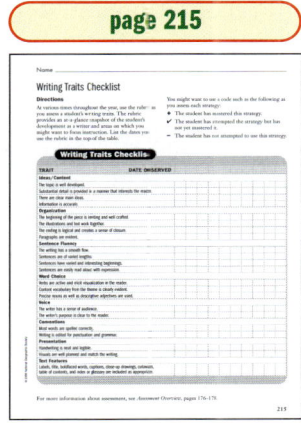

Assessment Overview *continued*

page 179

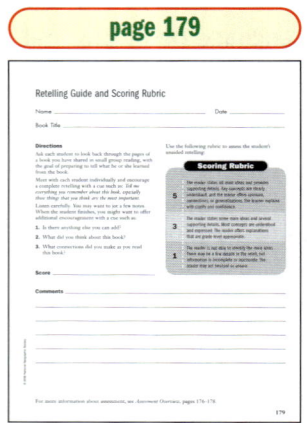

Retelling Guide and Scoring Rubric The Retelling Guide and Scoring Rubric will lead you through the evaluation of students' retelling of the theme selections, allowing you to assess how well students understood what they read. Work with individuals as you invite students to retell what they know about theme selections. As students tell about theme selections, listen for main ideas and supporting details in their retellings.

Fluency Scoring Guide (page 180) Use one of the theme selections to assess individual students' fluency development. If you have already assessed a student's fluency, you will be able to see progress over time. Consider using the Fluency Scoring Guide as students read aloud related texts, such as *Windows on Literacy* Content-Based Fiction. This will allow you to determine how well students adjust their reading for different purposes and for different types of material.

Oral Reading Record (page 185) Use the Oral Reading Record to assess a student's accuracy in word recognition and decoding strategies. If you met with students before reading theme materials, taking a running record after reading theme selections will allow you to determine how well students use newly-taught reading strategies as they work with the texts in the theme. The before-and-after snapshot will help you tailor instruction as you determine which strategies and concepts were learned and which still need reinforcement.

Learning Masters/page 6

What I Learned In What I Learned (*Learning Masters* p. 6), students list the information that they learned from the theme texts. Glancing over their learning masters will give you insight into what concepts were learned and which need reinforcement. For reinforcement of ideas in the theme, consider using the related *Windows on Literacy* titles listed in the Teacher's Guide in the Overview for each theme.

Learning Masters/page 7

How I Learned In How I Learned (*Learning Masters* p. 7), students use a checklist of strategies to highlight the strategies they used to better comprehend the text. Look over students' checklists to determine which strategies students are skilled at using and which strategies need extra reinforcement as you move into new themes. Allow time for students to explain to partners strategies they used to understand the text.

Retelling Guide and Scoring Rubric

Name _____   Date _____

Book Title _____

Directions

Ask each student to look back through the pages of a book you have shared in small group reading, with the goal of preparing to tell what he or she learned from the book.

Meet with each student individually and encourage a complete retelling with a cue such as: *Tell me everything you remember about this book, especially those things that you think are the most important.*

Listen carefully. You may want to jot a few notes. When the student finishes, you might want to offer additional encouragement with a cue such as:

1. Is there anything else you can add?

2. What did you think about this book?

3. What connections did you make as you read this book?

Score _____

Comments _____

_____

_____

_____

_____

_____

Use the following rubric to assess the student's unaided retelling:

Scoring Rubric

5 The reader states all main ideas and provides supporting details. Key concepts are clearly understood, and the reader offers opinions, connections, or generalizations. The learner explains with clarity and confidence.

3 The reader states some main ideas and several supporting details. Most concepts are understood and expressed. The reader offers explanations that are grade-level appropriate.

1 The reader is not able to identify the main ideas. There may be a few details in the retell, but information is incomplete or inaccurate. The reader may act hesitant or unsure.

For more information about assessment, see *Assessment Overview*, pages 176–178.

Fluency Scoring Guide

Name _____ Date _____

Book Title _____

Fluency refers to a reader's ability to interpret print through expressive oral reading. Fluency is not just about reading quickly. Fluency refers to a reader's ability to read in a way that sounds like language and to represent the author's message at a pace that matches the meaning. This means that the reader needs to pause in response to punctuation, phrasing, or powerful images and select a pace that matches the kind of text and the purpose for the reading. With this in mind, a set of directions may be read very slowly as the reader concentrates on visualizing and internalizing the steps of a process, while a lively poem may be read at a much faster pace as the language is savored and enjoyed.

Directions

Choose a selection for the student to read aloud. As the student reads, use the rubric to assess the student's ability to read fluently.

Score _____

Comments _____

_____

_____

_____

_____

_____

_____

Scoring Rubric

5
- The reader reads with expression.
- The rate matches the style of the text.
- The reader adjusts tone and emphasis to reflect meaning.
- The reading reflects an understanding of audience.
- Pauses are used for emphasis.
- Self-corrections and fix-up strategies are employed so smoothly that the listener does not notice them.

3
- There is some expressiveness in the reading.
- There is an attempt to match the rate to the kind of text being read.
- The reader may over-exaggerate tone in an attempt to be dramatic.
- The reader is so focused on print that the audience may be forgotten.
- Pauses are focused on word recognition rather than emphasis of meaning.

1
- The reader reads slowly and in a monotone.
- There is no evidence of shifts in tone, speed, or inflection in response to meaning.
- There are frequent pauses for sound-outs and repeats of words.
- Time is taken to look at pictures to construct meaning.

For more information about assessment, see *Assessment Overview*, pages 176–178.

Oral Reading Records

Oral reading records, also called running records, are powerful tools that provide a framework for teachers to systematically observe and interpret a student's reading behaviors. They give insight into how a student is using reading strategies and cueing systems.

Although taking oral reading records does require some practice, once teachers become comfortable with the technique, most find these to be relatively easy to do. More importantly, they provide information that helps to monitor individual growth and to plan instruction.

Taking Oral Reading Records

1 Establish a Rotating Schedule

Plan to take oral reading records for each student frequently so that you can monitor progress and adjust instruction as needed. A goal might be to record each student's reading every few weeks. Set up a rotating schedule so that you spend some time each day taking oral reading records.

2 Learn the Coding System

Oral reading records use a standard set of conventions to record a student's reading behaviors as he or she reads. You need to become comfortable with these to feel confident in taking oral reading records. These include:

- Using a check mark (✔) for each word read correctly.

- For each miscue, draw a horizontal line above the miscue. Write the reader's behavior above the line. If the student self-corrects the miscue, add *sc* to show the self-correction. For example, for a student who reads *posters* for *signs* and then self-corrects, you would write

sc

✔   ✔   ✔   ✔ *posters*

Carla and Jason make ~~signs.~~

- If the student omits a word, draw a line through the omitted word.

- If the student inserts a word, insert a ∧ and write the inserted word above the text.

- If the student substitutes a word, draw a line through the original word and write the substituted word above it.

3 Select the Text

You can use a book that the student has already read to evaluate how well the student is using those strategies that have been taught. You can use a text that is new to the student to evaluate the student's use of cueing systems. The text needs to provide enough challenges so that the student makes some miscues; otherwise, no information is gathered from the experience.

4 Observe the Student Reading

Use the oral reading records provided in this book to record observations. For each theme, the text of one of the two nonfiction selections is printed on a form. The blank form provided on page 184 can be used with other books from *Windows on Literacy: Language, Literacy & Vocabulary*. Sit beside or behind the student so that you can observe the reading. Avoid teaching, but you can provide a word when asked or suggest that the student try it again if you think a reread of some text would be helpful.

5 Have the Student Retell

After the reading, ask the student to retell everything he or she can remember about the text. Record your impressions of the retelling. See *Retelling Guide* on page 179.

6 Analyze the Oral Reading Record

An analysis of the record helps you determine the difficulty level of the text for that student and also provides insight into the student's use of strategies and cueing systems.

Understanding a student's use of strategies and cueing systems requires a careful analysis of each error and each self-correction. You will be judging whether the student is using one or more of these cueing systems.

- **Meaning** Meaning, or semantic, cues are those based on the context of the text. A student who substitutes *posters* for *signs* is using the meaning of what was read to predict text.

- **Structure** Structure, or syntactic, cues are those based on grammar, syntax, and language structure. A student who substitutes *went* for *wanted* knows that a past tense verb is correct but is not using meaning to confirm the correct verb.

- **Visual Information** Graphic cues are based on visual information and/or phonic cues. A student who reads *closed* for *closing* is not paying attention to word endings.

7 Using the Reading Record Summary

The form on page 183 allows you to compile information and analyze the results of the Oral Reading Record. This form allows you to note general print awareness and strategies used when encountering unknown words and when making an error.

The second section of the form will help you to determine the student's reading level, which is important in choosing books for individuals.

- To determine the error rate, divide the total number of words read by the total number of errors made. Use this information to get a ratio. For example, a student who read a total of 60 words and made 4 errors has an error rate of 1:15. The student made one error for every 15 words read.

- The accuracy rate is the percentage of words read correctly. So a student reading 56 words correctly out of a total of 60 words is reading at a 93% accuracy rate. This helps to determine the level of reading.

- 95%–100% is an independent or easy reading level.

- 90%–94% is an instructional level.

- Below 90% is a difficult or frustration level.

- Self-corrections are positive reading behaviors. To determine a student's self-correction rate, add the number of errors and the number of self-corrections. Then divide this total by the number of self-corrections. This will give you a ratio. For example, a student who has a self-correction rate of 1:3 is able to recognize an error and correct it one out of every three times. A self-correct rate of 1:3 to 1:5 is considered good.

The form also allows you to add notes on the student's retelling and make notes on your overall analysis of reading behaviors.

8 Use the Results

Oral Reading Records yield a wealth of information about individual readers. Use the results from the accuracy and error rate scores to determine if a text is too difficult for a student. Use the analysis of errors and self-corrections to plan instruction for individuals or groups. This analysis is also useful in talking with parents and other teachers.

For more information about assessment, see *Assessment Overview*, pages 176–178.

Name _____   Age _____   Date _____

Text _____   Level _____   Seen/Unseen

Reading Record Summary

Strategies Used

Directionality   1-to-1 Matching   Phrased Reading (using punctuation)   Fluent Reading

At an Unknown Word		**After an Error**	
Makes No Attempt	Attempts by Using:	Ignores	Self-corrects Using:
Seeks Help	_____ Letter/Sound Knowledge	Seeks Help	_____ Letter/Sound Knowledge
Reruns	_____ Meaning	Reruns	_____ Meaning
Reads On	_____ Syntax	Attempts SC	_____ Syntax

Reading Level

Error Rate $\dfrac{\text{No. of Words}}{\text{No. of Errors}}$ = 1: _____   _____ Easy/Independent

Accuracy %   _____ Instructional

S/C $\dfrac{(ER + SC)}{SC}$ = 1: _____   _____ Difficult/Frustration

Notes on Oral Retelling

Analysis of Reading Behaviors

Recommendations:

Teacher _____   Date _____

Name _____   Age _____   Date _____

Book Title _____   Level _____   Words _____

Accuracy _____   S.C. Rate _____

Oral Reading Record

PAGE	TEXT	ER	SC	ER MSV	SC MSV
	TOTAL				

Book Title **Big Red Tomatoes** _____   Level _____ **13** _____   Words _____ **168** _____

Accuracy _____   S.C. Rate _____

Oral Reading Record

PAGE	TEXT	ER	SC	ER MSV	SC MSV
2	Big red tomatoes are smooth and round and juicy.				
4	They taste good in a salad.				
	They taste good in a sandwich.				
5	They taste good in a sauce.				
6	Where do tomatoes come from?				
	They are grown on farms.				
7	They are grown from seeds.				
8	Farmers put the tomato seeds into pots of soil.				
9	Soon, the seeds sprout.				
	Tiny leaves push up through the soil.				
10	The little tomato plants are called seedlings.				
	SUBTOTAL				

Oral Reading Record *continued*

PAGE	TEXT	ER	SC	ER MSV	SC MSV
11	The seedlings grow into plants. Farmers plant the tomato plants in long rows on their farms.				
12	Water and sunshine help the plants grow. Little yellow flowers start to grow among the leaves.				
14	A tiny tomato forms in the middle of the flower.				
15	At first the tomato is green.				
16	It grows bigger and bigger. Then, as it ripens, it turns red.				
18	People pick the tomatoes.				
20	The tomatoes are packed into boxes. Then they are sent to markets.				
21	People buy big red tomatoes.				
22	They mix them in a salad. They eat them in a sandwich.				
23	They cook them in a sauce.				
	TOTAL				

Name		Age		Date	

Book Title **Thomas Edison**   Level **14**   Words **145**

Accuracy _____   S.C. Rate _____

Oral Reading Record

PAGE	TEXT	ER	SC	ER MSV	SC MSV
3	Thomas Edison was an inventor.				
	He invented many famous things over 100 years ago.				
	People still use things that Thomas Edison first invented.				
4	Thomas Edison invented a music player called a phonograph.				
	People could use the phonograph to listen to music.				
5	Music players have changed since they were first invented.				
	Today, people listen to music on machines that look like this.				
6	Thomas Edison invented the lightbulb.				
	People could use lightbulbs to light their homes at night.				
7	Lightbulbs have changed since they were first invented.				
	Today, people use lightbulbs that look like this.				
	SUBTOTAL				

PAGE	TEXT	ER	SC	ER MSV	SC MSV
8	Thomas Edison invented a movie camera. People could use the movie camera to make silent movies.				
9	Movie cameras have changed since they were first invented. Today, people use movie cameras that look like this.				
10	Lightbulbs, music players and movie cameras have all changed since Thomas Edison invented them. But his ideas are everywhere.				
	TOTAL				

Book Title **From Field to Florist** _____   Level _____ **14** _____   Words _____ **140** _____

Accuracy _____   S.C. Rate _____

Oral Reading Record

PAGE	TEXT	ER	SC	ER MSV	SC MSV
2	Look at the flowers.				
	They are for sale in a flower store.				
3	A person who sells flowers is called a florist.				
	Where does the florist get all the flowers?				
4	Farmers grow the flowers.				
	Some of the flowers are grown in large fields.				
5	Some of the flowers are grown in greenhouses.				
6	In the morning, farmers pick the flowers				
	they will sell at the market.				
	They put the flowers in their truck.				
7	They take their flowers to the market.				
	SUBTOTAL				

PAGE	TEXT	ER	SC	ER MSV	SC MSV
8	At the market the flowers are kept in buckets full of water.				
	The water helps keep the flowers fresh.				
9	Florists visit the market.				
	This is where they get the flowers to sell in their stores.				
10	The florist gets the flowers ready to sell at the store.				
	Some of the flowers are made up into bunches.				
11	People buy flowers at the flower store.				
	TOTAL				

Name			Age	Date

Book Title **Gingerbread** Level **14** Words **134**

Accuracy _____ S.C. Rate _____

Oral Reading Record

PAGE	TEXT	ER	SC	ER MSV	SC MSV
2	Mom and I are going to make gingerbread.				
3	We need all of these things.				
4	I measure a half cup of butter.				
5	We measure a half cup of sugar.				
6	We measure one cup of molasses.				
7	Mom melts the butter in a saucepan.				
	She adds the molasses and sugar.				
8	I use a whisk to beat two eggs.				
	Then Mom adds the eggs to the saucepan.				
	SUBTOTAL				

Oral Reading Record continued

PAGE	TEXT	ER	SC	ER MSV	SC MSV
9	I measure two cups of flour.				
	I measure one tablespoon of ginger.				
	I measure one teaspoon of baking soda.				
10	Mom adds the butter, molasses, and sugar to the mixing bowl.				
11	Mom uses butter to grease a baking pan.				
12	Mom pours the mixture into the baking pan.				
13	We bake the gingerbread for 30 minutes.				
14	We decorate the gingerbread.				
	We cut the gingerbread into squares.				
15	Now the gingerbread is ready to eat.				
	Yum!				
	TOTAL				

Name _____

Book Title **Sun Power** _____

Age _____

Level **15**

Accuracy _____

Date _____

Words **78**

S.C. Rate _____

Oral Reading Record

PAGE	TEXT	ER	SC	ER MSV	SC MSV
2	What helps plants grow?				
4	Sun power!				
	Plants need sunlight to grow.				
6	What melts the ice?				
8	Sun power!				
	Heat from the sun melts the ice.				
10	What makes this car go?				
12	Sun power!				
	This car uses sunlight to make the car go.				
14	What heats the houses?				
	SUBTOTAL				

Oral Reading Record *continued*

PAGE	TEXT	ER	SC	ER MSV	SC MSV
16	Sun power!				
	The panels on the roofs use sunlight to heat the houses.				
18	What helps dry the clothes?				
20	Sun power!				
	Heat from the sun dries the clothes.				
22	What helps keep you warm?				
23	Sun power!				
	TOTAL				

Name		Age		Date	

Book Title **Exploring Fossils**　　Level　**16**　　Words　**257**

　　Accuracy　　　　　S.C. Rate

Oral Reading Record

PAGE	TEXT	ER	SC	ER MSV	SC MSV
3	Fossils				
	Look at these pictures.				
	Can you see a leaf?				
	What else can you see?				
4	The remains of things that lived millions of years ago				
	are called fossils.				
	Many fossils are found in rocks.				
6	How Was This Plant Fossil Formed?				
	Millions of years ago, parts of a plant fell onto wet ground.				
	They were quickly buried by layers of soft mud.				
7	Over many millions of years, the mud turned to rock.				
	The shape of the plant stayed in the rock.				
	That's how this plant fossil was formed.				
	SUBTOTAL				

Oral Reading Record continued

PAGE	TEXT	ER	SC	ER MSV	SC MSV
8	How Was This Animal Fossil Formed?				
	Millions of years ago, this lizard died.				
	Its body was quickly buried by layers of soft mud.				
9	Over many millions of years, the mud turned to rock.				
	The lizard's skeleton also turned to rock.				
	That's how this animal fossil was formed.				
10	Finding Fossils				
	Scientists go to many different places to look for fossils in rocks.				
11	When scientists find fossils, they use special tools to remove the fossils from the rocks.				
12	Sometimes scientists take the fossils they find to laboratories.				
13	They study the fossils very carefully.				
	They prepare some of the fossils for display in museums.				
	SUBTOTAL				

PAGE	TEXT	ER	SC	ER MSV	SC MSV
14	Some people like to look for fossils when they are at the beach or when they are out hiking. Sometimes people find fossils even when they are not looking for them!				
16	One day, you might find a rock that contains a fossil. If you do, think about what the plant or animal looked like when it was alive. Fossils help all of us learn about prehistoric life on Earth.				
	TOTAL				

Name _____   Age _____   Date _____

Book Title **All Kinds of Maps** _____   Level ___**15**___   Words ___**164**___

Accuracy _____   S.C. Rate _____

Oral Reading Record

PAGE	TEXT	ER	SC	ER MSV	SC MSV
2	You can learn a lot about a place by looking at a map.				
	Different kinds of maps show different things.				
4	This is a political map of the United States.				
	It shows how people have divided the land into 50 states.				
	Two of the states are not connected to the others.				
6	This is a physical map of the United States.				
	It shows physical features of the land such as mountains				
	and rivers.				
8	This is a population map of the United States.				
	It shows which parts of the country are most populated.				
	Some places have a lot more people than others.				
	SUBTOTAL				

Oral Reading Record *continued*

PAGE	TEXT	ER	SC	ER MSV	SC MSV
10	This is a climate map of the United States. It shows what the climate is like in different parts of the country.				
12	This is a land use map of the United States. It shows how the land is used in different parts of the country.				
14	This is a road map of the United States. It shows where the major highways in the country are located.				
	TOTAL				

Name _____ Age _____ Date _____

Book Title **Looking for Symmetry** Level **16** Words **224**

Accuracy _____ S.C. Rate _____

Oral Reading Record

PAGE	TEXT	ER	SC	ER MSV	SC MSV
2	What Is Symmetry?				
	Look at the line on the picture of the spider.				
	The line is in a special place.				
	The line is drawn so the spider looks the same on both sides				
	of the line.				
	This is called symmetry.				
	The line is called a line of symmetry.				
4	Look at the line on the picture of the sunflower.				
	Is this a line of symmetry?				
	Yes, this is a line of symmetry.				
	The sunflower looks the same on both sides of the line.				
	The two sides match.				
	SUBTOTAL				

PAGE	TEXT	ER	SC	ER MSV	SC MSV
6	Look at the line on the picture of the crab.				
	Is this a line of symmetry?				
	No, this is not a line of symmetry.				
	The crab does not look the same on both sides of the line.				
	The two sides do not match.				
8	Look at the line on the picture of the butterfly.				
	Is this a line of symmetry?				
	Yes, this is a line of symmetry.				
	The butterfly looks the same on both sides of the line.				
	The two sides match.				
10	Look at the line on the picture of the sea star.				
	Is this a line of symmetry?				
	No, this is not a line of symmetry.				
	SUBTOTAL				

Oral Reading Record continued

PAGE	TEXT	ER	SC	ER MSV	SC MSV
	The sea star does not look the same on both sides of the line.				
	The two sides do not match.				
12	Look at the sea star again.				
	Is this a line of symmetry?				
	TOTAL				

Name _____   Age _____   Date _____

Book Title **Water Can Change** _____   Level **17**   Words **140**

Accuracy _____   S.C. Rate _____

Oral Reading Record

PAGE	TEXT	ER	SC	ER MSV	SC MSV
3	Ice Ice is hard and cold. Ice is a solid. A solid has its own shape.				
4	What happens when you put ice in the sun? The heat from the sun melts the ice.				
5	The hard ice changes. The ice becomes water.				
6	Water Water is a liquid. The heat changed the ice to water. The heat changed the solid to a liquid.				
	SUBTOTAL				

Oral Reading Record *continued*

PAGE	TEXT	ER	SC	ER MSV	SC MSV
	A liquid is runny.				
	It flows easily.				
	A liquid takes the shape of its container.				
8	What happens when you heat water?				
	The heat makes the water boil.				
9	The water changes.				
	The water becomes steam.				
10	Steam				
	Steam is a gas.				
	The heat changed the water to steam.				
	The heat changed the liquid to a gas.				
	It is hard to see most gases.				
	A gas goes into the air.				
	A gas spreads to fill any space.				
12	Heat can make things change.				
	SUBTOTAL				

Name		Age	Date

Book Title **Life in the Ocean**　　Level **18**　　Words **371**

Accuracy _____　　S.C. Rate _____

Oral Reading Record

PAGE	TEXT	ER	SC	ER MSV	SC MSV
2	Many strange and amazing animals live in the ocean.				
	Some animals live close to the surface.				
	Others live in very deep water.				
	Scientists have divided the ocean into different parts,				
	called zones.				
4	At the top of the ocean is the Sunlit Zone.				
	The light is bright in this zone.				
	The water is warmer than in the other parts of the ocean.				
	Most of the animals you know live here.				
5	Flying fish live in the Sunlit Zone.				
	A flying fish has large fins that are like wings.				
	It uses the fins to fly out of the water if it is in danger.				
	SUBTOTAL				

Oral Reading Record *continued*

PAGE	TEXT	ER	SC	ER MSV	SC MSV
7	Dolphins live in the Sunlit Zone. A dolphin has a hole in its head. It uses the hole to breathe when it comes above the water.				
9	Sea turtles live in the Sunlit Zone. A sea turtle has strong flippers. It uses the flippers to swim quickly through the water.				
10	Deeper down is the Twilight Zone. The light is dim in this zone. The water is very cold.				
11	Hatchet fish live in the Twilight Zone. A hatchet fish has large eyes. It uses its large eyes to find food in the dark.				
13	Lanternfish live in the Twilight Zone. A lanternfish has lights on its body. It uses the lights to see in the dark and find food.				
	SUBTOTAL				

Oral Reading Record *continued*

PAGE	TEXT	ER	SC	ER MSV	SC MSV
14	Even deeper down is the Midnight Zone.				
	There is very little light in this zone.				
	The water is icy cold.				
15	Gulper eels live in the Midnight Zone.				
	A gulper eel has a wide mouth and a stretchy stomach.				
	It uses its wide mouth to swallow fish larger than itself.				
17	Anglerfish live in the Midnight Zone.				
	An anglerfish has a flashing light on its head.				
	It uses the flashing light to find food.				
18	At the bottom of the ocean is the Trench Zone.				
	There is no light in this zone.				
	The water is near freezing.				
19	Rattails live in the Trench Zone.				
	A rattail has a long tail.				
	It uses its tail to search for food on the bottom of the ocean.				
	SUBTOTAL				

Oral Reading Record *continued*

PAGE	TEXT	ER	SC	ER MSV	SC MSV
20	Tripod fish live in the Trench Zone.				
	A tripod fish has three long fins to rest on.				
	It uses its fins to keep from sinking into the ooze on the bottom				
	of the ocean.				
	TOTAL				

Book Title **Wool Keeps Me Warm**   Level _____ **17** _____   Words _____ **147** _____

Accuracy _____   S.C. Rate _____

Oral Reading Record

PAGE	TEXT	ER	SC	ER MSV	SC MSV
2	We wear warm clothes when the weather is cold.				
	We wear sock, sweaters, scarves, and hats.				
	These clothes are often made from wool.				
	Where does wool come from?				
4	Wool comes from sheep.				
	Sheep grow a thick wool coat.				
	How does the wool on sheep become the wool that we wear?				
6	Once a year people cut the wool off the sheep.				
	This is called shearing.				
	What happens to the wool next?				
8	The wool is packed into bales and put on a truck.				
	The truck takes the wool to a factory.				
	SUBTOTAL				

Oral Reading Record *continued*

PAGE	TEXT	ER	SC	ER MSV	SC MSV
10	At the factory the wool is cleaned and combed.				
	Combing the wool makes it straight and smooth.				
12	A machine spins the wool to make yarn.				
	The yarn is long, thin, and strong.				
14	Now the yarn can be knitted together.				
	A knitting machine can make socks, sweaters, scarves,				
	and hats.				
16	Now the wool is ready for us to wear!				
	TOTAL				

Name _____ Age _____ Date _____

Book Title **Places to Visit** _____ Level _____**17**_____ Words _____**202**_____

Accuracy _____ S.C. Rate _____

Oral Reading Record

PAGE	TEXT	ER	SC	ER MSV	SC MSV
2	There are many famous places to visit in the United States.				
	Have you been to the Grand Canyon?				
	It is in Arizona.				
3	The Grand Canyon is a deep valley with steep sides.				
	In some places it is 18 miles wide.				
	Other places are less than one mile wide.				
4	Have you been to Yellowstone Nat onal Park?				
	It is in Wyoming, Idaho, and Montana.				
5	Yellowstone is the oldest National Park in the world.				
	It is one of the largest safe areas for wildlife in the				
	Jnited States.				
	SUBTOTAL				

Oral Reading Record *continued*

PAGE	TEXT	ER	SC	ER MSV	SC MSV
6	Have you been to Niagara Falls? It is in New York.				
7	Niagara Falls is the largest waterfall in North America. It is made up of two waterfalls, the Horseshoe Falls and the American Falls.				
8	Have you been to Mount St. Helens? It is in Washington.				
9	Mount St. Helens is a volcano. It erupted in 1980 forming a crater on top.				
10	Have you been to Mammoth Cave? It is in Kentucky.				
11	Mammoth Cave is a huge underground cave. There are stalactites and underground lakes in the cave.				
	SUBTOTAL				

Oral Reading Record *continued*

PAGE	TEXT	ER	SC	ER MSV	SC MSV
12	Have you been to the Everglades?				
	It is in Florida.				
13	The Everglades is a huge marsh.				
	It is known as a river of grass.				
14	Have you been to these famous places?				
	TOTAL				

Writing Rubric

Directions

Record the student's name, the date, and the name of the Theme or assignment. Circle the most appropriate items in columns one, two, or three to assess your student's writing.

Name _____ Date _____

Theme/Assignment _____

Writing Rubric

Very good	Average	Needs Work
Content • The writing topic is well developed. • The writing reflects strong knowledge of the content of the book or books. • The writing has clear main ideas. • The writing provides substantial detail in an interesting manner. • The writing has accurate information.	**Content** • The writing topic is somewhat developed. • The writing reflects some knowledge of the content of the book or books. • The writing has some clear main ideas. • The writing provides some detail in an interesting manner. • The writing has an inaccuracy.	**Content** • The writing topic is not well developed. • The writing reflects little knowledge of the content of the book or books. • The writing does not have clear main ideas. • The writing does not provide details. • The writing presents much inaccurate information.
Organization • The beginning is inviting and well crafted. • The illustrations and text work well together. • The ending is logical and creates a sense of closure. • Paragraphs are evident.	**Organization** • The beginning is clear but not especially well crafted. • The text usually matches or connects to the illustrations. • The ending makes sense but does not create a sense of closure. • The student has indented but has not created logical paragraphs.	**Organization** • The beginning simply starts. • The text rarely connects to the illustrations. • The ending is abrupt or absent. • The student has not used paragraphs.
Sentence Fluency • The writing has a smooth flow. • Sentences are of varied lengths. • Sentences have varied and interesting beginnings. • Sentences are easily read aloud with expression.	**Sentence Fluency** • The writing flow is uneven. • Most sentences are the same length. • A few sentences have interesting beginnings. • Some sentences are easily read aloud with expression.	**Sentence Fluency** • The writing does not flow. • One sentence length is used throughout. • Sentences all begin the same way. • Sentences cannot be read aloud with expression.
Word Choice • Verbs are active and elicit visualization from the reader. • Content vocabulary from the theme is clearly evident. • Precise nouns are used as well as descriptive adjectives.	**Word Choice** • Some verbs are active and elicit visualization from the reader. • Some content vocabulary from the theme is used. • A few precise nouns and descriptive adjectives are used.	**Word Choice** • Verbs are not active. • Content vocabulary from the theme is not used. • Precise nouns and descriptive adjectives are not used.
Voice • The writer has a sense of audience. • The writer's purpose is clear.	**Voice** • The audience for the writing is not clear throughout. • The writer's purpose is not always clear.	**Voice** • The audience for the writing is not clear. • The writer's purpose is unclear.
Conventions • Most words are spelled correctly. • Writing is edited for punctuation and grammar.	**Conventions** • Several words are misspelled. • Writing is partially edited for punctuation and grammar.	**Conventions** • There are many misspellings. • Writing is not edited for punctuation and grammar.
Presentation • Handwriting is neat and legible. • Visuals are well planned and match the writing.	**Presentation** • Handwriting is legible. • Visuals match the writing.	**Presentation** • Handwriting is barely legible. • Visuals do not match the writing.
Text Features • Labels, title, boldfaced words, captions, close-up drawings, cutaways, table of contents, and index or glossary are included as appropriate.	**Text Features** • A few appropriate text features are included.	**Text Features** • No text features are included.

For more information about assessment, see *Assessment Overview*, pages 176–178.

Writing Traits Checklist

Directions

At various times throughout the year, use the rubric as you assess a student's writing traits. The rubric provides an at-a-glance snapshot of the student's development as a writer and areas on which you might want to focus instruction. List the dates you use the rubric in the top of the table.

You might want to use a code such as the following as you assess each strategy:

+ The student has mastered this strategy.

✔ The student has attempted the strategy but has not yet mastered it.

− The student has not attempted to use this strategy.

Writing Traits Checklist

TRAIT DATE OBSERVED								
Ideas/Content								
The topic is well developed.								
Substantial detail is provided in a manner that interests the reader.								
There are clear main ideas.								
Information is accurate.								
Organization								
The beginning of the piece is inviting and well crafted.								
The illustrations and text work together.								
The ending is logical and creates a sense of closure.								
Paragraphs are evident.								
Sentence Fluency								
The writing has a smooth flow.								
Sentences are of varied lengths.								
Sentences have varied and interesting beginnings.								
Sentences are easily read aloud with expression.								
Word Choice								
Verbs are active and elicit visualization in the reader.								
Content vocabulary from the theme is clearly evident.								
Precise nouns as well as descriptive adjectives are used.								
Voice								
The writer has a sense of audience.								
The writer's purpose is clear to the reader.								
Conventions								
Most words are spelled correctly.								
Writing is edited for punctuation and grammar.								
Presentation								
Handwriting is neat and legible.								
Visuals are well planned and match the writing.								
Text Features								
Labels, title, boldfaced words, captions, close-up drawings, cutaways, table of contents, and index or glossary are included as appropriate.								

For more information about assessment, see *Assessment Overview*, pages 176–178.

Theme **Plant Life** _____

Content Vocabulary Checklist

Read each word. Write a number on the line.

1 = I know this word and can use it.

2 = I have heard this word before.

3 = I don't know this word.

_____ flowers   _____ leaves   _____ seeds   _____ soil

_____ fruit   _____ root   _____ shoot   _____ stem

Label this picture.
Use the words from the Word Bank.

Word Bank

| flowers |
| leaves |
| root |
| soil |
| stem |

Theme **Then and Now** _____

Content Vocabulary Checklist

Read each word. Write a number on the line.
1 = I know this word and can use it.
2 = I have heard this word before.
3 = I don't know this word.

_____ change   _____ long ago   _____ the past

_____ invent   _____ machine   _____ school

Complete the sentences.
Use words from the Word Bank.

Word Bank

change	machine
invent	the past
long ago	school

_____ people washed their

clothes in a tub. Now, people use a washing

_____.

Inventors are always thinking of new ways to do things. They

_____.

In _____, children in _____ learned only from

the teacher and books. But there has been a _____. Now,

many children can also learn from computers.

Content Vocabulary Checklist

Read each word. Write a number on the line.
1 = I know this word and can use it.
2 = I have heard this word before.
3 = I don't know this word.

_____ buy   _____ stores

_____ goods   _____ transport

_____ move   _____ truck

_____ sell   _____ warehouse

Word Bank

buy	sell	transport
goods	store	warehouse

Complete the graphic organizer at right. Use words from the Word Bank

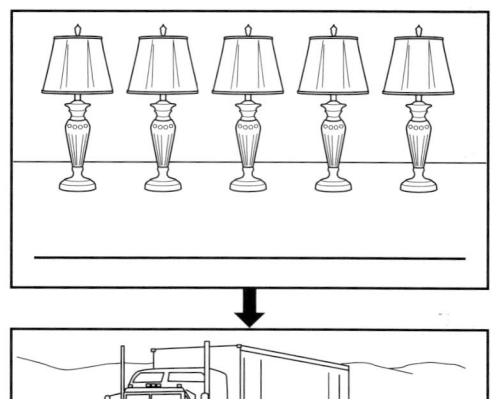

_____

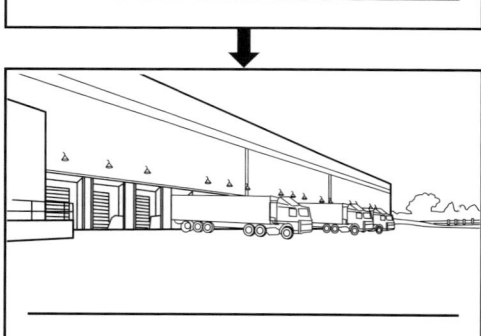

_____

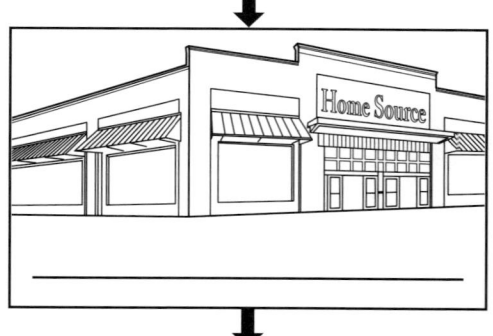

_____

_____

_____ and _____

Theme **Measurement** _____

Content Vocabulary Checklist

Read each word. Write a number on the line.
1 = I know this word and can use it.
2 = I have heard this word before.
3 = I don't know this word.

_____ inch	_____ ounce	_____ teaspoon	_____ quart
_____ foot	_____ pound	_____ tablespoon	_____ gallon
_____ centimeter	_____ gram	_____ cup	_____ liter
_____ meter	_____ kilogram	_____ pint	

Complete each sentence.
Use words from the Word Bank.

Word Bank

Word Bank
inches
teaspoon
tablespoon
kilograms
cup
feet
grams

1. I can measure how tall someone is in

_____ and _____.

2. _____ and _____ tell

how heavy something is.

3. Three measuring tools are a _____,

a _____, and a _____.

Theme **Wind, Water, and Sunlight** _____

Content Vocabulary Checklist

Read each word. Write a number on the line.

1 = I know this word and can use it.

2 = I have heard this word before.

3 = I don't know this word.

_____ heat   _____ power   _____ water

_____ melts   _____ sunlight   _____ wind

Complete each sentence.
It will show a cause or an effect.
Use words from the Word Bank.

Word Bank

heat	power
melts	wind

Sunlight gives _____.

Sunlight _____ ice.

_____ makes sailboats move.

Sunlight, wind, and water can help make electric _____.

Draw a picture. Show
the power of wind,
water, or sunlight.

Theme **Prehistoric Life** _____

Content Vocabulary Checklist

Read each word. Write a number on the line.
1 = I know this word and can use it.
2 = I have heard this word before.
3 = I don't know this word.

_____ dinosaur   _____ paleontologist   _____ skeleton

_____ extinct   _____ prehistoric

_____ fossil   _____ remains

Complete the sentences.
Use words from the Word Bank.

Word Bank

| dinosaur |
| extinct |
| fossils |
| prehistoric |
| skeleton |

Welcome to the museum! You will learn about

plants and animals from long ago. These are

_____ plants and animals. They no

longer live on Earth. They are _____.

You will see bones fitted together into a huge _____. This

animal looked like a giant lizard. Can you guess what it was? It was

a _____.

The bones from long ago are _____.

Theme **Maps** _____

Content Vocabulary Checklist

Read each word. Write a number on the line.

1 = I know this word and can use it.

2 = I have heard this word before.

3 = I don't know this word.

_____ border	_____ highway	_____ ocean
_____ continent	_____ landforms	_____ river
_____ country	_____ mountain	_____ road

Complete the labels with words from the Word Bank.

Word Bank

border	mountain
country	ocean
lake	river

N ↑

Border

Mountains

River

Name _____   Date _____

Theme **Patterns, Shapes, and Symmetry** _____

Content Vocabulary Checklist

Read each word. Write a number on the line.

1 = I know this word and can use it.

2 = I have heard this word before.

3 = I don't know this word.

_____ circle	_____ pattern	_____ square
_____ half	_____ rectangle	_____ symmetry
_____ line of symmetry	_____ shape	_____ triangle

Look at the names of shapes in the Word Bank. Draw one shape in each box below. Write the name of the shape beneath the picture.

Word Bank

circle	square
rectangle	triangle

_____   _____   _____   _____

Draw a line of symmetry on this starfish.

Tell what a line of symmetry is. _____

_____

Content Vocabulary Checklist

Read each word. Write a number on the line.

1 = I know this word and can use it.
2 = I have heard this word before.
3 = I don't know this word.

_____ change   _____ ice   _____ melt   _____ temperature

_____ gas   _____ liquid   _____ solid

_____ heat   _____ matter   _____ steam

Complete the sentences.
Use words from the Word Bank.

Word Bank

heat	melt
ice	temperature

The _____ is 38 degrees Fahrenheit (F). The sun gives

_____ . The _____ on the sidewalk changes.

The ice begins to _____ .

Theme **Animal Habitats** _____

Content Vocabulary Checklist

Read each word. Write a number on the line.

1 = I know this word and can use it.

2 = I have heard this word before.

3 = I don't know this word.

_____ Arctic   _____ habitat   _____ ocean   _____ rain forest

_____ desert   _____ level   _____ prairie   _____ zone

Draw a picture of one of the habitats in the Word Bank.

Word Bank

Arctic	prairie
desert	rain forest

Write two sentences that tell about the habitat you drew.

_____

_____

Content Vocabulary Checklist

Read each word. Write a number on the line.

1 = I know this word and can use it.

2 = I have heard this word before.

3 = I don't know this word.

_____ factory		_____ machine	
_____ goods		_____ product	
_____ harvest		_____ raw material	

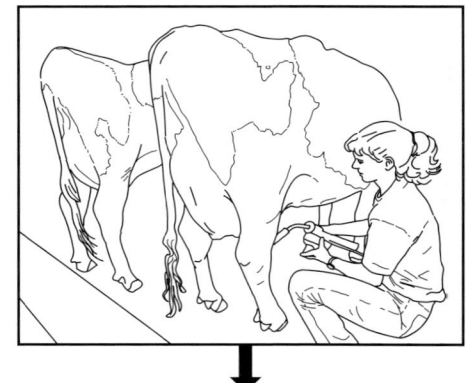

Complete the sentences. Use the Word Bank.

Word Bank

factory	product
machines	raw material

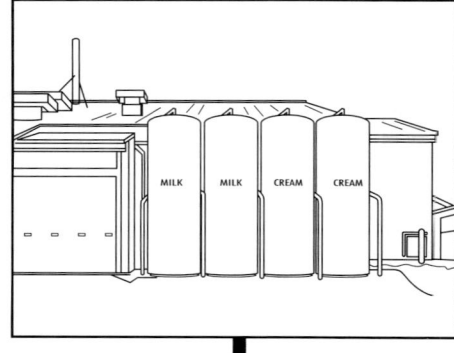

Here's how milk becomes ice cream:

Milk is a _____ for making ice cream.

Milk is taken to a _____.

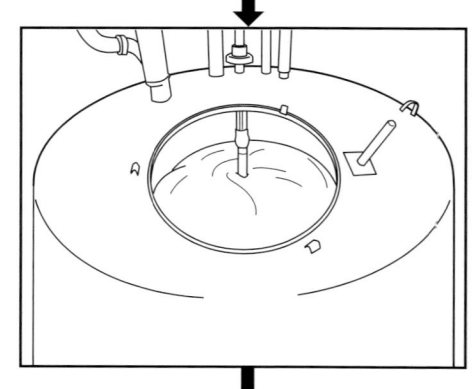

_____ turn the milk into ice cream.

Ice cream is a _____. People

buy ice cream, and then they eat it!

Content Vocabulary Checklist

Read each word. Write a number on the line.
1 = I know this word and can use it.
2 = I have heard this word before.
3 = I don't know this word.

_____ canyon   _____ landmark   _____ volcano

_____ cave   _____ monument   _____ waterfall

_____ geography   _____ national park

Label each picture.
Use words from the Word Bank.

Word Bank

canyon

cave

monument

volcano

waterfall

Name _____

Oral Language Developmental Checklist

Directions

At various times throughout the year, use the rubric as you assess a student's proficiency with language. At the top of the table, list the dates you use the rubric.

You might want to use a code such as the following as you assess each strategy:

+ The student has mastered this strategy.

✔ The student has attempted the strategy but has not yet mastered it.

— The student has not attempted to use this strategy.

Oral Language Developmental Checklist

	DATE OBSERVED								
Uses language to explain or inquire									
Can clearly describe events, places, and understandings, using adjectives and related verbs									
Uses connectives such as *because, if, after*									
Uses content-related vocabulary to express understanding									
Makes connections linking learning with a prior experience or related reading									
Uses correct verb tense and English word order when talking about content									
Uses abstract verbs such as *think, like, hope, believe,* and *understand* to express thinking									
Makes cohesive statements that are connected to the topic									
Asks questions to clarify vocabulary and concepts									
Asks questions to deepen and extend content understanding									
Understands literal-level concepts									
Uses language to predict and infer									
Uses language to argue a point or persuade; expresses an opinion									
Understands cause/effect and comparison									
Summarizes main ideas from reading									
Compares and contrasts during discussions									
Uses language to help a listener visualize									
Cites evidence from a text to support a point									
Can consider information from more than one source and make a generalization or draw a conclusion									
Makes thoughtful choices about vocabulary that best reflects a topic of conversation									
Can shift language to reflect many genre (personal narrative, directions, explanation, and so on)									

For more information about assessment, see *Assessment Overview*, pages 176–178.